Gentle but firm. Compassionate yet incisive. Abounding in understanding.

Colin Dye
Senior Pastor, Kensington Temple
London, England

Mike Bickle's practical wisdom will serve the body of Christ well.

Terry Virgo
Leader of Pioneer International
London, England

A man of transparent integrity shows us the way forward into areas where angels have feared to tread.

R. T. Kendall
Senior Pastor, Westminster Chapel
London, England

Mike Bickle is a man with a remarkable teaching gift, quick to acknowledge past mistakes which he has clearly learned from. This is a book every charismatic should read if we are going to increase our ability to hear from God, speak to Him and remain committed to Christ, to Scripture and to one another.

Gerald Coates
Leader of Pioneer International
London, England

At a time when the Spirit is speaking strongly to the churches about the gift of prophecy and the office of prophet, *Growing in the Prophetic* is an extremely important book. Mike Bickle brings an enviable combination of maturity and transparency to his exposition of biblical principles molding the prophetic along with valuable lessons learned, both positive and negative, through his ministry to the "Kansas City prophets."

C. Peter Wagner
Professor of Church Growth
Fuller Theological Seminary
Pasadena, California

Growing in the
PROPHETIC

Mike Bickle

with Michael Sullivant

CREATION
HOUSE
BOOKS ABOUT SPIRIT-LED LIVING
ORLANDO, FLORIDA

Creation House
Strang Communications Company
600 Rinehart Road
Lake Mary, FL 32746
Phone: 407- 333-3132
Fax: 407-333-7100
Web site: http://www.strang.com

Unless otherwise noted, all Scripture quotations are from the New
King James Version of the Bible. Copyright © 1979, 1980, 1982 by
Thomas Nelson Inc., publishers. Used by permission.

Scripture quotations marked NAS are from the New American
Standard Bible. Copyright © 1960, 1962, 1963, 1968, 1971, 1972,
1973, 1975, 1977 by the Lockman Foundation. Used by permission.

Scripture quotations marked NIV are from the Holy Bible, New
International Version. Copyright © 1973, 1978, 1984, International
Bible Society. Used by permission.

First printing, May 1996
Second printing, August 1996
Third printing, November 1996
Fourth printing, July 1997
Fifth printing, February 1998

I want to dedicate this book to the faithful congregation of Metro Vineyard Fellowship, who courageously stuck by me for the last twelve years as we continued on the journey to be a prophetic church. They have seen God's glory on several occasions and yet endured many perils because I had neither the maturity nor the wisdom to pastor prophetic people in a proper way. I thank you, Metro Vineyard Fellowship.

Also, I want to thank Paul Cain whose fatherly love and wisdom have made a real difference in my life. Paul's exceptional prophetic gifts have astounded me on many occasions. His mature wisdom has helped me through seasons of perplexity time and time again. His godly example of meekness and kindness has challenged me to follow him as he follows Christ. As a spiritual father, his love has given me the security and courage not to give up. Thank you, Paul.

Acknowledgments

I want to express my deep appreciation to Walter Walker who initially came up with the idea for this book. He relentlessly pursued me to meet deadlines and to get this book finished. He interviewed Michael Sullivant and me for many hours, then took the transcriptions and turned them into the pages of this book. God has greatly blessed me with such a skilled and yet humble ghostwriter for this book. Thank you, Walter, for your abilities and your great heart.

Also, I want to thank Jane Joseph for the timeless hours of overtime that she has dedicated to this book. A prophetic secretary is as valuable as a prophetic ghostwriter. She too is a gift of God.

Last but not least, I want to thank my precious wife, Diane, and my two most wonderful sons, Luke and Paul, for allowing me to sacrifice some of our time together to write this book.

CONTENTS

W hy another book on the prophetic ministry? I've read several books on the prophetic over the years. Some focus on the various biblical categories of prophets and the supernatural manifestations which occur through them. Others focus on how to prophesy and then what to do with prophetic words.

This book touches on those subjects, but it also frankly discusses the joy and the pain of prophetic people in a local church context. I relate the perils, perplexities and tensions involved in nurturing prophetic people among non-prophetic people. When Holy Spirit activity happens among weak people like us, the clash between selfish ambition and lack of wisdom is inevitable. Many tensions arise. Plus, we encounter Holy Spirit experiences that are foreign to us. All this makes for a challenging experience in our church life.

David Pytches wrote some of the prophetic history of our local church in a book called *Some Said It Thundered*. I appreciated his book. Since then, someone suggested that I write a follow-up book that revealed all our mistakes in the prophetic ministry. He suggested I call it *Some Said We Blundered*. I almost agreed. Indeed, we've made many mistakes on our journey in the prophetic ministry.

The future of the church will be exciting as well as challenging. New dimensions of the Holy Spirit's ministry are certainly going to continue. This is not a good time for a know-it-all, but rather it's the proper time for the virtue of humility expressed in a teachable spirit.

I want to mention one more thing. Michael Sullivant helped me write this book. He has been an associate in ministry with me at Metro Vineyard Fellowship since 1987. He is a trusted friend with godly character and a prophetic gifting that continually increases. His wisdom to pastor the prophetic people at our home church is proven. He travels throughout the United States and internationally teaching and demonstrating the prophetic ministry in a style that is devoid of hype — which is exactly what we need.

This book is written in first person, but know that Michael has been at my side contributing significantly throughout the whole process. His contribution comes out of experience as both a prophetic person and a pastor of prophetic people. He knows the joys and sorrows firsthand. He is more than qualified to write his own book on prophetic ministry. Thus I feel honored to have him as my coauthor.

CHAPTER 1

"THERE'S BEEN A TERRIBLE MISTAKE"

John Wimber had set it all up. It was July 1989, and four thousand people had crowded into a warehouse which had been converted into a church building by the Vineyard Christian Fellowship in Anaheim, California.

John had spoken a couple of times at the conference, then had introduced Paul Cain, me and others who were going to bring messages on the prophetic ministry. I taught on the nurturing and administration of the prophetic ministry in the local church and offered some practical advice to encourage laymen with prophetic giftings. These two ideas are the main topics of this book. I also related some stories about how we had periodically experienced God's use of dreams, visions, angels and His audible voice to accomplish His purposes in our church life. I even shared a few stories about how God confirmed some of these prophetic revelations with signs in nature — comets, earthquakes, droughts and floods occurring at precisely predicted times.

I guess I should have been clearer about the fact that seldom do any of these supernatural experiences ever happen through me. For over a decade I have been mostly a spectator of the prophetic ministry and, initially, a reluctant one at that.

In my early days of ministry, I was a young, conservative evangelical pastor hoping one day to attend Dallas Theological Seminary. I was anti-charismatic and proud of it. Within a few short years, I found myself surrounded by and caught up with a small group of unusual people who some referred to as prophets. "Why me, Lord?" I asked many times.

Paul Cain is a grand old saint and a dear friend whose prophetic ministry is nothing short of astounding. His ministry earlier in that conference, along with my prophetic stories, must have overloaded some people's spiritual circuits. These were predominately conservative evangelical church people who had been blessed by Wimber's theology on healing, but who for the most part had not been exposed to any kind of prophetic ministry.

There is, I have discovered, a great longing throughout the body of Christ to hear from God in a personal way.

I finished my session, and we were about to break for lunch. At the last minute John Wimber came up on the platform and whispered in my ear, "Would you pray and ask the Holy Spirit to release the gift of prophecy to people?"

If you've been around John Wimber at all, you know that there's not an ounce of hype or showmanship in him. He'll invite the Holy Spirit to move over an audience and touch thousands of people with the same tone of voice that he'll give the last announcement. It was in that matter-of-fact way that he asked me to pray for the people to receive what I had just been describing.

With four thousand spiritually hungry people watching us, I whispered back to John, "Can I do that since I'm not prophetically gifted myself?"

John responded, "Just go ahead and pray for the release, and let the Lord touch whomever He touches."

"Why am *I* praying for these people?" I thought. I started looking around for help from Paul Cain, John Paul Jackson or someone who might know what he was doing. But I was obviously on my own.

"Well, OK, John, if you want me to," I thought. It would be a harm-less prayer.

John announced that I was going to ask the Holy Spirit to release the gift of prophecy in people's lives. So I prayed. As soon as the meet-ing was over a long line of people formed, anxiously waiting to talk with me. Some wanted me to pray personally for the prophetic gift to be imparted to them. Others wanted me to give them a "word from the Lord," that is, to prophecy what God wanted to say about them and His plan for their lives.

I had recently introduced Paul Cain, Bob Jones and the other prophetic ministers to the Vineyard, men who for years had operated in prophetic ministry in ways that had amazed me. But, perhaps because I prayed for everyone, some of the people attending the conference had mistakenly determined that I was an anointed prophet and certainly the man to see if they wanted the prophetic gift released in them.

I noticed Bob Scott, my brother-in-law who helped me start the church, at the back of the room pointing at me and quietly laughing. He knew I was not a prophet, and he also knew that I was in deep waters.

Over and over I explained to the people lined up to see me, "No, I don't have a word for you. No, I can't impart prophetic gifts. No, I'm not prophetically gifted."

I looked around for John but could not find him. After spending some time explaining this individually to about twenty-five people in line, I simply stood up on the stage and made a loud announcement, "There's been a terrible mistake! I don't have a prophetic ministry!" Then I slipped away.

The previous day John Wimber had introduced me to Richard Foster, author of *Celebration of Discipline*. Richard had been waiting for me to finish praying for people so that we could go to lunch. I was starving; besides, I wanted us to get as far away as possible as fast as possible. Heading for the car, I was stopped by several people in the parking lot who also wanted me to prophesy to them. Of course, I had no prophetic words for them.

Finally, we made our escape and found a restaurant about ten miles from the meeting place. But to my surprise, while I was standing at the salad bar with a plate of food in my hand, I was asked by two different people who attended the conference to prophesy to them. Then a couple came over to my table wondering if I had a prophetic word for them.

I then wished that I had made it clearer during my session that I was not a prophet nor the son of a prophet. Actually, I am the son of a professional boxer.

Many people know about God only in the context of things far away and long ago. They are hungry to know that God is involved with their lives in an intimate way in the present. When that knowledge is dramatically awakened for the first time, people, myself included, often overreact for a short season.

Those who are either excited or desperate to hear from God are seldom restrained and polite. I was getting impatient and exasperated with people's persistence. The fact that I was with Richard Foster, whom I had wanted to meet for a long time, increased my irritation. It was very embarrassing.

You'd never guess by reading *Celebration of Discipline* that Richard is a spontaneous comedian. He roared with laughter when I laid my plate down and said to him, "Richard, I'm not a prophetic person! A terrible mistake has been made today."

Yet, that situation was insignificant compared to the uproar that was to come a few years later. It was neither the first time nor the last time I felt that God had picked the wrong man to pastor a team of prophetic people.

A RELUCTANT INTRODUCTION TO PROPHETIC MINISTRY

Our experience has been that many people, both leaders and laymen, who have involved themselves with ministries that embrace the prophetic, have been brought in kicking and screaming. A good example of this is my close friend Dr. Jack Deere. He was formerly a professor at Dallas Theological Seminary and a committed cessationist before he met John Wimber and experienced the demonstrations of God's power. A cessationist believes the supernatural gifts of the Holy Spirit manifested during the first century have ceased. He also went through a difficult, soul-searching journey as he came to embrace the prophetic ministry.

With the attention we have received over the last few years in regard to the prophetic giftings in our church, some people are amazed to discover the type of people the Lord has brought to work with us. Eight of the men on our staff have master's degrees, plus another four have earned doctorates — all from conservative evangelical, non-charismatic seminaries. The personality profiles of these men are in strong contrast to that of the prophetic ministers, but the diversity is essential.

The Lord has helped us to establish an academically challenging, full-time Bible school called the Grace Training Center of Kansas City. The scholarly types and the prophetic ministers teach side by side as one ministry team who has learned to work in unity. We want to combine the gifts of the Spirit with a responsible scholarship in the Scriptures, and our students have given us encouraging reviews regarding the spiritual and biblical training that they have received.

Like most people in our church, most of these seminary-educated staff members of the Metro Vineyard leadership team are not highly prophetic. They are pastors and teachers who have felt a strong calling to be a part of a ministry that embraces, among other things, the prophetic ministry. The same is true for the majority of laymen in our church who have prophetic giftings. Their involvement in this type of ministry is often a contradiction to their early training against the spiritual gifts.

So many times God's calling cuts directly across the grain of our natural strengths and previous doctrinal training. We believe that God wants to integrate strong evangelical training in the Scriptures with supernatural manifestations of the Holy Spirit. This is one of the main reasons that we started Grace Training Center.[1]

Paul told the Corinthians that God's strength was made perfect in his weakness (2 Cor. 12:9). It is common for God to call people to something for which they are not naturally equipped.

Peter, the uneducated fisherman, was called as an apostle to the educated Jews. Paul, the self-righteous Pharisee, was called as an apostle to the pagan gentiles.

To be called in weakness to do something needing great strength is similar to being called as a theological skeptic to be a part of something supernatural. I certainly fit into that category as do some of the people on the Metro Vineyard staff and many people in our church. No one would have ever suspected from our early religious training and affiliations that we would ever have become remotely involved in a prophetic ministry. God must have a sense of humor.

BECOMING ANTI-CHARISMATIC

In February 1972, at the age of sixteen, I was touched by the Holy

16

Spirit's power. At an Assembly of God church in Kansas City named Evangel Temple, the Holy Spirit seemed to engulf me, and I spoke in tongues for the first time. Before that experience, I had never even heard of the gift of tongues. I had no idea what had happened to me. I asked the people who prayed for me to help me understand what happened. They said I spoke in tongues. I asked, "What is that?" They told me I could learn more about it at the next meeting.

Though I had a powerful encounter with God, I was immediately convinced by my Presbyterian leaders that the experience was a demonic counterfeit. I eventually concluded that I had been deceived by this counterfeit experience, so I fully renounced the experience. I committed myself to resist anything charismatic. I reasoned that anything that seemed so real could easily deceive other people.

I set out to warn other "innocent" believers to beware of "counterfeit" experiences such as speaking in tongues. So for the next several years it became my personal mission to debunk charismatic theology and rescue from deception anyone who had also been led astray by such a "counterfeit" experience.

I didn't like charismatic people any more than I liked charismatic theology. The ones I had met seemed to boast of *having it all.* I felt they were proud and arrogant. In my estimation, they were lacking in many things, especially in passion for the Scriptures and personal holiness. Besides, their theology was not evangelically orthodox.

As a young Christian I was a committed student of evangelical greats, absorbing myself in the writings of J. I. Packer, John Stott, Stuart Briscoe, Jonathan Edwards, Dr. Martyn Lloyd-Jones and others. I took my zeal for evangelical orthodoxy and my crusade against supernatural gifts of the Spirit with me everywhere I ministered God's Word. I spoke at a number of college campus ministries throughout the Midwest.

ANOTHER TERRIBLE MISTAKE

In April 1976, I was invited to a small town in Missouri to give a trial sermon for a little Lutheran house church of twenty-five people who were searching for a pastor. They were interested in the renewal going on in the Lutheran church. I preached one of my favorite messages, an anti-charismatic version of the baptism of the Holy Spirit.

This was a sermon I had preached many times on college campuses. I took it straight from John Stott's little book on the baptism of the Holy Spirit. I wanted to make it clear from the beginning that I didn't want anything to do with charismatic heresies.

Though these people seemed to love the Lord, they were not aware of all the various theological arguments against tongues. They were interested in my becoming their pastor, but the doctrinal implications of my sermon went right over their heads.

At the same time I was unaware that most of them were enjoying the Lutheran renewal movement. Their reserved demeanor fooled me.

Some of the leading people in their prayer group were out of town that weekend. When they got back, they heard that the young preacher had spoken on the baptism of the Spirit. Well, that was good enough for them, and I was hired.

Those leaders who were out of town during my sermon assumed I was in agreement with their *charismatic* theology, and I assumed they had heard that my sermon was filled with *anti-charismatic* theology. I was totally unsuspecting of what would happen next.

About six months later, approximately seventy-five people were attending the new little church plant. One of the leaders, a man who had been out of town during that original baptism-in-the-Spirit sermon, pointed out to me that some of the newcomers had not yet received the baptism of the Spirit. He wanted me to extend the invitation and pray for them.

"But I do that every Sunday morning at the altar call for salvation," I explained.

"No, no," he said. "We want the tongues part."

"I don't believe in tongues," I answered. We hadn't talked much longer before I realized what had happened. It became clear that they had totally misunderstood my early arguments against charismatic doctrines. I groaned, "Oh, there's been a terrible mistake!"

A part of me wanted to run away as fast as I could. "I'm the pastor of a charismatic church!" I grimaced to myself.

I couldn't believe it. How could I have gotten myself into this mess? In retrospect, there was no doubt that God Himself got me into it. By now I really liked these people and trusted their genuineness, their humility and their love for the Scriptures and for evangelism. How could such good people be charismatics?

My experience with this church was God's way of breaking down some of my prejudices against charismatics. I now had a category of people I respected and accepted as authentic Christians, but who, in my mind, happened to be a little off theologically. Mike Bickle was now tolerating charismatics. That was OK for now since I had made plans to go to Mexico as a missionary. I thought to myself, "I can endure anything for a short season."

AMBUSHED BY GOD

I continued with the church for a few more months before I encountered the first prophetic word aimed at me, which, of course, I didn't believe in.

One evening some men from the church and I went to hear the president of the Full Gospel Businessmen's Fellowship speak at a meeting. This man called me out and said, "Young man at the back. God's going to shift you from where you are, and you are going to stand before hundreds of young people — immediately."

"Not me," I thought to myself. I had already made the arrangements to work with a missionary organization in Mexico. I thought I was saying good-bye to Western Christianity and going where the harvest was — Latin America. I had already set my heart on spending my life in Mexico and South America. I was upset at that prophetic word and said to myself, "This cannot be."

Then the man said, "Even though you say in your heart this very moment, 'This cannot be,' God will do it immediately."

People were clapping and hugging me, but I was angry and just wanted to get out of there.

The very next week I was in St. Louis with a friend, and I accidentally met the pastor of a large charismatic church in St. Louis. He looked at me and said, "I know we are strangers, but I have an unusual request for you. The Spirit of God just spoke to me and said that you're the one who's supposed to preach at our youth service where over one thousand young people gather every Saturday night." Before I could think about it, I heard myself say yes.

I was shocked and confused in my own heart that I had spontaneously agreed to preach in this radical charismatic church. I was embarrassed at myself. What would my friends think?

The Saturday night meeting went pretty well. At the end, the pastor stood up in front of the one thousand applauding young people and asked if I would come back the following week. Under the pressure of the moment, I agreed to be the speaker the next week, and the same thing happened on the following Saturday. I found myself agreeing to come several more times. They were so receptive to me that I thought I could change their theology.

The next month, on my wedding day, my elders had a private meeting with this pastor during the wedding reception and agreed that I should be the next youth pastor at this large charismatic church. Without ever consulting me, they simply made this announcement at the end of the wedding reception. I was so excited to be married to my wonderful wife, Diane, that I simply responded, "Great, I'll do anything you want!"

During my honeymoon, I realized how easily I had agreed to leave my new little church and become a youth pastor at a charismatic church — and I couldn't believe I did it. I asked myself, "How could I let this happen?" It seemed I was constantly being ambushed by God to do things I had prejudices against.

I felt a desperate need to reassert control of my life. I was now, of all things, *on the pastoral staff* of New Covenant Fellowship, a radical charismatic church in St. Louis, Missouri. How much worse could things get?

At New Covenant Fellowship I shared an office with an ex-Lutheran pastor named Tim Gustafson, who helped me process this strange, new charismatic environment. Little did either of us realize that my reluctant journey into the gifts of the Spirit had only begun.

I was still unsettled about the gift of tongues. The prophecy that I received at the Full Gospel Businessmen's Fellowship meeting saying that I would immediately stand in front of hundreds of young people had been fulfilled within two months by my becoming the youth pastor of this large church in St. Louis. However, I still didn't believe in prophecy, so I could have never imagined what would happen in the years ahead.

I chose to ignore the prophecy I had received. I thought it was a coincidence. I still had plans to go to Mexico, so I would simply be patient with this charismatic church like I was with the last one.

Little did I realize that I, a conservative evangelical, was about to get involved with spiritual gifts, particularly the gift of prophecy, on a level that seemed very unusual even to many charismatics.

In the spring of 1979, the church leadership asked me to consider turning over the youth ministry to start a new sister church which would relate to them. So, in September 1979, I became the pastor of a new church plant in South St. Louis County. The church was growing, and my wife, Diane, and I assumed that we would serve there for many years. I was beginning to give up the idea of being a missionary to Mexico. That God would have a different plan for us wasn't so strange, but the way He communicated His plan to us presented another great challenge to our faith.

THE NEXT STEP OF FAITH

In June 1982, three years after the new church was founded, I was confronted by people who claimed to have had divine encounters with God. First it was Augustine Alcala, an itinerant prophetic minister, and later Bob Jones, who joined our church and ministered among us for several years. They talked about unusual experiences which included audible voices, angelic visitations, Technicolor visions and signs in the heavens, to name a few of the more spectacular ones.

Some of these divine communiqués seemed to have major implications for the direction of my life and ministry. If God was so interested in getting my attention, I wondered why He didn't just give me my own vision, despite the fact that I didn't have much faith in the validity of such experiences. I had fully accepted the idea of God healing the sick, but I wasn't prepared for such prophetic experiences.

At first these men's claims seemed to me to be the stuff of vivid but misguided imaginations and not genuine revelations from God. But as I listened and prayed, the Holy Spirit began to confirm their genuineness. At the same time, my most trusted friends and coworkers also began believing these were true prophecies. Though all of this ran contrary to my long-term reservations about this kind of thing, I decided to take a step of faith and allow for the prophetic ministry in our church.

The Lord used prophetic words confirmed in some extraordinary ways to relocate us from St. Louis to the Kansas City area. There we began another church plant in December 1982. In 1990, we became affiliated with the Association of Vineyard Churches and are now known as Metro Vineyard Fellowship.

Since 1983, our leadership team has discovered that prophetic ministry can bring great blessing to the church. We have also come to realize that it can cause confusion and condemnation and be counter-productive to God's purposes if not administrated properly.

In our early days, David Parker, who is currently an excellent pastor of a large Vineyard church in Lancaster, California, was on our staff. He helped our church immensely by putting a sound theological framework around the prophetic ministry. He has a mature ability to embrace the ministry of the Holy Spirit in a context of responsible biblical scholarship.

There were a few people with prophetic ministries who ministered among us during the first couple of years in this new church. They no longer do so. There were various reasons for their departure. Some of these were painful but necessary confrontations that our fellowship weathered and from which we have emerged wiser and more seasoned.

Through this book we hope to share insights we have painfully but joyfully gathered. It's been a very unusual journey. I could never have imagined the dramatic unfolding of events that were to come.

CHAPTER 2

THE COMING GREAT VISITATION

I am thankful that God never intended the prophetic ministry at our church in Kansas City to become a "prophetic movement." It was referred to in that manner by people who later became opponents and critics. We saw ourselves as simply a church-planting team that contained some prophetic ministers, just as it contained pastors, teachers, evangelists and administrators. In my mind, the predominant features were to be passion for Jesus and intercession for revival.

Nevertheless, the prophetic people who wound up ministering among us seemed so extraordinary that their contributions became the notable feature, especially to those who viewed us from the outside.

The events associated with the prophetic seemed so unusual and intriguing that the message of holy passion, intercession and revival was sometimes overshadowed. Thus it was negatively tagged a "prophetic movement," and we were called "the Kansas City prophets."

Inside our local church the prophetic also gained too high a profile, but it was still not the primary emphasis of our leadership team. I was continually seeking to keep our church focused on one of our primary purposes: interceding for the great revival I believe is still to come — a revival that will see countless multitudes of new believers coming into the church; a revival that will see the church restored to the passion, purity, power and unity of the New Testament.

Prophecy is not something in which a church should major. It's one of the many tools used to build the house, but it's not the house. When you construct a building you don't call a hammer a *movement*. The hammer is just one of the many significant tools.

We first moved to Kansas City in November 1982 to start the church. Several weeks before we had our first Sunday service, we began nightly intercessory prayer meetings. We had about fifteen people, and we met from 7:00 P.M. to 10:00 P.M., seven nights a week. These prayer meetings continued every night for ten years, with exceptions for holidays like Thanksgiving and Christmas.

In October 1984, when our church was almost two years old, we added two more daily intercessory prayer meetings. We met three times each day, 6:30 A.M. to 8:30 A.M., 11:30 A.M. to 1:00 P.M. and 7:00 P.M. to 10:00 P.M. Most of these intercessory prayer meetings had between twenty and fifty people in attendance. For over six hours a day we interceded, first for revival in Kansas City and America. Then the Lord spoke to us to pray for key places like England, Germany and Israel.

From 1987 to 1989, we multiplied into six different congregations throughout the city. We sought to function as one church structure that was meeting in six places. Each congregation would take some of the responsibility for these daily prayer meetings.

In 1992, we released three of those congregations to operate as independent churches. The other two merged back into the central worship center. Today at Metro Vineyard Fellowship we still have intercessory prayer meetings three times a day on Mondays, Wednesdays and Fridays.

Throughout our church's life we have been heavily committed to intercession for a coming great visitation of God. I say all this because intercession is one of the primary purposes of the prophetic ministry in

Kansas City. Regrettably, we did an inaccurate job pastoring our people and evangelizing our community.

Today our church is based on small fellowship groups. We encourage everyone to participate in these home groups and to be involved in our regular servant evangelism projects. Consequently, we cannot maintain the same level of commitment to intercession that we did during the first ten years of our church's history. Things are more balanced now between pastoral care and evangelism; yet we need to be inspired continually by the prophetic ministry in order to maintain the intercessory prayer meetings three times a day for three days a week.

In the past, to people who were viewing our ministry from the outside, the prophetic ministry was powerful and intriguing. Consequently, it took on a certain notoriety, and our church became identified with it. But to us, the prophetic ministry — even with its astounding features and prophecies confirmed by things like comets, droughts and earthquakes — was aimed mainly at one thing: encouraging and sustaining our intercession for revival for the church. God wants the church to experience a great harvest of new souls who come to maturity in the grace of God and specifically in their passionate affection for Jesus.

Prophecy should never be an end in itself. The prophecies encouraged us to stay faithful to the daily prayer meetings and to focus on a life of loving passion for Jesus. I believe prophetic ministry is the gas that fuels the tank of intercession and purity. It's the prophetic hope that causes our prayers for a coming great visitation of God to be persistent through the many years and the diverse seasons of hardship.

THE ACTS 2 MODEL: WIND, FIRE AND WINE

I believe that Acts 2 is a divine pattern of how God visits His church in power. Many elements in this passage reveal how God started His church on the day of Pentecost. I want to highlight three of these.

First, God sent the "wind" of the Spirit, then the "fire" of the Spirit, and then the "wine" of the Spirit. The wind of the Spirit involves the release of the miraculous. I believe angels are definitely involved in this. Hebrews 1:7 relates the ministry of angels to the wind. On the day of Pentecost, those present heard the sound of a mighty rushing wind. Later in Acts 4 the building they were praying in shook.

When God sends the wind of the Spirit, we can expect to see great signs and wonders such as the sound of rushing wind and the shaking of buildings as well as extraordinary healings — raising the dead and the recovery of paralytics. A great harvest of souls will come as a result of this.

The fire of God came next in Acts 2. This baptism of fire will enlarge our hearts in the love of God. We will receive a deeper understanding of God's love, which will result in a fiery passion for Jesus and compassion for people. This new passion for God energized by the Holy Spirit will cause the atmosphere in the body of Christ to be dramatically different. The focus will be on how to love Jesus with all our hearts and strength. Included in this particular aspect of the Spirit's ministry will be anointed intercession for the lost and the beginning of new souls coming powerfully into the kingdom of God.

The wine of God is linked in the book of Joel to the outpouring of the Holy Spirit. It is God's ministry through the Spirit of bringing joy inexpressible and refreshment to weary, burdened souls.

In April 1984, an amazing thing happened to us — the Lord spoke audibly to two members of our prophetic team in Kansas City on the same morning. These two people were not together, but in separate places when each of them heard God speak. He said several things, but I will highlight only one of them now.

The Lord spoke in a thunderous voice and said, "In ten years I will *begin* to release the wine of My Spirit."

Two things immediately struck us. First, what is the wine of the Spirit? Second, how will we ever be able to wait for ten years? I was twenty-eight years old at the time, and ten years seemed like a millennium.

Now it seems obvious what the wine of the Spirit actually is. One reason that God sends His wine is to refresh and renew the hearts of His people in the midst of the weariness and despair that is common today. God is currently releasing "His wine" throughout His church in many nations.

In January 1990, the Lord spoke to about five prophetic people within the time frame of one week. He said He would strategically visit London and then Germany with the manifest presence of the Spirit. He made it clear that from London the United Kingdom would be touched, just as the Germanic speaking nations would be touched as He visited Berlin. The Spirit will touch all of Europe and all of the world in the days ahead. We have sought to encourage many to intercede for His church in those two strategic cities. Reports from both

England and Germany indicate that we are beginning to witness the initial fulfillment of these prophecies.

In Acts 2, God first sent the wind, then the fire, then the wine. As God restores the church before the second coming, I believe the order will be reversed. First, He is sending the wine of the Spirit to refresh and heal the weary church. Then He will send the fire of the Spirit to enlarge our hearts in God's love. Last, He will send the wind of the Spirit, which includes a manifestation of the ministry of angels. This demonstration of the Holy Spirit's power will bring countless numbers of new people to saving faith in Jesus Christ.

The church truly has great things ahead. However, Satan will seek to challenge us like never before.

EXEGESIS AND PROPHETIC REVELATION

For us, the whole concept of nurturing and administrating the prophetic ministry in the local church is an outgrowth of our expectation of an outpouring of the Holy Spirit as foretold in Joel 2 and cited by Peter's first sermon on the day of Pentecost.

> And it shall come to pass in the last days, says God, that I will pour out of My Spirit on all flesh (Acts 2:17a).

Concerning a last-days outpouring of the Holy Spirit, the scriptural basis and historical precedents must always precede prophetic revelation and personal, subjective experience. The strongest kind of faith comes from both understanding based on the Scriptures and discernment by the Spirit.

Many Old Testament prophecies about God's kingdom are fulfilled in two ways. First, there was a local fulfillment in Israel. Many prophecies had their fulfillment during the first coming of Christ, the outpouring of the Spirit at Pentecost or the birth of the church. But the complete fulfillment of many prophecies will only be manifested with a worldwide scope just before the second coming of Christ.

Jesus spoke of the kingdom not only as if the kingdom had come, but also as if it was still yet to come. As George E. Ladd puts it, the kingdom was both already and not yet.[1] The kingdom has come with the advent of Christ, but the complete manifestation of prophecies concerning the kingdom of God will occur at the end of the age when Jesus Christ returns again.

For example, in the next to the last verse of the Old Testament, Malachi prophesied:

> Behold, I will send you Elijah the prophet before the coming of the great and dreadful day of the Lord (Mal. 4:5).

Jesus identified John as Elijah (Matt. 11:14) and later said of him:

> Indeed, Elijah is coming first and will restore all things. But I say to you that Elijah has come already, and they did not know him but did to him whatever they wished (Matt. 17:11-12).

We see an immediate local fulfillment of "Elijah's" coming in John the Baptist's ministry in Judea. However, we also see a future fulfillment when "Elijah" will come to restore all things at the end of the age.

In the same way, the Joel 2 prophecies concerning the outpouring of the Holy Spirit are partially fulfilled in Jerusalem on the day of Pentecost. Peter quotes the prophecies and says:

> These are not drunk, as you suppose, since it is only the third hour of the day. But this is what was spoken by the prophet Joel (Acts 2:15-16).

But, just because the outpouring at Pentecost was "that which was spoken through the prophet Joel" doesn't mean that was *all* of the outpouring. The Spirit fell on 120 people in a small room in Jerusalem. That's not big enough for the complete fulfillment — even if you include the three thousand who were converted and baptized that day. The prophecy of Joel says, "I will pour out My Spirit on *all flesh* (Joel 2:28, italics added).

I am convinced that the fullness of Joel 2 is yet to be seen. The prophecy will have a worldwide scope to it where all flesh — that is, all believers not just prophets — will have dreams and see visions. The greatest and fullest manifestation of the kingdom of God — the Day of the Lord, the restoration of all things and the outpouring of the Holy Spirit — is reserved for the consummation of all things at the end of the age. I believe there will be an unprecedented revival in which all believers will experience dreams, visions and everything Joel prophesied just before the second coming of Christ.

CHANGING THE FACE OF CHRISTIANITY IN ONE GENERATION

For years I had read Jonathan Edwards, David Brainerd, Dr. Martyn Lloyd-Jones, and some of the Puritan writers, and had adopted their theology of an unprecedented ingathering of souls at the end of the age.[2]

But it was years later in a dirty little motel room in Cairo, Egypt, that the belief in a last-days outpouring of the Holy Spirit became a personal issue. At that time I wholly committed my life to be a part of it.

By September 1982 I had resigned from South County Christian Fellowship in St. Louis after having planted that church three years earlier with my dear friend Harry Schroeder. We had not planned to arrive in Kansas City until early November. So I accepted an invitation to speak at a pastor's conference in India.

Since I had one of those thirty-day, go-anywhere-you-want tickets, I spent two weeks visiting five major cities in developing nations. These included cities such as Calcutta, India; Seoul, Korea and Cairo, Egypt. I wanted to use this opportunity to see the "poor of the earth," so I went to the slum areas.

I arrived in Cairo, Egypt, in mid-September. Following the suggestions of a taxi driver, I checked into a little hotel. The eight-by-eight-foot room was equipped with a small bed, squeaky ceiling fan, stone-age plumbing and an assortment of crawling things that periodically scampered across the concrete floor. It was primitive by Western standards.

I was spending time every day interceding for my future church plant in Kansas City. That was a continual burden on my heart. I began to pray at around 8:30 that first evening. I knelt on the cement floor by the rickety bed for about thirty minutes when I had one of the most incredible encounters that I've ever had.

I didn't see a vision, and I wasn't caught up into heaven. I simply heard God speak to me. It wasn't what some people call the audible voice. I call it the internal audible voice. I heard it as clearly as I would have heard it with my physical ears and, honestly, it was terrifying.

It came with such a feeling of cleanness, power and authority. In some ways I felt I was being crushed by it. I wanted to leave, but I didn't want to leave. I wanted it to be over, but I didn't want it to be over.

I only heard a few sentences, and it took just a few moments, but every word had great meaning. The awe of God flooded my soul as I experienced a little bit of the terror of the Lord. I literally trembled and wept as God Himself communicated to me in a way I've never know before or since. The Lord simply said, "I will change the understanding and expression of Christianity in the earth in one generation." It was a simple, straightforward statement, but I felt God's power with each word as I received the Spirit's interpretation.

I understood that this reformation/revival would be His sovereign initiative. God Himself was going to make this drastic change in Christianity across the world.

The phrase "the understanding of Christianity" meant the way Christianity is perceived by unbelievers. In the early church people were afraid to associate casually with believers partly because of the displays of supernatural power. In the 1990s most unbelievers consider the church to be irrelevant.

God will change the way unbelievers view the church. They once again will witness God's wonderful yet terrifying power in the church. They will have a very different understanding of Christianity before God is finished with this generation.

The phrase "the expression of Christianity" meant the way the body of Christ expresses its life together. God is powerfully going to change the church so that it functions effectively as a healthy body in the power and love of God instead of just having meetings and programs based on its design and structure.

Paul Cain says that there are three elements of this new understanding and expression of Christianity: unparalleled power, purity and unity. Christians' relationships with God and each other, the way they are perceived by unbelievers, and even the structure and functioning of the church will be radically and suddenly changed by God Himself.

This change will take place — not in a month, a year or a few years — but in one generation. That night in Cairo I had the sense that I was being invited to be a part of this.

The understanding and expression of Christianity is going to be changed by a great outpouring of the Spirit that will cross all kinds of national, social, ethnic and cultural barriers. It won't be just a Western world revival. The Joel 2/Acts 2 prophecy says that in the last days God will pour out of His Spirit on "all flesh" (Acts 2:17).

A lot of things will begin to happen as a result of this outpouring of the Spirit. It will have so many multidimensional expressions that it cannot be called simply an evangelism movement, a healing movement a prayer movement, a unity movement or a prophetic movement. It will be all of those and more. Above all things, it will impart and renew deep, affectionate passion for Jesus through the Holy Spirit.

The Holy Spirit longs above all things to glorify Jesus in the human heart (John 16:14). He wants to impart deep holy affections for Jesus in the bride of Christ. Speaking of this outpouring only in terms of a prophetic movement is a much too limited concept.

The increase of prophetic ministry in the local church involves more than verbal, inspirational prophecy. In my understanding, it includes angelic visitations, dreams, visions and signs and wonders in the sky, as well as an increase in prophetic revelation, even the kind given through the subtle impressions of the Holy Spirit.

My experience in the Cairo hotel room only lasted about thirty to sixty minutes, though it seemed like a couple of hours. I left the room and walked around the streets of downtown Cairo alone until about midnight, committing myself to the Lord and to whatever plans He had for me. The awe of God lingered in my soul for hours. I woke up the next day still feeling its impact.

This experience connected what I believed doctrinally about the fulfillment of the Joel 2/Acts 2 prophecy of a last-days outpouring of the Spirit and to my everyday life. I believe it relates to this generation. This personal and contemporary application of an end-times, dramatic, worldwide visitation of God is without doubt based partially on *my* subjective experience. But it is also based on the Scriptures.

Both the promise of Acts 2 and this experience impacted the way we started our new church plant in Kansas City. They are what initiated our commitment to intercession for a great coming visitation of God. The nurturing and administration of the prophetic ministry is a part of that and can only operate successfully in the context of building the local church. It is not an end unto itself.

GOD'S GLORY IN THE CHURCH

Supernatural events surrounded Paul Cain's birth. I will tell of these in chapter 9. By the age of thirty, Paul Cain had a very unusual prophetic ministry. In the early 1950s, he was on television and radio, and had ministered in several meetings in which twenty to thirty thousand people attended. He purchased a tent which seated twelve thousand for his traveling ministry.

But instead of releasing him to greater ministry, the Lord impressed upon him to withdraw from ministry for a season. That season lasted over twenty-five years.

Paul struggled through those years wondering why God had set him aside in the prime of his life and, after such a supernatural beginning, seemed to have forgotten him. What encouraged and sustained Paul more than anything else during those years was a recurring vision. Paul claims that it was an open vision, like a movie screen that appeared in front of him, and that this vision happened many times.

I believe Paul Cain's recurring vision gives us insight into aspects of the great end-times revival that will be the complete worldwide fulfillment of the Joel 2/Acts 2 prophecy.

In this vision, Paul saw large stadiums filled with people in cities all over the world. Great signs and wonders were taking place, and countless multitudes were being saved as God's glory was being manifest in His church.

In the last days, as in the first century, the increase of the prophetic ministry will not simply be a movement unto itself. It is only one of the aspects of a greater and more far-reaching outpouring of the Holy Spirit on all flesh.

One of the unique things about the last great revival will be the signs and wonders described in Acts 2:19 that will be displayed in nature, both on the earth and in the sky. I was awestruck by the personal visitation of God that I experienced in Cairo. I was surprised by the way God introduced me to the prophetic ministry. But the Lord was getting ready to completely overwhelm me by confirming prophetic words through the acts of God in nature.

CHAPTER 3

CONFIRMING PROPHECIES THROUGH THE ACTS OF GOD IN NATURE

The confirmation of prophetic words by the acts of God in nature is not a common topic in the church. But undoubtedly at the end of this age, signs in the heavens as well as the very forces of nature on earth will serve as a dramatic testimony both to the church and to unbelievers.

In Kansas City, we have seen these kinds of things happen only a few times, and we know of a few other instances. It is, however, our suspicion that the church in other parts of the world might be experiencing more of this than the Western church is.

When a balanced prophetic ministry flourishes, it is often followed by some form of signs and wonders. In his Pentecost sermon, Peter quoted the Joel 2 promise for a last-days revival. Of course, the last days began with the cross, the resurrection and the baptism of the Holy Spirit on the day of Pentecost.

The greatest fulfillment of the Joel 2 promise will be in the final years of the last days — those few years just prior to the second coming of Jesus Christ. This time period is commonly referred to as the "end times."

The first half of the passage in Acts 2 speaks of the outpouring of the Spirit and the increase of prophetic revelation on the entire body of Christ:

> And it shall come to pass in the last days, says God,
> That I will pour out of My Spirit on all flesh;
> Your sons and your daughters shall prophesy;
> Your young men shall see visions,
> Your old men shall dream dreams.
> And on My menservants and on My maidservants
> I will pour out My Spirit in those days;
> And they shall prophesy (Acts 2:17-18).

The second half of the passage is dedicated to the great increase of the acts of God in nature.

> I will show wonders in heaven above
> And signs in the earth beneath:
> Blood and fire and vapor of smoke.
> The sun shall be turned into darkness,
> And the moon into blood,
> Before the coming of the great
>   and awesome day of the Lord.
> And it shall come to pass
> That whoever calls on the name of the Lord
> Shall be saved (vv. 19-21).

There is a divine order and sequence in the text: the outpouring of the Spirit, followed by the increase of prophetic dreams and visions, followed by the occurring of confirming signs in the sky and on the earth. So the fact that we have witnessed a few of these kinds of supernatural confirmations in nature is related to the increase of the prophetic ministry.

We believe that what we have seen is only a small token of what

34

will happen in even more dramatic ways in many churches throughout the nations. The last days will be accompanied by a multiplication of all four elements of the Joel 2 prophecy: 1) the outpouring of the Spirit; 2) prophetic dreams and visions; 3) signs and wonders on earth and in the heavens and 4) a wholehearted turning to Jesus — first for salvation and then with extravagant love for Him and 100 percent obedience. This wholehearted calling on the name of the Lord is not only for unbelievers, but it includes the church growing in holy passion for Jesus.

This chapter is intended to encourage you about the future. In the end times, there will be awesome displays of prophetic visions and dreams with confirming signs and wonders in nature. These prophetic events will not take place simply within the confines of a few *prophetic-type* churches but before the eyes of all mankind, believers and unbelievers alike.

As we have worked through the meaning of our own prophetic experiences, we have concluded that there are perhaps several reasons the Lord gives confirmations of prophecies by supernatural acts of God in nature. People can get carried away when things like this happen. We have painfully learned that the church needs to deal with such displays of power and revelation in a careful way. The body of Christ, in the process of nurturing and administrating this increasing prophetic ministry, will be faced more and more with prophecies that are confirmed by an act of God in nature. Consequently, a second aim of this chapter is to comment on what we have learned in the process.

THE UNEXPECTED SNOWFALL

A traveling prophetic minister had given a prophetic word to me in St. Louis regarding the new church plant in South Kansas City before I moved there. In it, he warned of a false prophet who would be present in the early days of our new church.

In March 1983, not long after our arrival in Kansas City, a strange-looking fellow came into my office and introduced himself to me. I was at first skeptical about Bob Jones and thought that he was the false prophet I had been warned about. Ironically, at this first meeting, Bob Jones confirmed this prophecy by also warning me of a false prophet who would be in the midst of our new church plant. I wondered to myself, "Could Bob Jones be a false prophet himself and still give a warning about a false prophet?" This thought was enough to keep me in turmoil for several days!

I met with the pastor of the church Bob had previously attended for several years. This pastor told me that Bob was a godly man and a proven prophet with much good fruit. He also told me that Bob had prophesied in the spring of 1982 that a group of young people were going to come to the south side of Kansas City by the spring of 1983 and that they would be used in intercession for revival. Therefore, the pastor blessed Bob's decision to join our new church of young people.

When Bob Jones walked into my office on March 7, 1983, he was wearing a winter coat. This was strange because the snow was long gone, and the temperature was in the seventies in Kansas City the day we met.

In this first meeting, Bob prophesied that God was going to raise up a prophetic church in Kansas City and that he would be used in its foundation. During this meeting, he claimed that the Lord would confirm this prophecy with a sign in nature. He told me that on the first day of spring, a sudden snow would come, and at that time he would sit around a table with the leaders of our new church, and we would accept him.

I didn't take the prophecy seriously since I was sure Bob was the false prophet I had been warned about. I dismissed the matter, thinking that anyone who prophesied his own acceptance had to be a false prophet. But I still thought it was strange to see a man wearing a heavy winter coat during such warm weather.

Several weeks later, a friend named Art came to visit for a weekend. At the end of the Sunday morning service, I looked up and saw Bob Jones talking with Art. I fully expected Art to come over and inform me that I had a crazy man in the church. Instead, Art came back saying, "Mike, this man seems like a prophet of God. He told me the secrets of my heart!"

Art had intended to fly out Sunday after the church service, but his small private plane was grounded due to bad weather. About 9:00 P.M. that night, Art suddenly insisted on seeing Bob again.

We all gathered at my house from 10:00 P.M. until 3:00 A.M. It was an incredible evening. I was overwhelmed at some of the things God revealed to Bob about private issues and personal prayers in my life. I suddenly blurted out, "Bob, I'm thankful that Art insisted on our meeting tonight. I really believe that you are truly prophetic."

Bob smiled as he reminded me that he already knew we would accept him on the first day of spring, just as he had prophesied the first day we met.

It was a true prophecy. I suddenly realized that it was March 21, the first day of spring. Art had been delayed by the sudden snow. We were all sitting around the table fellowshipping, and I had just accepted Bob Jones with my own mouth. All of it happened just as Bob had said the Lord told him it would.

The unexpected snow on March 21 was precisely predicted by Bob to confirm the prophetic vision that God was raising up a prophetic church in Kansas City and that Bob Jones would be used in its foundation. The small but significant sign in the sky (heavens) was the prediction of a snow that would suddenly come exactly on March 21, the first day of spring. Now it had happened: This snow had surprised Kansas City after several weeks of unseasonably warm weather.[1]

THE UNEXPECTED COMET

A month had passed. I was a bit bewildered by the snow incident. We had continued to meet every night since November 1982, from 7:00 P.M. to 10:00 P.M. to pray for revival in Kansas City and across America. Then, on Wednesday evening, April 13, 1983, I had another unusual experience with God. For the second time I heard the internal audible voice of God saying something with unmistakable clarity.

God told me to call the church to a solemn assembly of fasting and prayer for twenty-one days. The story of the angel Gabriel (Daniel 9 –10) coming to help against the demonic Prince of Persia was deeply impressed upon my mind. I also felt that the Lord said that people from all over the city would join with me in twenty-one days of prayer and fasting for revival in our nation.

I had some serious reservations about this. How was I, a new young pastor in the area, going to call the city to prayer and fasting? Who would listen to me? The other pastors would think I was full of pride to presume such a thing!

My wife, Diane, wasn't very encouraging either. She was perplexed at the idea of announcing to the inhabitants of a city that they would be invited to twenty-one days of prayer and fasting for revival. She reminded me that I had no credibility in the city. We had lived in Kansas City for only six months.

Nevertheless, I was a little surprised at the resolve I felt in my own spirit. I was new at receiving these kinds of words from the Lord, and I was a little perplexed. So the next morning, I decided to call Bob Jones. Remember, at that time, I had believed he was a genuine prophet for about one month.

Over the telephone I explained, "Bob, I've received what I think is a word from the Lord, but it's pretty unusual. I guess I believe in prophets now, and I really need a prophet to confirm what I heard last night. Can you help?"

In his calm drawl Bob replied, "Yeah, I know all about it. God already told me what He told you last night."

This seemed a little bizarre to me, but strange and unusual things were becoming more common. How could Bob Jones know what God had spoken to me? I asked a couple of my friends to come along as witnesses, and we drove to Bob's house. On the way, I explained to them that God literally told me to call part of the church in Kansas City to twenty-one days of fasting and prayer. The passage I had received was Daniel 9, in which Gabriel spoke to Daniel about the visitation of God.

I arrived at Bob's house very anxious to see if he had received the same message from God that I had. If I ever needed a true prophetic word to confirm something, it was now. I put Bob to the test. I asked him to tell me what God had revealed to me the night before. With a big smile on his face, he told me with great accuracy what God had spoken to me. My friends and I sat there in awe. Then he proceeded to explain several other things that God had showed him.

Bob said that he literally saw the angel Gabriel in a dream early that morning. He also prophesied that God had already given me Daniel 9 and that God was calling us to pray for the visitation of God for our city and our nation. He told us that there would be an unpredicted comet in the sky (heavens) which would confirm that God was truly calling this solemn time of prayer and fasting. Bob also said that God was going to send revival to Kansas City and the entire nation just as He had told me.

We were astonished! I knew there was no way he could have known about the Daniel 9 scripture that I had received the night before. And the comet — that certainly would be beyond human knowledge. I thought, "I wonder where this new prophetic journey is going to lead. I will just have to wait and see."

38

Three weeks later, on May 7, 1983, the day our prayer and fasting began, the newspaper reported:

> Scientists will have a rare chance next week to study a recently discovered comet that is coming within the "extremely" close range of 3 million miles...Dr. Gerry Neugebauer, principal U.S. investigator on the international Infrared Astronomical Satellite Project (IRAS) said, "...It was sheer good luck we happened to be looking where the comet was passing."[2]

God gave a prophetic revelation that we were to pray and fast for twenty-one days with the expectancy of revival in His timing, and then He sent a confirmation of the revelation with a natural sign in the heavens: an unexpected comet sighting on the day that we were to begin the fast. The prophecy by Bob Jones about the comet was reported by the newspaper on the exact day that the fast began.

SIGNS IN THE EARTH BENEATH

Paul Cain, a seasoned prophetic minister, was introduced to John Wimber, leader of the Association of Vineyard Churches, on December 5, 1988, at John's home in Anaheim, California. A week or two before Paul's scheduled arrival, Dr. Jack Deere, who was at that time an associate pastor with John Wimber in Anaheim, asked Paul if God would grant a prophetic sign to confirm His message for John Wimber and the several hundred Vineyard churches under John's leadership.

Paul answered, "The day I arrive, there will be an earthquake in your area." That, however, is not an astounding prediction for southern California.

Jack asked, "Will this be the big one we've all been hearing about?"

"No," Paul answered, "but there will be a big earthquake elsewhere in the world on the day after I leave."

The prophetic word Paul had received for John was Jeremiah 33:8, which says, "I will cleanse them from all the sin they have committed against Me and will forgive all their sins of rebellion against Me" (NIV). Paul brought reassuring words to the Vineyard church movement that God was still with them and that the word of the Lord was "Grace, grace, grace."

At 3:38 A.M. on December 3, the day Paul arrived, there was an earthquake in Pasadena, which is in the Anaheim area. Occasionally the Lord will use the timing (3:38 A.M.) of an event as an added emphasis to the prophetic message (Jer. 33:8). I believe that this was more than a coincidence.

Paul left Anaheim on December 7, 1988. Another confirming sign from the Lord occurred the day *after* he left. There was a massive earthquake in Soviet Armenia on December 8, 1988, just as Paul had prophesied. There was no way that the fulfillment of such a sign in the earth could be brought to pass by human effort. [3]

John Wimber admitted that previously he had always taken the possibility of prophecy seriously. Many of the major events in the development of the Association of Vineyard Churches were prophesied in advance. But Paul Cain represented a new dimension of the prophetic ministry that they had never encountered before. Concerning the effects that these earthquakes had on John, he writes, "He [Paul Cain] had my full attention!"[4]

The Lord showed Paul that God would give mercy to the Vineyard as described in Jeremiah 33:8. God gives mercy and grace to enable us to walk in a more mature level of purity and holiness.

The prophetic symbolism seemed clear — God was speaking to the Vineyard churches through these events that He was going to shake the Anaheim Vineyard over the next season by prophetic ministry like the local earthquake shook Pasadena. The prophetic shaking would not merely be local, but would eventually cause a shaking internationally. This was pictured by the internationally known earthquake in Soviet Armenia.

This sign in the earth (the earthquake) was symbolic of the shaking that the Vineyard would experience as God renewed His mercy to them during the season that followed.

CONVINCING POWER, IRREFUTABLE TRUTH

Signs and wonders in nature are not to be taken lightly because they are not given for trivial reasons. Don't expect God to show a sign in the heavens concerning which car you are supposed to buy.

Fire fell from heaven and consumed Elijah's sacrifice, the Red Sea parted, and a star led the wise men to Bethlehem. These were not insignificant events in the progress of God's plan and purpose.

The comet was *not* to verify something that related only to us. It was bigger than that. Our understanding is that it was to confirm to us God's plans eventually to visit our nation with full-scale revival.

We deeply appreciate the fact that God has used many different ministries over the years to prophesy and to intercede concerning the coming revival in America. No one group or denomination is more significant to God than the others. He does not move stars or part the seas to show off for curious inquirers. The magnitude of His manifest power is usually proportional to the significance of His purpose.

God's power displayed by signs and wonders in nature in the last days will be unprecedented because it will serve to confirm and signify one of the greatest events of all time — the last ingathering of souls and the second coming of Jesus Christ. The purpose of the outpouring of the Spirit, the increase of the prophetic ministry and, finally, the signs and wonders in nature is to awaken the church to passionate Christianity and to bring people to salvation. The Joel 2 prophecy quoted by Peter in his first sermon makes this point with these words:

> And it shall come to pass that whoever calls on the name of the Lord shall be saved (Acts 2:21).

This applies to believers calling on the name of Jesus with great passion and to unbelievers calling on His name for salvation.

All of this will be a great benefit to mature the church, as well as a dramatic display of power to touch the lost, for the last great harvesting of souls. It will be an extravagant outpouring of His mercy and power.

Convincing power and irrefutable truth marked the spread of the gospel in the first century. The presence and power of the Spirit provided undeniable evidence of the truth the apostles proclaimed. An important element of the gospel message in those days was that the apostles were eyewitnesses to the fact that Jesus was risen from the dead. Firsthand eyewitness verification of this essential truth was of highest importance in the initial preaching of the gospel.

When the apostles assembled to choose a man to replace Judas, the stipulation was that he needed to have been with them from the beginning so, as Peter said, he could "become a witness with us of the resurrection" (Acts 1:22).

One fundamental job of the twelve apostles was to provide eyewitness verification to all that Jesus said and did. Whenever the preaching of the gospel is recorded in Acts, you find words similar to this: "and we are witnesses of these things" (see Acts 3:15; 5:32; 10:39; 13:31).

The church's message in the end times will not only be that Christ is risen from the dead, but that His return is imminent. Throughout history there have been great revivals in which the power and presence of the Holy Spirit seemed almost irresistible to some unbelievers.

But the ingathering of souls in the end times will be the greatest harvest of all time because the presence and power of the Holy Spirit will be accompanied by signs in the heavens and on the earth that will dramatically confirm the message of the gospel. This will be in a way that is similar to the apostles' eyewitness verification. Just as in the early days of the church, the gospel in the last days of the church will be preached with convincing power *and* irrefutable truth.

The Revelation of John is filled with passages that allude to the fact that in the last days, there will be signs in the heavens and on the earth given for the purpose of announcing both the return of Christ and the ingathering of new souls for the great harvest. Compare the events that occur when the Lamb opens the sixth seal to the signs and wonders prophesied in the Joel 2 prophecy (signs in the earth beneath, the darkened sun and the moon turned to blood):

> I looked when He opened the sixth seal, and behold, there was a great earthquake; and the sun became black as sackcloth of hair, and the moon became like blood. And the stars of heaven fell to the earth, as a fig tree drops its late figs when it is shaken by a mighty wind. Then the sky receded as a scroll when it is rolled up, and every mountain and island was moved out of its place (Rev. 6:12-14).

In Revelation 11, John records seeing two witnesses and says of them:

> And I will give power to my two witnesses, and they will prophesy one thousand two hundred and sixty days in sackcloth (Rev. 6:3).
>
> These have power to shut heaven, so that no rain falls in the days of their prophecy; and they have power over waters

to turn them to blood, and to strike the earth with plagues, as often as the desire (v. 6).

In Revelation 14 John sees one like the Son of man with a sharp sickle in his hand. An angel comes out of heaven and says to Him with a loud voice:

"Thrust in Your sickle and reap, for the time has come for You to reap, for the harvest of the earth is ripe." So He who sat on the cloud thrust in His sickle on the earth, and the earth was reaped (Rev. 14:15a-16).

It is difficult to know the exact interpretation of each of these passages, but it seems clear that the combination of signs in nature, the increase of prophetic ministry and the great ingathering of souls is spoken of not only by Peter in Acts 2 but by John in Revelation as well. In the Olivet discourse (Matt. 24-25), Jesus also uses the same language to describe the events immediately preceding His second coming.

Immediately after the tribulation of those days the sun will be darkened, and the moon will not give its light; the stars will fall from the heaven, and the powers of the heavens will be shaken. Then the sign of the Son of Man will appear in heaven, and then all the tribes of the earth will mourn, and they will see the Son of Man coming on the clouds of heaven with power and great glory (Matt. 24:29-30).

As we approach the end times, there will be a great increase of the prophecies confirmed by the acts of God in nature. The greatest prophecy and the greatest sign that will ever be seen in the heavens is the last one — the actual appearing of Jesus Christ.

IT SHALL NOT RAIN

On May 28, 1983, the last day of the twenty-one days of prayer and fasting, Bob Jones stood up in a group of about five hundred people and gave a dramatic prophetic word. He said that there would be a drought over Kansas City for three months during that summer. Indeed, a drought did occur from the end of June to the end of

September that year. He went on to say that it would rain, however, precisely on August 23. He said this was to be a prophetic sign to us that we should not grow weary in waiting for the precise timing of the spiritual drought over the nation to end.

Just as the natural drought over Kansas City was to be divinely interrupted on a predetermined day, the spiritual drought would also be divinely interrupted precisely at the appointed time. Consequently, our fasting and prayer, along with the intercession of many others across the nation, was not in vain. God wanted us to understand that there was a precise divine timing of the coming release of the Holy Spirit on the church in America and that this revival was strategically in His hands.

Although prophesying that involves the withholding of rain is unusual, it is certainly not without biblical precedent. Elijah prophesied to King Ahab:

> As the Lord God of Israel lives, before whom I stand, there shall not be dew nor rain these years, except at my word (1 Kin. 17:1).

Luke also records a similar event in the early church:

> And in these days prophets came from Jerusalem to Antioch. Then one of them, named Agabus, stood up and showed by the Spirit that there was going to be a great famine throughout all the world, which also happened in the days of Claudius Caesar (Acts 11:27-28).

Apparently, these prophetic ministers continued as a regular part of the leadership team in Antioch. Luke describes the young prophetic church in Antioch this way:

> Now in the church that was at Antioch there were certain prophets and teachers (13:1).

Though the drought in Kansas City did not begin immediately (there was rain in the month of June), by the end of June the heavens closed. For the month of July and for the first three weeks of August there was almost no rain. By that time I had become an expert weather watcher, and I knew that on August 23 there was no prediction for rain.

Much of the credibility of the prophetic ministry was on the line. I doubt if anyone was as tense as I was. Nevertheless, this thing wasn't my idea.

I called a friend in our church, Steve Lambert, at high noon. I said that it didn't look much like rain. Steve laughingly replied, "You better hope it rains, or you'll have to leave town." I couldn't see what was so funny.

Our church was scheduled to gather for a meeting the evening of August 23. Just before the church meeting began, there came a tremendous downpour of rain for almost an hour. Everyone was shouting and praising God. The drought continued the next day and lasted another five weeks — three months in all, as prophesied, with the exception of August 23. It was the third driest summer on record for Kansas City in approximately one hundred years.

While the unprecedented display of signs and wonders in the end times will be, in effect, the last and best invitation to the lost, the irrefutable confirmation of prophetic truth will also be a great source of encouragement to the church. It will enflame our fervency and passion for Jesus, strengthen our perseverance and enable us not to lose heart in the time of waiting or even suffering.

Because of this dramatic and unusual confirmation, we were greatly encouraged to continue to pray for the revival in Kansas City and in America and not to grow weary as we are waiting for our prayers to be answered. As I mentioned earlier, the Lord also specifically spoke to our team about interceding for revival in the United Kingdom, Germany and Israel. The confirmation of the prophetic word by acts of God in nature has strengthened our faith to believe that just as the rain came precisely on the day predicted, the spiritual rain will come precisely at the divinely appointed time.

PROPHETIC REVELATION AND SUFFERING

One principle to note is the connection between the abundance of revelation and a higher degree of suffering or testing. According to Paul, his thorn in the flesh was given to keep him from exalting himself in light of the abundance of revelation that he had received (2 Cor. 12:7). The thorn was given *because of* revelation.

On the other hand, it seems that God gives powerful revelation *because of* the testings that some are about to encounter. Paul received a prophetic vision instructing him to take his missionary efforts into

Macedonia rather than Bithynia. That decision resulted in Paul and Silas being arrested, dragged before the magistrate, severely beaten with rods, thrown into the inner prison and secured in stocks.

The clarity of their initial supernatural directions to go to Macedonia must have reassured them that God was still with them in the midst of their trial (Acts 16:6-24).

This revelation-before-tribulation principle is repeated many times in the Scriptures: the miracles of the Exodus before the wilderness testing, Joseph's dreams before being sold into slavery, David's supernatural military victories along with the prophet Samuel's words before the wilderness temptations and so on. Though the thorn can come because of revelation, so also revelation can come to prepare us for the future testings. A powerful prophetic revelation with undeniable confirmations stabilizes people in a time of severe testing.

In the end times, the awesome signs and wonders in the heavens will be much greater than these early experiences of the sudden snow, the comet, the earthquake and the rain storm. How greatly will the saints who are awaiting the physical and visible return of Jesus Christ be encouraged by the undeniable confirmations of His coming!

LEARNING LESSONS THE HARD WAY

Our church unfortunately got somewhat out of balance on this. Many stood in amazement at these natural confirmations — the comet, the earthquake and the drought.

However, some people became spiritually unbalanced in that they idolized some of the prophetic ministers like Paul Cain and Bob Jones. Paul didn't ever live in Kansas City, but his reputation was bigger than life because of what happened when he regularly visited.

The lack of balance in this area caused us to go through some painful but necessary correction. The Lord is jealous for His people and for their affections. He will not allow us to make weak and fallible leaders the source and focus of His work.

Some people may respond to this admission of our mistakes by saying, "Aha! That's the reason we shouldn't get involved in the prophetic. It will only get us off balance and our eyes off Jesus." I have had that argument with myself more than once, and these are my conclusions.

First, I reminded God that involvement in prophetic ministry was never my idea. What happened to us was a divine ambush. We could only say, "God, You got us into this!" It was obviously a sovereign orchestration of events.

We would have had to reject the Lord in order to lead the church in such a way that nothing unusual, risky, prophetic or supernatural was ever welcomed or accepted. Yes, there would have been less chance of people getting carried away, but the Lord would have been grieved.

I could have, perhaps, sought to minimize the ministry of the Holy Spirit so that people wouldn't become too excited or emotional. However, a church that resists the prophetic dynamic can easily get into a spiritual rut. God ordained that the church needs the input of the prophetic to stay properly encouraged so as to minimize the unbelief and boredom that plagues so much of the church today.

Second, I am convinced that the outpouring of the Spirit, the prophetic ministry and the signs and wonders in nature are clearly a part of God's agenda for the end times. Whether we like it or not, what we have experienced is only a drop in the bucket compared to the magnitude and the frequency of what is coming. This will become more obvious to the church as the Lord's return draws closer.

Third, one of the most important reasons for embracing the prophetic is simply that the Scripture teaches us to "pursue love, and desire spiritual gifts, but especially that you may prophesy" (1 Cor. 14:1); "Therefore, brethren, desire earnestly to prophesy" (1 Cor. 14:39); and "Do not despise prophecies" (1 Thess. 5:20). It is easy to despise prophecies, and we are commanded by God not to allow such a mind-set to dominate our church life.

LEARNING FROM MISTAKES

Because we believe that what we have experienced is only a small token of what the whole church will experience in abundance, it is worth sharing some of the insights we so awkwardly stumbled into. We have learned a few simple lessons about prophecies confirmed by signs and wonders of nature.

1. Do not assume that such dramatic events mean that your church will be the center for God's purpose and plan for your area.

That sounds simple, but throughout history people who have witnessed displays of God's power have concluded that their group was the focus of God's plan for their generation. At Jesus' birth, the shepherds saw the angels sing in the sky and the magi witnessed the moving star, but probably neither group was present to participate in the day of Pentecost thirty-three years later.

God is committed to using the whole church in unity in each area. Although we never bought into the idea that we were the only ones God would use, we definitely fell into spiritual pride and became intoxicated by the "heady wine" of this kind of revelatory experience.

The prophetic confirmations in nature we witnessed were related to prophetic words concerning what God is going to do beyond the boundaries of Kansas City. We were allowed to witness the prophetic signs in order to strengthen and encourage our call to intercession for revival.

2. Do not put undue emphasis on the prophetic vessels God uses.

We gave too much attention to people like Paul Cain and Bob Jones. Some assumed that because they were so dramatically used that they certainly must be right in everything they said and did. The Lord lovingly chastised us because He is jealous for His Son to be the central focus.

By the way, Paul and Bob are very different from one another and have rarely spent time together. I have spent a lot of time with each of them, but they never connected relationally with each other in a significant way. Their personalities and ministry styles are quite different from each other. They relate to us differently and even believe differently on various subjects.

3. On some occasions unusual revelation combined with extraordinary confirmation can be used to validate certain prophetic ministers.

Such was the case with Bob Jones and the sudden snow in the spring of 1983. We feel that this was God's way of preparing us for some specific thing God wants to speak to us through Bob Jones. Even if this does happen, the church needs to proceed carefully. Confirmation of a man as a valid prophetic person is not a universal endorsement of all he says and does.

48

Occasionally, the Lord may give directions to a church that would be difficult to act on without a strong prophetic confirmation. One such event is recorded by Eusebius, the third century church historian. According to Eusebius, the entire body of believers in the city of Jerusalem picked up and left the city because of a prophetic revelation, and, consequently, their lives were spared.

> The whole body, however, of the church at Jerusalem, having been commanded by a divine revelation, given to men of approved piety there before the war, removed from the city, and dwelt at a certain town beyond the Jordan, called Pella.[5]

Immediately after their departure Jerusalem was put under siege by Titus, the Roman general, and was destroyed in A.D. 70.

Surely God established the credibility of these prophetic messengers in the eyes of the church before the coming crisis. I don't know how He confirmed the prophetic message that they quickly leave Jerusalem before Titus destroyed the city in A.D. 70. I do know people aren't easily persuaded to leave their city and houses. So it must have been a strong enough confirmation to be believed.

I believe that there is a quality of prophetic ministry emerging in the body of Christ in our day that will achieve a similar kind of credibility in the eyes of both the church and, to a degree, even secular leaders and society. Many may scoff at this idea, but someday God might use prophetic ministry to actually save them from disaster!

The earthquake, the snowfall, the comet and the rainstorm were natural phenomena that we interpreted as prophetic confirmations because they were predicted to the precise day in relation to a prophetic vision. Some think that these events happened coincidentally.

The point of this chapter is not to provide lengthy data to prove the validity of these events in our experience. Rather, I want to highlight two things: in the end times there will be undeniable prophetic signs in the heavens and on the earth, and the magnitude and the frequency of these future events will far outweigh anything that has ever been seen before.

I encourage you to think through what the Bible says about these prophetic signs in the last days. What exciting times lie ahead for the body of Christ!

CHAPTER 4

FALSE EQUATIONS ABOUT
PROPHETIC GIFTINGS

It's too bad, Richard," I replied. "I'm sorry you feel that way." My friend Richard is a dedicated and godly Nazarene pastor with an earned seminary degree. We pretty much are in agreement now, but at first he was absolutely shocked and offended at the idea that prophetic persons may be incorrect in some of their doctrines.

Richard used an easy but inaccurate equation to judge spiritual gifts. He thought that a man with a history of accurate prophesies also must be uniquely godly and biblically sound on most areas of doctrine. I disagreed with him.

He had no experience with prophetic people, yet he had his theories clearly worked out. I had much experience with prophetic people and was receiving an ongoing education with regard to most of my old

50

theories. Yes, prophetic people must be clear about major doctrines like the person and work of Christ and the place of the Scriptures. But on lesser points of doctrine, they might be misinformed.

One of the most surprising and enlightening things I share with conservative evangelical pastors is that there are people with valid gifts of the Spirit who are themselves still carnal. This challenges a commonly held idea that it is greater truth, wisdom and character that produce greater power.

Many think that only godly, mature people are used by God in demonstrations of power, but there are many exceptions. What is often surprising to both charismatic and non-charismatic pastors is that people can express valid gifts of the Spirit, yet have some pretty significant hang-ups and unresolved issues in their lives.

Many leaders have assumed that if there is a definite flaw in a person's doctrine, wisdom or character, then that is proof positive that the gifts and power in their ministries must not really be from God after all.

Another false assumption comes from the way some look at Paul's first letter to the Corinthians. Since in that letter we find a lot of instruction about carnality, as well as the majority of Paul's instruction about spiritual gifts, they assume carnality must be the cause of the emphasis on spiritual gifts, or vice versa — spiritual gifts must have caused the carnality. There are a couple of things wrong with that conclusion.

First of all, it is based on a faulty equation. Spiritual gifts are not always proven invalid by carnality. There is no suggestion in 1 Corinthians that the gifts being misused made them invalid. Notwithstanding the Corinthians' abuse of certain gifts, Paul continued to adamantly exhort them, "Pursue love, and desire spiritual gifts, but especially that you may prophesy" (1 Cor. 14:1).

Second, the suggestion has been made that since Corinth was the only church to whom Paul wrote at length concerning spiritual gifts, the gifts must not have been present in the other Pauline churches. The nature of the New Testament is such that you must be very careful how you mount an argument from silence, such as saying that Pauline churches didn't know about spiritual gifts since Paul did not mention them in the letter he wrote to those churches. Most of us understand that Paul's letters were written to address matters at hand and were not constructed as a catechism.

The thing I conclude from his silence about spiritual gifts in some of his other letters is that he obviously felt they were already being used correctly. There was probably no need for additional instruction or correction on the subject of spiritual gifts in these other churches.

Since Paul didn't mention the Lord's table in many of his letters, it might likewise be argued that none of the other Pauline churches knew about communion or practiced it. First Corinthians is the only letter in which Paul mentions holy communion, yet it was undoubtedly practiced regularly in all the churches if not at most meetings.

Abuses did not disqualify either the practice of the Lord's table or the practice of spiritual gifts. First Corinthians teaches us that valid gifts are not always a function of mature, wise and 100 percent doctrinally correct people.

GIFTS OF GRACE

The word used in the New Testament for spiritual gifts is *charisma* or literally, "gifts of grace." In other words, these gifts are given freely and are not earned.

It was Simon the sorcerer who misunderstood the gifts and power of the Holy Spirit, thinking they could be purchased (Acts 8:18-24). What a terrible thing, we think. No doubt Simon had a wrong equation, and Peter severely rebuked him because of the wickedness in his heart that would allow him even to consider buying the power of God. But there's not much difference between earning gifts and buying them. Money is only a function of effort and labor.

Contrary to some commonly held equations, the gifts and power of God are distributed at the will of the Holy Spirit.

> But one and the same Spirit works all these things, distributing to each one individually as He wills (1 Cor. 12:11).

They are not given as a token or a badge of God's approval of a person's level of spiritual maturity. Neither are they earned by our consecration. They are grace gifts.

Paul wrote to the Galatians who had difficulties understanding grace and who kept putting law and works back into their equation:

> O foolish Galatians! Who has bewitched you...? This only I want to learn from you: Did you receive the Spirit by the

works of the law, or by the hearing of faith? Are you so foolish? Having begun in the Spirit, are you now being made perfect by the flesh? (Gal. 3:1-3).

Apparently, the Galatians had experienced a filling of the Holy Spirit, and with it, certain manifestations of spiritual gifts. Paul reminded them that just as being spiritually gifted is by grace, so justification is by grace. You can turn that idea around as well. Just as we are saved by grace, not by works of merit, we receive the gifts of the Spirit by grace, not works.

The lame man who begged for alms was commanded by Peter and John to walk in the name of Jesus. When Peter saw how amazed the people were about the healing, he said:

Men of Israel, why do you marvel at this? Or why look so intently at us, as though by our own power or godliness we had made this man walk? (Acts 3:12).

Peter wanted to make that point clearly and quickly before there were any false assumptions. The manifestation of God's power was not a sign of his personal godliness. He went on to say:

And on the basis of faith in His name, it is the name of Jesus which has strengthened this man whom you see and know; and the faith which comes through Him has given him this perfect health in the presence of you all (Acts 3:16, NAS).

The healing was the result of God's purpose in His timing by means of faith in Jesus' name, a faith that comes through Him. That passage contains many implications. But if it says anything, it is that the miracle was not about Peter or about promoting his spirituality. It had to do with God and His purposes.

BECOMING THE GIFT

Paul writes to the Ephesians, "But to each one of us grace was given according to the measure of Christ's gift" (4:7). What Paul says in the following verse makes it clear that the *gift* he was referring to is a *ministry gift*:

> And He Himself gave some to be apostles, some prophets, some evangelists, and some pastors and teachers (v. 11).

We can't help but notice the misconception about the anointed people referred to in this passage. We commonly assume that people are given the gift of being a prophet, pastor or evangelist.

Paul saw it differently. "He gave some *to be* apostles...prophets...evangelists...pastors...teachers." Clearly, the minister *was the gift* to the church. It was not an issue of the anointed gift being for the benefit of the minister.

That really changes the way we look at it. God's giftings are not about our promotions and esteem. God's gifts are distributed to people who become vessels and conduits of His mercy for the benefit of others.

The gifts of God in a person's life are not merit badges signifying that person's consecration, wisdom or 100 percent doctrinal truth. You might interpret the meaning of Ephesians 4:7 like this: Out of unmerited grace, each person is given gifts for the purpose of being used to bless others.

Gifts of the Holy Spirit, whether they are in the form of manifestations of power and revelation or in the form of people given as ministers, are for the purpose of blessing the church. Yet, most of us can hardly avoid the temptation of seeing supernatural power gifts working through an individual as a symbol of God's approval of that person's life, spiritual maturity and doctrine. The more significant the giftings and power, the more approval from God — or so it would seem.

If we understood that the manifestations of the Spirit are for the common good and not for the good of the individual whom God uses, we would be less likely to stumble over the idea that God uses imperfect, often immature people to bless the church.

By Grace Through Faith Alone

I am not suggesting an antinomian (lawless) approach to the use of spiritual gifts any more than those who preach salvation and justification by faith alone suggest living a lawless life falsely dependent on grace as an easy way out. I'm desirous of strengthening our conviction to examine all things carefully even if they are from a famous prophetic vessel who is powerfully anointed.

In his rebuke to the Galatians, Paul used the idea of receiving the

54

gifts of the Spirit by faith and not works as analogous to receiving justification by faith and not works (Gal. 3:1-5). In my mind there is a great difference between immature, unwise and even carnal servants and those who are in deliberate rebellion and defiance against God. People in rebellion and defiance toward God should seriously be held in question if they claim to be used by the Holy Spirit in prophecy and healing or other spiritual gifts.

This whole idea of grace is completely contrary to our natural way of thinking — the idea that the gifts, even the gift of salvation, can be given on the basis of grace through faith alone and not with reference or regard to meritorious efforts. Every other religion besides Christianity has at its core a prescription for some kind of salvation or union with God based on works. In this most commonly held false equation, man must earn his forgiveness, striving diligently to bridge the separation between God and man. Indeed, it is hard to understand it being any other way.

The point of this chapter is not justification, but giftings and manifestations of the Holy Spirit's power in the church. However, the same principle applies. There is no way anyone will understand justification by grace appropriated only through faith without looking at it from God's perspective.

When we see the holiness of God, on one hand, and the depth of mankind's sin on the other, a lot of things come into a new light. Justification by faith alone makes sense only when you realize that no amount of human effort could bridge that immeasurable gap. God's solution on the cross makes sense when you realize that the human effort equation is hopelessly flawed.

No amount of consecration or sanctification could earn the right to the gifts of the Spirit any more than indulgences could gain forgiveness or Simon's money could purchase God's power. Gifts of the Spirit are given based on the grace of God, not on the maturity, wisdom and character of the vessel.

Consequently, we need to learn to recognize valid gifts of the Spirit in people's lives even though the people are a long way from being perfected. Careful nurturing and administrating of those gifts enables us to enjoy the benefit of the deposits God has made in the lives of immature believers. These deposits have been made for the purpose of blessing the church.

When compared to the purity and holiness of God, the differences between the best of us and the worst of us are not as great as some of us might like to imagine. The life and ministry of Jesus showed us what God was really like. Nevertheless, we still hold on to misconceived ideas about God's ranking of sins.

Throughout Bible times, God forgave and extended great mercy to people who, by our standards, did some pretty despicable things. Without diminishing the gravity of some of the more serious sins on our list, Jesus showed everyone that God's opinion about things like pride, hypocrisy, treatment of the poor, unforgiveness and self-righteousness were more serious to Him than we could have ever imagined. This violates some of our preconceived notions and our ranking of the "really bad sins."

"Man looks at the outward appearance, but the Lord looks at the heart," the Bible says (1 Sam. 16:7). It seems He is rather patient and merciful with people who do bad things due to the fact that they are unwise, immature or just weak. But to those who continue to deliberately disobey God, attempting to misuse God's grace and turn it into an excuse for sin, He often exercises His judgment, exposing such deliberate rebellion.

The problem for us is that it is very hard to know what is really in someone's heart or how God perceives them. We need to be careful about judging spiritual gifts as invalid because of people's weaknesses and immaturity. God may be more concerned about what He has set out to accomplish in the life of the prophetic vessel than about passing full judgment on that person.

FALSE EQUATION #1: CHARACTER EQUALS ANOINTING

Equations work backward as well as forward, even misconceived equations. So, those who wrongly assume that spiritual giftings and anointings endorse character will also conclude that it is character that produces spiritual gifts.

This encourages people in some circles to "fake it" so as not to appear "ungifted." It also implies that the most spiritual, mature and righteous people are those who have the most prolific gifts. If as a church you start down a road with this assumption, you are in for a bizarre ride.

This kind of thinking also sets people up for a great deal of condemnation, especially when everyone else seems to be prophesying, having prophetic dreams and seeing visions. I can say from experience that this can put a lot of pressure on people if they feel they are less spiritual than those with greater gifts of power.

I felt this way for a season, and the result was that I abdicated my position of leadership to those with powerful prophetic gifts. The church was bruised and hurt by that decision, which came out of my insecurity and false humility.

Remember, most prophetic people don't have the gift of leadership that is essential for a church to be healthy, balanced and safe. A church led only by prophets is not a safe environment for God's people.

One of the most important things to do in a church that wants to nurture and administrate prophetic ministry is to dial down the mysticism and the carnal desire to look superspiritual. We need to keep our eyes off people and remain focused on Jesus and His purpose for us. This is not a spiritual beauty contest, but it can turn into one very quickly if people see gifts as merit badges rather than something to bless the church. It is not about the vessel. It's about loving the Lord and building up His church.

The fact that power and revelation flow through prophetic ministers is not necessarily a sign that God is pleased with the other areas of their lives. Sometimes the prophetic gifts will continue to operate even when there is an inner crumbling taking place in their private lives.

People with prominent spiritual giftings, as well as those with callings to leadership, must constantly guard against high-mindedness. High-mindedness is simply considering that you, your position or your purpose are so important that you are judged more leniently. High-minded people are those who consider that because they are doing such an important work for God and because His power is manifest through them, they are not accountable for things like integrity, honesty and kindness — especially in the small and unseen matters of life.

It is this temptation to self-deception that plagues many people in positions of power and influence. It is a great deception because, in actuality, the opposite is true. To whom much is given, much will be required (Luke 12:48).

Every person through whom spiritual gifts operate, as well as every person in a position of privilege or leadership, needs to be acutely aware that a day of reckoning is coming. We will all stand before God one day for a final evaluation of our lives and ministries (1 Cor. 3:11-15).

God has mercy on weak vessels and will manifest His gifts through them even when things are not totally right inside. But don't be deceived. This will not go on forever. It's like a dog on a long leash. He can chase after a cat to a limit, but eventually — and suddenly — he'll come to the end of the leash.

Some of God's people have been displayed as examples that He is patient with their sin and that His gifts are without repentance. Others are examples of another fact — that God eventually calls His servants to give account of their stewardship. God's disciplines are manifest more openly to this group, and it causes us to fear God (1 Tim. 5:20-24).

Saul was a picture of both ways that God chooses to deal with His servants. Saul remained as king of Israel in his sin and rebellion and was patiently used by God to win great battles. God partially blessed Israel under Saul even with his sinful failing, but only up to a point. Saul had lost both the fear of the Lord and his awareness that God was watching and weighing his actions. Eventually, he crossed the line with God.

The message for prophets, leaders and church people is this: God's gifts are freely given as a sign of His mercy, not His approval. Don't disdain valid spiritual gifts manifested through spiritually immature people. But also, do not be fooled by God's grace and patience with prophetic vessels who remain anointed for a season as they continue in their carnality. Eventually He will call us all to account as stewards of the gifts He has entrusted to us.

FALSE EQUATION #2: ANOINTING EQUALS DIVINE ENDORSEMENT OF MINISTRY STYLE

The benefits that have come to our church as a result of the prophetic ministry have naturally been accompanied by some headaches. The greatest difficulties have had to do with ministry styles and methodologies.

In chapter 5, I will talk about some of the things God does that seem strange and unusual. He sometimes offends the mind to reveal the heart. The point here, however, is the unorthodox style and methodology which prophetic people may adopt because of their own weaknesses.

I have had some long and painful discussions about this with some of the prophetic people in our church — from the most experienced to those just beginning to experience the prophetic gifts. In the most problematic cases, the people and even the particular prophetic word seemed to be anointed by the Holy Spirit, but their style of delivering it was really off.

If people are not held accountable, what begins as an unusual methodology can turn into exaggeration and manipulation. In several cases I have simply had to say, "You must stop it."

Prophetic people are often tempted to think that their particular method and style is essential to the anointing working through their lives. They will sometimes say, "No, I have to do it this way or the anointing of God won't be manifest through me."

Methodology or ministry style does not produce power or anointing. That's another false equation that some people fall prey to. Because you were standing in a certain place doing a certain thing when God spoke, moved or healed doesn't mean that the circumstances had anything to do with it. Nevertheless, people find themselves trying to recreate the setting so they can see God's power again.

The Lord often used Bob Jones by having him lay his hands on people's hands. He would sometimes put his fingers against their fingers and, somewhere in the process, God would reveal specific things by the Holy Spirit that He wanted Bob to speak to that person. Bob Jones was consistently accurate in his prophetic ministry. But before long the finger-to-finger method became the way others sought Holy Spirit discernment for people. This is, of course, ridiculous. The discernment came from the Holy Spirit, not from the methodology.

I've seen all kinds of people from all over the body of Christ imitating styles and methods because they think that the method is the key. But the person of the Holy Spirit is the key to operating in the power of God. We have to beware constantly of thinking that if we get the early morning prayer meeting going just the way it was before and the same worship leader back up there with those same anointed songs, then maybe God will do the comet-thing again. That's spiritual superstition.

Some prophetic ministers have these bizarre equations in their mind. The room has to be just such a way. The music has to be just right. There should be no crying babies who would cause the Holy Spirit to lift. It can get to be like a ball player before a game, wearing the same socks or going through the same superstitious routine.

So what if the baby cries or if the room is not in the right configuration? What does that have to do with the personality of the Holy Spirit and His anointing? The Holy Spirit is probably not as skittish and easily quenched by the lack of "ambiance" within a particular setting as some people think He is.

What we call an "anointed" meeting often refers to creating and maintaining the right *mood* or *atmosphere.* Conservative evangelicals often work at this; some of them seek to know exactly which words and songs set the mood for the altar call. If the lights can be dimmed, that's even better.

We all need to be careful to avoid thinking that methodology releases God's power or that the Spirit can't move without the right human methods.

Music can be arranged in a way that makes it more enjoyable and pleasant. It's OK to do that, but it is not necessarily the same as the blessing of the Holy Spirit or the presence of God. In some churches they turn the amps up and get the saxophone going, and, they will tell you, it is hot!

There is the natural tendency in some of us to try to systematize spontaneous experiences. We sometimes think that if we discover the method-key, then we can control it. If people are successful in their ministry (or only appear to be), then they might start using the methods to manipulate people as well. I have had to warn some of our prophetic people to change their methods because they were basically manipulative and controlling even though it was unintentional.

People who are perceived as anointed men or women of God possess a potential for the power of suggestion. A leader succumbing to such suggestion and manipulation might speak to people in this manner:

> Come up if you want to be touched by God. We are going to
> pray, and if you are really sensitive to the Spirit, you will
> fall under the power of God.

Whether it is being suggested that people will fall down, get a prophetic word or speak in tongues, this is manipulative power of suggestion. I've seen a well-known minister rebuke people because they wouldn't fall down when he prayed for them. He told one woman, "Listen, just receive."

The lady replied, "I am receiving."

But the minister said, "Don't tell me you are receiving. You're just standing there resisting." They got in an argument, right on the spot. He really wanted her to fall down as a sign that God was touching her.

Ministers with power and prophetic giftings who are not in relationship with a balanced local church team often allow their method-as-power tendencies to dominate their ministry. It is simply much more difficult to get away with manipulation and pretense when you relate closely to a balanced team of people who live in the real world.

Some people in ministry will push and lean until the person they are praying for goes down. To them it has become a personal mission because their public image is on the line. This is high-octane manipulation.

Miscalculations and false equations about methodology lead to hype and exaggeration. The methods become a false prop. The methods of ministry are operating in high gear, but nothing holy and supernatural is actually taking place. The minister's credibility, however, is on the line, and he feels he has to produce. He may believe that the sure proof of a formula or method is that it works every time.

When people have gone this far, they feel pressured to say that God is working even when He isn't. This is a critical mistake.

These ministers have started down a road of hype and institutionalized methodology. They are afraid to say God is not moving in a particular ministry setting, because if they do, they feel like everything falls apart. There is too much vested interest in preserving the formula or the image.

Some people build organizations around the particular brand of methodology they have become famous for. They hire staffs, build organizations and work to keep the machine going. But one day everybody will finally realize and admit that the king has no clothes. Nothing is really happening. It has become a conspiracy of pretense.

The gifts and manifestations are given as the Holy Spirit desires. We can pray, dance and shout all night like the prophets of Baal, and if the Holy Spirit doesn't want to move, He's not going to move. That is His business.

God sometimes pops a surprise test by withholding His power in a key ministry time to see if the leader will humbly trust Him instead of always trying to appear anointed. In His mercy, He gives us a spiritual pop quiz that reveals our motives to help prepare us for the final exam on the last day.

We want to undermine the false equation that says if you follow a formula, God will manifest His power every time. I believe that on certain occasions He strategically does not manifest His power in order to win people's hearts away from the minister and his methods. Sometimes He will withdraw His Spirit in order to keep from perpetuating our confidence in methodology. Our desire is never to look weak, but Paul's testimony was that he delighted in weakness, that the true power of Christ might work through him (2 Cor. 12:9-10).

A spiritual mystique is intrinsically woven into prophetic ministry. After all, hearing directly from the living God about anything is a rather awesome thing. When open and hungry people get around a prophetically anointed person, they are both hopeful and fearful that this person will reveal secrets and divine perspectives to them. They often cling to every word such a person may utter. This dynamic makes both parties vulnerable to unique temptations.

However, I believe that it is a carnal thing to utilize any mystique that may surround the prophetic ministry in order to influence people. Unfortunately, this happens all too often. Many prophetic folks begin to take themselves too seriously, or they love the feeling of having such influence over others. They are tempted to make themselves look and sound more spiritual, holy and sensitive than they really are.

I have observed that it is easier to get one's identity wrapped around the prophetic ministry more than any other role one may have in the body of Christ. Prophetic people often submit to other's expectations that they constantly hear from God — whether God is saying anything to them or not!

I believe there is a sense in which we should make things a little "harder on God" when it comes to showing His power. Let me explain.

I have pondered how Elijah poured water on the sacrifices on Mt. Carmel (1 Kin. 18). He didn't put on lighter fluid and strike a match behind his back! He was confident that if the genuine fire of God fell, then it could consume even a wet sacrifice.

I would challenge prophetic ministers to put some "water on the sacrifices" they prepare and really trust God to prove His power without their feeling the pressure of trying to help God out so much. Then when His power is demonstrated, the people will not glorify the prophet of God, but the God of the prophet.

I encourage them to throw a cloak over their prophetic mystique and deliberately refuse to utilize it to gain favor, praise, opportunities, sympathy, trust, affection or money. I appeal to them to stay impressed with God and His power without becoming impressed with themselves.

FALSE EQUATION #3: ANOINTING EQUALS 100 PERCENT DOCTRINAL ACCURACY

Throughout church history there have been a lot of anointed people who have wound up with strange doctrines. Their constituency bought into the false assumption that a person whom God uses in a genuine prophetic or healing ministry *must* be 100 percent doctrinally correct. The most notable example in recent history is William Branham.

Branham, poor and uneducated, began his ministry in 1933. He was a traveling Baptist evangelist, and his meetings were frequently attended by thousands, sometimes over twenty thousand. His ministry was characterized by amazing manifestations of healing and the word of knowledge.

Very often, when people would approach him in a healing line, Branham would describe their diseases, give other facts and information about them, and sometimes even call them by their names. The gift, many people insisted, was 100 percent accurate.

An interpreter for Branham in Switzerland who later became an historian said, "I am not aware of any case in which he was mistaken in the often detailed statements he made."[1] The healings were also both numerous and astonishing.

Branham ended up in some doctrinal heresy, although never to the extent of denying Jesus Christ as Lord and Savior or doubting the authority of the Scriptures. While affirming the deity of Christ, he denied the trinity. He allowed himself to be spoken of as the "angel" to the seventh church referred to in Revelation 3. This caused great confusion among his followers. They reasoned that if God could give him genuine prophetic information about people's lives, then why didn't God in the same way give him sound doctrine? But the gift of prophesy doesn't at all ensure that you will have the gift of teaching or vice versa.

The problem is that people with strong power and prophetic ministries often aren't satisfied. Being used by God in prophecy and healing miracles becomes common to them, and they don't get a zing out of prophesying anymore. They often want to become teachers.

One of the tough parts of effective prophetic ministry is keeping personal opinions out of the way. On the other hand, teachers have a platform on which to declare many of their own thoughts. Prophetic people often chafe against this restraint on them that is not upon teachers.

It is so important that prophetic ministers are part of a local church team that includes gifted teachers. If they are not in a team, then they are often tempted to assume too much responsibility and thereby venture outside their calling.

When prophetic people and evangelists become separate from the local church, they are often tempted to establish doctrine, just as a gifted teacher with a large following sometimes does. Some of the unbalanced doctrine so widespread in the body of Christ has come from such people who have a large following through television and radio. They teach the multitudes who have gathered because of the supernatural gifts of the Spirit that operate through them.

However, if they don't have a teaching gift that has been cultivated through proper training in the Scriptures, they are sure to teach unbalanced doctrine to their followers.

The most common example of this that I know of is the problem of "gift projection." Many anointed prophetic leaders have conveyed this notion to their followers: "If you were really close to the Lord and sensitive to the Spirit like I am, you would be doing the things I am doing."

People who imply this have often failed to perceive the sophisticated and beautiful diversity of the body of Christ. In their attempt to encourage believers, they have unwittingly discouraged them.

Prophetic ministers need to be wary of many possible pitfalls. In order to lend credibility to what they are teaching, they can be tempted to be unclear about whose authorization they are working under. I've heard some people start out by declaring what the Holy Spirit said to them, then immediately proceed into their own ideas under the guise of prophesying. The problem comes when they fail to distinguish between a Holy Spirit inspired revelation and their own teaching or opinion.

Most of the congregation can't tell where one stops and the other starts. The pastor/teachers in the local church should watch that very carefully in prophetically gifted ministers.

Pastors need to be careful not to allow the presupposition that miraculous power and revelation validate the truth and accuracy in whatever else is said by the prophetic members of their team.

FOR THE PROFIT OF ALL

False assumptions about spiritual gifts and what they signify can eventually cause us to throw out something good or accept something bad. Power gifts do not necessarily endorse character or methodology. Neither do a prophet's great miracles validate all his doctrine.

The most important thing to remember is that "the manifestation of the Spirit is given to each one for the profit of all" (1 Cor. 12:7). Spiritual gifts are for the purpose of blessing the body of Christ, not exalting the person through whom they come.

An appropriate scripture prophetic people should allow to govern their gifts is in 1 Corinthians:

> So also you, since you are zealous of spiritual gifts, seek to abound for the edification of the church (14:12, NAS).

God delights in using weak and imperfect vessels in order that He might receive the glory.

CHAPTER 5

GOD OFFENDS THE MIND
TO REVEAL THE HEART

T he introduction of prophetic ministry into our home church was difficult for me because I despised the weirdness of some of the people God used. I was also bothered by some of their bizarre methods which were totally foreign to anything in my previous evangelical background and experience.

It was not just the prophetic ministry that bothered me; the other manifestations of the work of the Holy Spirit often seemed contrary to my sense of orderliness and respectability as well. Before I could move forward with what God wanted to do with us, I had to deal with what caused me to be offended in my mind.

We Christians have created a lot of religious assumptions about how God deals with us. He is a gentleman, we say, who will never barge in, but who politely stands at the door, quietly knocking and patiently waiting.

The Holy Spirit is often thought of as being extremely shy or skittish. If we want the Holy Spirit to move, we get very quiet and still. If a baby cries, some think, the Spirit might be quenched or perhaps scared off. This sounds ridiculous, but some Pentecostals and conservative evangelicals alike operate under notions such as these.

Paul instructed the Corinthians not to forbid tongues or prophecy, but to "let all things be done decently and in order" (1 Cor. 14:40). Our leadership team has worked hard at creating an atmosphere in which the free flow of spiritual gifts can take place "decently and in order."

But Paul's instructions to bridle people who are operating in the flesh have been interpreted in such a way as to suggest that the Holy Spirit will operate only in ways that conform to our sense of order and respectability. That was not the case in the Old Testament, in the early church or in revivals throughout history.

Two facts are clear. First, *the Holy Spirit does not appear to be overly concerned about our reputations.*

The outpouring of the Spirit didn't do much for the respectability of those in the upper room. "These men are not drunk as you suppose," said Peter. Some people seem to be drunk as a result of the filling of the Holy Spirit. I can imagine Peter preaching his Acts 2 sermon while still feeling the effects of some of the holy hilarity of heaven himself.

Peter directed his first sermon to the out-of-town visitors who were in Jerusalem for the feast of Pentecost. Many of those were the people who were amazed and perplexed at hearing praises to God in their own language (Acts 2:8-12).

But Peter also preached to those who were the most religious of all, the Hebraic Pharisees of Judea who, being offended in their minds, scoffed, "They are full of new wine" (v. 13). The disciples' behavior might have seemed out of order to these religious leaders, but it was, nevertheless, the work of the Holy Spirit.

A second fact about the Spirit's dealing with us is this: In contrast to the polite, shy, gentlemanly image we have of Him, *He intentionally offends people.*

It pleased God that the Gentiles were offended by the foolishness of the gospel message and that the Jews were tripped up by the stumbling block of the cross (1 Cor. 1:21-23). Paul warned the Galatians that if they required circumcision as demanded by the Jews, then "the offense of the cross has ceased" (Gal. 5:11). The implication is that the gospel is sometimes offensive by God's design.

THE INTENTIONAL OFFENSE

A good example of God intentionally offending people is in John 6. Jesus had fed five thousand people with the multiplied fish and loaves. Now they expected that the Messiah would prove Himself with some great sign, something more than multiplying bread or healing people. They anticipated something comparable to the parting of the Red Sea, the splitting of the Mount of Olives or the calling of fire down from heaven. The people asked Jesus:

> What sign will You perform then, that we may see it and believe You? What will you do? Our fathers ate the manna in the desert (John 6:30-31a).

In other words, they were asking Jesus to do something like the manna-from-heaven thing again. Jesus didn't give them their desired sign, but responded by saying:

> I am the living bread which came down from heaven (v. 51a).
>   Most assuredly, I say to you, unless you eat the flesh of the Son of Man and drink His blood, you have no life in you. Whoever eats My flesh and drinks My blood has eternal life, and I will raise him up at the last day (vv. 53-54).

Jesus offended them in their minds theologically by saying that He was the Bread that came down from heaven (John 6:33-35). He offended their expectations by refusing to give them the expected sign (Matt. 12:39-40). He offended their sensibility and their dignity by suggesting that they eat His flesh and drink His blood (John 6:53-54).

The first response was that they "complained about Him" (John 6:41). Then they "quarreled amongst themselves" (v. 52). Even His disciples were baffled and said, "This is a hard saying; who can understand it?" (v. 60).

Knowing their murmurings Jesus asked, "Does this offend you?" (v. 61). Because they were offended in their minds, even many of His disciples went back and walked away from the Son of God (v. 66).

Throughout the Bible, God is revealed as One who offends and confounds those who think they have everything figured out, those who are bound by their traditions and expectations of how God operates. You might say they have "hardening of the heart." The words of Isaiah are referred to several times in the New Testament (see 1 Pet. 2:8; 1 Cor. 1:23):

> He will be as a stone of stumbling and a rock of offense
> (Is. 8:14a).

Jesus knew their hearts — that most of them loved their tradition more than God. He also knew that those who followed Him as told in John 6 did so with mixed motives. He revealed their hearts by intentionally offending their minds.

By offending people with His methods, God reveals the pride, self-sufficiency and feigned obedience that lies hidden in people's hearts.

General Naaman, the commander of the Syrian army, was plagued with leprosy. He had come out of desperation to see the prophet of God in Israel. Israel was a military enemy of Syria.

But Elisha just sent out a message to Naaman saying, "Go and wash in the Jordan seven times, and your flesh shall be restored to you, and you shall be clean" (2 Kin. 5:10). The prophet didn't even bother to come out of his house to see Naaman who had traveled so far. Needless to say, Naaman, a prominent military leader in Syria, was so offended by this that he said:

> "Are not the Abanah and the Pharpar, the rivers of Damascus, better than all the waters of Israel? Could I not wash in them and be clean?" So he turned and went away in a rage (v. 12).

I know some obnoxious individuals who make it a practice to offend people. God's offense, on the contrary, is redemptive. He offends people's minds in order to reveal their hearts. The Bible teaches that God gives grace to the humble but resists the proud (Prov. 3:34, James 4:6, 1 Pet. 5:5-6). Dealing with Naaman's stumbling block of pride was the first and essential step to his healing, which he received when he was humbly obedient to Elisha's words.

OFFENDED AT THE PEOPLE GOD USES

Paul wrote that God offends people not only by His message, but by His messengers as well.

> But God has chosen the foolish things of the world to put to shame the wise, and God has chosen the weak things of the world to put to shame the things which are mighty; and the base things of the world and the things which are despised God has chosen, and the things which are not, to bring to nothing the things that are, that no flesh should glory in His presence (1 Cor. 1:27-29).

I understand that the context of this principle (God's intentional offense) relates to issues much broader than strange prophets and bizarre manifestations. But in these instances, the principle can be clearly applied.

While I was still pastoring in St. Louis, the idea that God offends the mind to reveal the heart became very real to me. I preached on it several times. I thought God was preparing us for an outpouring of the Spirit that might include some unusual things. I strongly believed in God's desire and power to heal the sick. I thought there might be some unusual healings. I had no experience with the prophetic ministry as I know it today.

Looking back, I see that He was preparing me so that I would not stumble over the strangeness of the prophetic people I was about to meet in the months to come in Kansas City.

OFFENDED AT BIZARRE PROPHETIC METHODS

Some people are different by their very personality and culture, but God has called them nonetheless. Others are led to do strange things by the prophetic call and ministry.

Compared to your normal guy working down at the plant, some prophetic people can seem pretty eccentric. It took me a while to get used to some of their idiosyncrasies which greatly offended my mind at first. The truth is that some of their idiosyncrasies still irritate me, but I've learned to look past them for the sake of receiving God's blessings through them.

When I first met Bob Jones, I was completely convinced he was

70

not of God. I did not desire to talk to him ever again. I had very little experience with prophetic people and no thought-out theology on the subject. Yet I had a firm conviction that he was surely a false prophet.

I'm surprised now at how authoritative I was about things I didn't understand or hadn't experienced. I think they call that pride. Looking back, I realize that one of the principal factors that influenced me was that Bob looked and acted so strangely.

He spoke in parables constantly. I knew God spoke to us in parables, too, but this was *really* strange stuff. Bob would tell me symbolic stories filled with word pictures for which I had no interpretation. Then he would claim that God told him those parables. I didn't have any gridwork or paradigm on which to base his claim that God speaks in such abstract ways to people today.

His ministry style was like nothing I had ever seen before. He would talk about feeling the wind of the Spirit or his hands getting hot during a ministry time.

His language was that of an uneducated person. His appearance was such that no one could ever have accused him of vanity or of being too caught up in the fashions of the day. Occasionally his shirt and pants were too short. Sometimes his stomach showed slightly when he stood, and when he sat, his pants legs sometimes went three inches above his socks.

These things about Bob Jones somewhat offended me — his appearance, his language, his revelation and his ministry style. Initially, I could not imagine his being a genuine prophetic person and could not believe he was inspired by the God of the Bible. Only after I had seen the accuracy of Bob Jones' prophetic ministry over time did I finally begin to think his strange ministry style might be acceptable. His love for Jesus and the Scriptures also became very apparent. Eventually, I found him endearing. There are several things to keep in mind as we examine prophetic methods.

UNBALANCED PEOPLE

Some unbalanced people are simply trying to be weird because of their misconceptions of prophetic ministry. They are excited about the idea of mystical prophets, and they intentionally act out of order. They suppose their strangeness will make them more anointed.

I don't believe the idea that because someone is prophetic they *should* be strange or *should* be persecuted. People will try to get away with all kinds of things based on that idea, claiming that others can't understand them unless the others are also prophetic. I don't buy that for a second.

Some people enjoy the strange actions of Bob Jones and try to imitate them because they think it's really spiritual when, in fact, some of it is just his personality and upbringing. Sometimes strange methods are just strange. It is not a case of God offending people's minds, but rather of the prophetic person having unusual styles and methods. Such things need to be corrected gently if the prophets want to function in public settings.

ARE PROPHETIC PEOPLE LONERS?

The Bible speaks of "schools" or "companies" of prophets (1 Sam. 10:10; 2 Kin. 4:1; 5:22). This reminds us that there is a corporate dimension to developing prophetic gifting among believers. It is not always necessary for a prophetic person to hear from God alone and then deliver his word in public. Other more mature Christians can help those with less experience to sharpen their listening and discerning skills when prophetic ministry is developed among believers.

UNCONVENTIONAL MINISTRY STYLES

Unconventional styles don't necessarily invalidate a prophet's message. Don't dismiss something simply because it's unconventional.

There wasn't an Old Testament biblical precedent for Paul to send out handkerchiefs to sick people (Acts 19:12) or for Jesus to put mud on a blind person's eyes. Jesus said we were to judge the fruit of a prophet, not his methodology — unless, of course, his methods violate a clear biblical text or principle (Matt. 7:15-20).

If people have a track record of being accurate prophetically, you can take them more seriously when their methodology is a little unorthodox. Sometimes their "methodology" is nothing less than following specific instructions from the Holy Spirit. It took some time for each member of our prophetic team to develop credibility with us. People without a proven prophetic gifting do not seem to have as much latitude with other believers to do unconventional things.

PROCESS OF CORRECTION

Pastors have to be careful about correcting people too abruptly, especially in public meetings. We must deal with them in love; first, because they are important to God, and second, because if we don't correct them properly, others will not feel the confidence to step out in faith to minister in the church.

At our church we go through a series of corrective steps. If someone prophesies something that we discern is fleshly, we will let it pass the first time unless it is clearly unbiblical or destructive in nature. People need to have room to make mistakes without the fear of being too quickly corrected.

If the problem happens again, then we talk with them very gently and suggest that they need to be a little more restrained. If they do it a third time, then we tell them privately to stop it and warn them that we will publicly stop them the next time. If they do it again, we will confront the issue publicly.

We will then publicly explain the entire process we have gone through. This helps people realize the correction was not an abrupt and harsh correction. We tell the rest of the congregation that this person was instructed and warned repeatedly. Others need to be assured that they will not suddenly be corrected publicly without prior warnings.

Most of God's people really want to bless others in godly order. Communicating the whole process publicly keeps people from being afraid to step out in faith, and it also reinforces the fact that the church leadership will deal directly with these kind of situations.

THE "NOW-NESS" OF THE SPIRIT

Prophetic ministry cannot be an end in itself. Its purpose is always to strengthen and promote something greater and more valuable than itself. As I indicated previously, one significant impact of the prophetic ministry at Metro Vineyard in Kansas City was strengthening our endurance and commitment to intercession for citywide and national revival.

People get off track when they allow themselves to become more focused on the unusual means of the message rather than God's purpose in that message. It is not so important whether the message comes from a five-star prophet with mountain-moving confirmations, or if it is something that simply seems good to everyone involved. The message is always more important than the method.

When I talk about nurturing and administrating the prophetic ministry in the local church, it is always in view of what God wants to accomplish through the prophetic; we do not just promote prophetic vessels. Experience has shown me that the very nature of the prophetic ministry is to alert the church to the "now-ness" of the Holy Spirit. It awakens us to the will and purpose of God for us in the *present* — what He specifically wants to do in us and through us.

This aspect of now-ness is a compliment to the other dimension of our faith and relationship to God which is forever established — Jesus' work on the cross and the Scriptures. While prophetic people enlighten us to the "now-word" (as some people call it), the pastor-teachers should ground us in the Word of God which is forever settled in heaven.

I love both of these dimensions. I love doctrine and theology, especially theology about the loveliness and majesty of God's attributes. I also long for the manifest presence and purpose of God displayed in our midst by those more prophetically gifted. Who can be satisfied with static religion that works whether God is actively present or not? Genuine Christianity is both doctrinally sound and vibrantly experiential.

The subjective side of our faith is always to be scrutinized in the light of the objective side, but both are essential. God is always working to bring the Word and the Spirit together. Someone has said, "If we have the Word without the Spirit, we dry up. If we have the Spirit without the Word, we blow up. But if we have the Word and the Spirit, we grow up."

Our desire is for *God,* not just knowledge about Him. I am hungry for the fresh wind of God's Spirit moving on our hearts and in our midst.

Nurturing and administrating prophetic ministry among us is only a secondary concern — a means to an end. What I am really concerned about is nurturing and administrating the free and fresh move of the Holy Spirit in the lives of all the people in our church.

The "problem," as you are probably aware, is that you cannot predict, administrate or control the moving of the Holy Spirit. You cannot force your programs, your preconceived expectations and your requirements upon the sovereignty of God that is manifest through the Holy Spirit.

OFFENDED AT THE OUTPOURING OF THE HOLY SPIRIT

People are offended in several ways by the Lord. Some are offended by the message of the cross itself. Some are offended by the type of people God uses. Others are offended by the way the Holy Spirit moves. I was not prepared for unusual manifestations of the Spirit, but I was even less prepared for the unusual people that God joined to our team.

When the power of the Holy Spirit is poured out, it is sometimes in an unexpected way; consequently, it is ridiculed and rejected. In the first Great Awakening in America, as on the day of Pentecost, a lot of strange things took place.

In October 1741, the Rev. Samuel Johnson, acting dean of Yale College, was suspicious of the revival then sweeping New England which was led by the itinerant preacher George Whitefield. He wrote an anxious letter to a friend in England:

> But this new enthusiasm, in consequence of Whitefield's preaching through the country, has got great footing in the College (Yale)...Many scholars have been possessed of it, and two of this year's candidates were denied their degrees for their disorderly and restless endeavors to propagate it...We have now prevailing among us the most odd and unaccountable enthusiasm than perhaps obtained in any age or nation. For not only the minds of many people are at once struck with prodigious distresses upon their hearing the hideous outcries of our itinerant preachers, but even their bodies are frequently in a moment affected with the strangest convulsions and involuntary agitations and cramps, which also have sometimes happened to those who came as mere spectators.[1]

Jonathan Edwards' wife, Sarah, was also profoundly affected by the power and presence of the Holy Spirit. In her own words, she describes how for a period of time lasting more than seventeen days she was so overcome with the presence of God that all her strength would leave her and she would collapse. At other times she could not restrain herself from leaping and shouting for joy.[2]

Jonathan Edwards was a defender of the move of the Spirit, but the extreme manner in which people were affected was too much for the conservative Christian leaders of New England. Their respectability was offended, and they completely condemned the movement, primarily for the excessive enthusiasm and unconventional manifestations of the power of the Spirit.

Dr. Sam Storms joined our staff in August 1993 as the President of Grace Training Center, our full-time Bible school in Kansas City. Dr. Storms obtained a Th.M. degree from Dallas Theological Seminary and a Ph.D. in intellectual history from the University of Texas at Dallas. Sam was somewhat skeptical about these spontaneous outbursts by people who were supposedly influenced by the Holy Spirit.

At the April 1994 Vineyard conference in Dallas, his skepticism was removed. Sam was at the back of the room when the power of the Holy Spirit fell on him. He first began to pray and weep as the Lord was ministering to some deeper needs in his heart. Shortly after this He abruptly tumbled out of his chair laughing hysterically, even though he was trying desperately to control himself.

After the conference ended, he was still incapacitated by the presence of God. Finally his strength returned, and some of us helped Sam up and started for the car. But in the parking lot it happened to him again. Sam repeatedly fell down, thus running the risk of ruining his yuppie clothes.

Twenty minutes later we got him to the restaurant, where God's power hit him again. We thought it was all over until we got up to our hotel room and realized Sam was missing. He was still in the stairwell, incapacitated by the Holy Spirit.

The fruit of Sam's encounter with the Holy Spirit was renewed faith, greater reverence for the power of God, and what the apostle Peter described as "joy inexpressible and full of glory" (1 Pet. 1:8).

BLESSED IS HE WHO IS NOT OFFENDED

The Pharisees and the disciples both misunderstood Jesus, and consequently, they were both offended.

We usually think of Pharisees as the really bad guys. Actually, they were the conservative intellectuals who were the defenders of the faith, who held to orthodoxy against the corrupting influence of Greek culture. But their stumbling block was pride in the accuracy of their interpretation (tradition of the elders). They were content with their orthodoxy but did not hunger for God Himself.

The disciples were offended as well. Throughout the synoptic Gospels (Matthew, Mark and Luke), we see an underlying theme of the disciples' profound inability to understand what was going on.

Those who were offended and who turned away from Jesus when He said, "I am the living bread which came down from heaven" (John 6:51a), were not Pharisees, but His disciples (followers other than the twelve). Though He taught with great wisdom and did a few mighty works in His hometown, His friends "were offended at Him" (Matt. 13:57).

The most commonly used Greek word in the New Testament for "offend" is also translated "to stumble." The Greek word is *skandalizo,* from which our English word *scandal* is derived. God even scandalizes or offends His own people's minds. By offending people's minds, He reveals the things in their hearts that cause them to stumble. Jesus is revealed in the Bible as the Way, the Truth, the Bread of Life and the Door. He is also "a stone of stumbling and a rock of offense" (Is. 8:14).

What is most revealed in the offended heart is a lack of hunger for God and a lack of humility. In God's eyes, these are two important characteristics of the heart.

Neither functioning in New Testament prophetic ministry nor moving in the supernatural ministry of the Holy Spirit is an exact science. These things challenge our improper control issues and our religious codes. They've been designed by God for this very purpose!

True Christianity is a dynamic relationship with a living God, and it cannot be reduced to formulas and dry orthodoxy. We are called to embrace the mystery of God and not to lust after neatly tying up every doctrinal or philosophical loose end that we encounter. Our hunger for a personal relationship with God Himself should overpower this drive within us to perfectly comprehend every fact.

Our humility before God should instruct us that we will never have all the answers, at least not in this age. We are hard enough to live with as it is. As long as we're in this flesh, I don't think possessing omniscience would help us be any easier to live with.

SELF-SATISFIED RELIGIOUS PRIDE

Jesus directly addresses the root problems of self-satisfaction and religious pride:

You search the Scriptures, for in them you think you have

eternal life; and these are they which testify of Me. But you are not willing to come to Me that you may have life.

I do not receive honor from men. But I know you, that you do not have the love of God in you (John 5:39-42).

How can you believe, who receive honor from one another, and do not seek the honor that comes from the only God? (v. 44).

These religious Jews were deceived by equating their knowledge of Scripture and their association with the religious community with the knowledge of God. Yet, truthfully, they were stubbornly refusing to enter into a personal relationship with God through His personal representative, Jesus. They boasted in their knowledge of Scripture while rejecting the author of Scripture.

When the Lord was beginning to challenge Michael Sullivant to be willing to move down the pathway of his prophetic calling, he had a vivid spiritual dream which touched these issues in his heart. The Lord appeared to him, looked him in the eye and said, "You have been waiting to obey Me until you had comprehensive plans. I want you to obey Me without comprehensive plans."

As Michael was kneeling before Jesus, a stack of transparencies came out of his belly and landed in his hands. He understood that these represented his own plans which the Lord could see right through. Michael felt chagrined and deeply sorrowful; he bowed his head and began weeping and repenting. He was saying, "Lord, I don't want to be disobedient to you."

After this, he looked up at the Lord through his tears, and Jesus was smiling at him.

To submit to this calling on his life, Michael has had to go through some rather stiff dealings of God regarding some intellectualism and self-reliance in his ministry and style of relating. This has included private corrections and even a degree of public humiliation to help him humble himself before the Lord.

A few years ago while Michael was functioning as a lead pastor at Metro Vineyard Fellowship, the Lord lifted the anointing for pastoral preaching and teaching off of him for a season. This change was obvious to almost everyone in the church, and it led to a shift in Michael's role in which he wasn't required to preach so often.

A few days after this, Paul Cain, who knew nothing of this situation, publicly prophesied to Michael and his wife, Terri, that God's intention was to "change his vocation" and lead them down a prophetic pathway. He assured them that the changes that had been occurring were not a demotion, but a plan designed to bring greater glory to God through their lives.

Any of us should welcome whatever it takes to enter into and enjoy a more intimate relationship with the Father, Son and Holy Spirit. God puts before us strategic stumbling blocks in the gospel and in our walks with the Holy Spirit to test our hearts. If we become hungry for God and humble in heart, these stumbling blocks actually become the stepping stones that lead us forward in His purposes for our lives.

CHAPTER 6

EMBODYING THE PROPHETIC MESSAGE

Along with prophetic ministry comes the prophetic standard. The Lord wants His ministers to embody the message they preach; He will "wink" at their carnality only for a season before disciplining them.

In this chapter I will discuss the fierce controversy that surrounded Kansas City Fellowship (now called Metro Vineyard Fellowship of Kansas City) beginning in 1990. We realize now that it was authentic, divine discipline of our ministry and our prophetic team, though most of what was said by our accusers was inaccurate. They misrepresented our doctrines and practices, and fabricated stories to validate their accusations. It was a terrible season of attack and turmoil for our church.

That does not excuse the fact, however, that there were three or four important issues in our midst that God was determined to address and correct.

EMBODYING THE MESSAGE

God will often make the lives of His prophetic vessels prophetic illustrations of the messages they are called to proclaim.

Ezekiel was instructed by the Lord to take a clay tablet, portray it as Jerusalem and lay siege against it as a sign to the house of Israel. He was also to lie on his left side for 390 days according to the years of Israel's iniquity, then forty days on his right side for Judah's iniquity (Ezek. 4:1-8).

Sometimes God deals with His servants in a way that is hard for us to understand. That is one of the burdens of the prophetic calling.

When people's lives are used to illustrate God's point, these message-bearers feel God's heart in the matter. The prophet Hosea is one of the best examples of this.

God instructed him to embrace and marry a harlot. In doing so, Hosea demonstrated God's love and forbearance toward the harlot nation of Israel. This was undoubtedly a painful thing for Hosea, but it enabled him to feel the heart of God (Hos. 3).

God wants His servants not only to *say* what He is like, but to *be* like Him; not only to *say* what He wants, but to *do* and *demonstrate* His will; not only to *declare* His heart, but to *feel* His heart.

The true nature of prophetic ministry, in my way of thinking, is passion for the heart of God. The apostle John records the angel saying to him, "Worship God! For the testimony of Jesus is the spirit of prophecy" (Rev. 19:10). Bringing the fresh revelation of the heart of Jesus (the testimony of Jesus) to us is the focus and motivation of the prophetic ministry. It involves more than simply communicating His ideas. It is feeling and revealing His heart.

The Lord spoke audibly to two members of our prophetic team on the same morning in April 1984. In essence, He said that He had placed an emphasis and requirement of humility upon the leadership in the church.

Most of us at Metro Vineyard, of course, thought of it in terms of emphasizing the *doctrine* of humility without really considering the implementation of it in our everyday lifestyle. Since God spoke audibly to two people at the same time, you would think we would have taken the message to heart in the fullest way possible. But God was also referring to the fact that He would dramatically confront our pride and selfish ambition. One way in which the Lord did this was by allowing us to be severely mistreated and then requiring us to bless our enemies. In this, we saw degrees of pride and selfish ambition in our hearts that we never imagined possible.

The reason for that, as I see it now, is that He not only wants us to preach the doctrine of humility that resists selfish ambition, but to be living demonstrations of the message. If you're going to preach it, you have to live it. We haven't done a good job of demonstrating humility, but it is something God will continue to deal with us about throughout the coming years.

THORNS IN THE FLESH

When God communicates a purpose and message with dramatic supernatural manifestations (angelic visitations, audible voices and signs in the heavens), then we know the Lord is urgent about making the message apply to our lives. If necessary, He will deal severely with us on those issues. God will challenge the areas in our lives that are inconsistent with the message He has given us to proclaim.

God often sends a thorn in the flesh to those to whom He gives abundant revelation, in order to protect their hearts from destructive pride. The apostle Paul said that he had been given a "thorn in the flesh" in order that he would not exalt himself. This was due to the fact that his ministry was surrounded by an "abundance of the revelations" (2 Cor. 12:7).

God has purposed to work a life message through each of us. For some, the beauty of God's work in them is never put on a public stage and is seldom noticed, except by a few. In such cases, those peoples' lives are perfected for God's pleasure and the impact on individuals around them.

Sometimes the Holy Spirit works inwardly for almost a lifetime before that person is given the full platform to release the message.

Still others are called to be proclaimers of the message. Some have been given an early platform and are allowed to preach beyond the maturing work of the Holy Spirit in their lives.

That has been our situation, to one degree or another. We were called to proclaim a message of humility that we ourselves did not yet possess. The discipline of the Lord was then released to equip our hearts in purity and humility.

God desires that all of us examine ourselves carefully in the light of His Word and become sensitive to the Holy Spirit's conviction in areas that need to change. But eventually, if we don't recognize the problems and deal with them, all kinds of external circumstances can be used to bring to light the unresolved or carnal issues in our lives. The thorn in the flesh produces humility over time in the lives of sincere yet immature followers of Christ Jesus.

The Scriptures suggest in several places that God extends His grace to people and patiently waits for them to change:

> Truly, these times of ignorance God overlooked, but now commands all men everywhere to repent, because He has appointed a day on which He will judge the world (Acts 17:30-31a).

> Do you despise the riches of His goodness, forbearance, and longsuffering, not knowing that the goodness of God leads you to repentance? (Rom. 2:4).

> The Lord is not slack concerning His promise, as some count slackness, but is longsuffering toward us, not willing that any should perish but that all should come to repentance (2 Pet. 3:9).

If we really love God, He gives us the chance to respond voluntarily to the Spirit. But if we don't respond, He will often extract submission from us.

The prophetic controversy we were about to find ourselves in the middle of was (in retrospect) God's way of extracting that kind of compliance. God was forcing an issue with us — that we would embody the message we were called to proclaim.

WATCHING THE WRONG GAUGES

In 1989, we seemed to be eating with a golden spoon. I was traveling with John Wimber and speaking regularly to crowds of thousands at international conferences. After a while I grew tired of it physically and emotionally. However, I enjoyed the attention and honor more than I realized.

People loved the messages and stood in lines to buy our tapes. I was meeting prominent Christian leaders from different nations. One of them said that what was happening in Kansas City was the freshest thing in a decade. My pride was being stroked and strengthened. I was overwhelmed with the invitations to preach and requests for interviews. A dozen publishers wanted me to write books for them. Several companies sent proposals to distribute our tapes in their nations.

It was physically impossible to answer the multitudes of letters and phone calls that came monthly. We were completely overwhelmed and in over our heads. We complained about the pressures, but actually our team enjoyed the attention more than we cared to admit.

We were out of touch with our pride, our limitations and exactly what it was that God wanted to do in us.

For a short season, whatever we touched seemed to prosper, so we figured God was excited about everything just as it was. There were some warning signals going off. However, we were moving too fast to recognize them.

In our early stages of growth we didn't have enough spiritual maturity to discern some basic warnings about our pride. If someone would have said, "You have pride," we would have gone overboard repenting of pride. But that's not the same as actually seeing our pride from God's perspective or even from the perspective of other people

WARNING SIGNS

One of the warning signs we missed was that we were "partying alone." We were so happy about the seemingly great things that were beginning to happen in the midst of our ministry that we didn't even notice that some other ministries were not having such a great time. We were rejoicing in our increase, but we ignored the fact that other ministries were having a difficult time.

Meanwhile, we partied on. We didn't see or feel their pain. We saw only our increase. If another church struggled or even disbanded, it was no concern to us as long as we continued to grow.

We now lament over having been so self-absorbed. Currently, we are more aware of these sinful tendencies in our hearts than we were in our early days. We now have more of a burden for other congregations in our city. We don't want to celebrate alone. When the Lord says that He is going to visit us, we ask, "But what about the other churches in the city? Are you going to visit them, too?"

We need to have Moses' point of view. God told Moses that He would make from Moses' descendants a great nation after He first destroyed the nation of Israel. Perhaps that was a test for Moses.

Whatever the case, Moses pleaded with the Lord to forgive the sins of the children of Israel (Ex. 32). Moses had no desire to see Israel destroyed and himself made the head of a new nation. A Moses-type leader would intercede until God included more of His people in the blessing.

On the other hand, Elijah didn't ask God to extend mercy to others; instead he declared that he was the only faithful servant left and wondered why God did not treat him better (1 Kin. 19). The same is true for Jonah who was bitter at God for extending His mercy to the Ninevites (Jon. 4).

A major warning sign we missed was that we felt no desire to include others because we were completely satisfied as long as our ministry was being blessed. That revealed a deeply ingrained pride and self-centeredness.

The second warning sign was our lack of perception that we needed other ministries. A lot of people around the body of Christ had much to contribute to what we were doing, but we didn't realize our need for their insight and input. They could have showed us how to do a lot of things better, but we were too busy and too caught up in the euphoria of our seemingly early success to realize this.

THE TEMPTATIONS OF OPPOSITION

Things seemed to be going so well through 1989, but in January 1990, our status suddenly changed. It was as if we tripped a bomb wire when we stepped into the 1990s.

We were soon being aggressively attacked by ten to twelve different ministries. To our knowledge, none of these ministries were connected and, for the most part, they didn't even know each other. Most of them were passing along lies about our doctrines and practices and presenting us as an extreme cult group that was deceived by demons. It was terribly humiliating.

In the midst of this painful situation, there were two main issues, two temptations we had to face regarding how we would respond to our accusers.

TEMPTATION TO RETALIATE

At first there was the temptation to retaliate. We had people from several places encouraging us to stand up and set the record straight. This would involve revealing certain negative things about these groups.

We were not comfortable spending our time and resources in attacking other Christians. Many people felt it was our responsibility to "defend the purpose of God." Deciding what to do was a difficult struggle amongst our staff, but there were several factors that helped us decide to remain silent.

Years before, the Lord told several prophetic people through dreams and visions that we would face this controversy. In September 1984, the Lord plainly revealed to us who one of the principal accusers would be. The Lord added that we were not to strike back. At that same time, the Lord even told us when the attack would be.

Five years later, in December 1989, some of our staff pastors discussed the fact that an attack would probably soon follow since the timing that God spoke about had been fulfilled. The attacks started immediately in January 1990. Having this information on the back burner for just over five years helped us to know that God was in control.

We also had some good advice. Early on the prophetic people had spoken very clearly about how this would happen and what our response should be. But it was John Wimber whose advice impacted our decision in the very hour it happened.

John used the illustration of Solomon and the two women claiming to be the mother of the same child. When Solomon pretended he was about to divide the child with a sword, the true mother gave up her rights to the baby and allowed the lying woman to have the child. By this, the true mother was revealed (1 Kin. 3:16-28).

John said that if we really cared about the bigger purpose of God, we would not retaliate. It would only create a destructive fury, and the purpose of God (the child) would be divided. It was in our anger and desire for revenge that we discovered our selfish ambition. The things that were being said were false, and I was growing increasingly angry.

About that same time I received a clear communication from the Lord. He said, "The measure of your anger toward these men is the measure of your unperceived ambition."

I reacted and said out loud, "No! It's not my unperceived ambition. Lord, I care about Your kingdom and Your name being defamed."

Then the Lord asked me a question, "Why then aren't you this angry when My name gets defamed as other ministries are maliciously attacked?" I had to be honest and admit that I was not mad when other Christian leaders were being criticized. It was the blow to my reputation that really bothered me. I saw with greater clarity that I had a selfish agenda which I was afraid might be hindered if the attacks persisted.

After struggling with it for a while, I realized that what the Lord said was very true: *The measure of my anger toward these men was the measure of my unperceived ambition.* We were inaccurately monitoring our ministry by the gauge of numerical and financial success.

But then I realized that there was an important indicator to which we had paid little attention — the fault line of selfish ambition hiding beneath our surface. Just as earthquakes expose the fault lines that lie deep below the surface, so also the current pressures on us were exposing our hidden fault lines of ambition and anger. We only had to be honest enough to admit it.

The true gauges of successful ministry are those issues that pertain to our becoming Christlike. Were our hearts growing in tender affection for Jesus? Were we growing in our ability to endure hardship with love? Could we bless our enemies with joy? These are the issues that God wants the prophetic ministry to impart successfully. We discovered that we were not very successful by God's gauges.

TEMPTATION TO BLAME THE DEVIL

Second, we faced the temptation to say that the attacks were all of the devil. In retrospect, we see that God's hand was in all of this — even using the things that came from Satan's hand.

Most of the accusations were drawn from inaccurate information. The methods used by our accusers were often unrighteous. There was tension in our church body from trying to decide whether the critics were totally misguided or partially right. Our present conclusion is that it was some of both.

The lack of wisdom and humility in us provoked certain things in them. In addition to that, some of the things they were pointing out were true — especially regarding our pride.

In any case, the uproar that ensued stopped us in our tracks and forced us to confront some of our problems. In that sense, we have come to see the redemptive hand of God in the whole mess.

There is a great danger in blaming everything on the devil. Some immature prophetic people tend to have a persecution complex. They feel the very nature of their calling means they are going to be persecuted. Consequently, whenever a genuine word of correction comes, some bristle and think to themselves, "Yes, we expected this because true prophets are always persecuted."

I know of a large Christian group that was being harshly criticized by those some call "cult-watchers" and "heresy hunters." It seems the methods and most of the data used against them were, in fact, questionable. That Christian ministry determined that the critics were from the devil and were simply persecuting the move of God.

But because of their initial perception that the critics were solely the devil's instruments of persecution, they didn't receive the divine correction. They have since disbanded over the very issues that were being pointed out to them by the cult-watchers.

Though they still see the methods used against them as inappropriate, many of the leaders of that organization now admit that some of the things they were accused of were accurate and, perhaps, were God's way of bringing correction.

SIX LESSONS LEARNED THE HARD WAY

God used this painful series of events to bring correction to us in several ways. It didn't do a whole lot for our reputation, but I've learned that God is more concerned that we embody the message than that we preserve our reputation. Let me share the lessons I learned.

1. REMOVING PRIDE

The first area of correction was definitely pride. We were caught up in the early increase and popularity of our ministry. God can change that pretty quickly. Some of the things we said came off sounding as if we were the spiritually elite. John Wimber confronted our know-it-all attitude, and we eventually agreed with our critics that we wrongly desired to be the center of some of the revival we prophesied about.

2. RECOGNIZING OUR DESPERATE NEED FOR OTHER MINISTRIES IN THE BODY OF CHRIST WHO WERE DIFFERENT FROM US

If I ever doubted there were spiritual fathers in America, I found them through this. A number of older mature men of God spoke into our situation. We grew to appreciate deeply parts of the body of Christ for whom we had no real honor in our earlier days. For years John Wimber has taught the Vineyard pastors to "love the whole church," not just those who look and act like us.

3. GAINING GREATER WISDOM AND UNDERSTANDING OF THE PROPHETIC PROCESS

We had an immature and naive view of the prophetic ministry. We underestimated the fact that it can have negative as well as positive effects. We also found some elements of manipulation and control in some members of our team. Some of us were brokering revelational knowledge with an attitude of spiritual pride for which we are now regretful. This can be very painful and even destructive to people's faith.

Inappropriate expectations were, in some instances, sown into people through inaccurate interpretation and the resulting application of prophetic revelations. It revealed a lack of wisdom and a great need for a more mature administration of the prophetic ministry in our midst.

4. CHANGING OUR CONCEPT OF THE CITYWIDE CHURCH

We had taught that the entire city would come under one governing eldership. We put too much emphasis on structure as the basis of future unity. We now focus on citywide unity through relationship instead of through structure.

5. BECOMING ACCOUNTABLE

We saw our need for input from people who had authority to correct us. As a result, we at Kansas City Fellowship submitted ourselves to John Wimber's oversight and became a part of the Association of Vineyard Churches. A couple of our prophetic ministers moved to the leading church in Anaheim for more theological training and oversight.

I strongly believe in the need for all churches and traveling ministries to be accountable to people both inside and outside of their immediate local setting.

Under John's direction, we put some restraints on Bob Jones. The purpose was to set some safe boundaries with regard to things he would say publicly. Bob didn't agree, and consequently, was less than diligent in staying within those restraints.

Some other problems followed in Bob's life which caused John Wimber to place Bob under a season of discipline. Bob moved from Kansas City to fulfill that season, and I understand he is doing much better. He is ministering again but is no longer under the covering of our church here or any other in the Vineyard movement.

6. NEEDING A BALANCED MINISTRY TEAM

Every church needs balanced input to maintain stability as well as zeal and motivation within the church. We all need the high-octane prophetic people with the more unusual supernatural manifestations, but we also need the dedicated theologians, compassionate pastors and all the other ministries.

Some ministries provide stability to a church and others, like the prophetic ministries, add zeal and motivation. Some contribute by inspiring people to greater devotion to the Lord.

My ministry is certainly not characterized by any unusual power or prophetic giftings nor am I a theologian. My focus is inspirational in nature. I specifically seek to stir up renewed love for Jesus in the churches I visit. We have several theologians on our staff who relate with our prophetic ministers. Currently, we have four people with earned doctorates and eight with master's degrees from various conservative evangelical seminaries. We must diligently seek to integrate these trained teachers with prophetic ministers. I feel very strongly about this. It is not easy, but it is vital to see this diversity in the churches.

Alongside these seminary trained pastors and teachers, we have a fluctuating number of prophetic people and gifted musicians. This combination is very necessary but at times very turbulent. I mention the musicians because they are absolutely vital to cultivating a prophetic church and can sometimes be as great a challenge to a pastor as the prophetic people can be. The continual challenges of integrating such diverse people is well worth the tremendous benefit they bring to the church community.

By the way, the whole team doesn't need to live in one city. A church doesn't need to have a full-time prophetic minister on its staff to have the benefit of the prophetic ministry. We often help local churches locate a proven prophetic team to visit them. Churches can use outside sources to create diversity.

THE DISCIPLINE OF THE LORD

The following scriptures in Hebrews 12 point out two obvious carnal reactions and then another more subtle reaction to the redemptive discipline of God in our lives.

> For consider Him who endured such hostility from sinners against Himself, lest you become weary and discouraged in your souls. You have not yet resisted to bloodshed, striving against sin. And you have forgotten the exhortation which speaks to you as sons: My son, do not despise the chastening of the Lord, Nor be discouraged when you are rebuked by Him; For whom the Lord loves He chastens, And scourges every son whom He receives (Heb. 12:3-6).

> ...lest any root of bitterness springing up cause trouble, and by this many become defiled (Heb. 12:15).

The first wrong response is to despise His correction by embracing some form of denial concerning our need for adjustment. We despise God's discipline when we think of all of our problems as being only the attack of Satan without any regard for God's redemptive discipline. Thus, we regard His discipline too lightly.

The second carnal reaction is to be discouraged under His loving reproof and fall into a paralyzing self-condemnation and hopelessness. Those who are overly discouraged by God's redemptive disciplines decide to quit following hard after God. It is too painful and the cost is too great. They decide that it is no longer worth it. Both of these extremes speak of a spiritual immaturity which we desperately need to outgrow.

The third improper reaction to discipline is to become embittered at God for His dealings in our lives. This is probably the most dangerous reaction of all because bitterness is a deadly spiritual poison that deeply affects all of our relationships.

I don't think contemporary Western Christians typically relate in a healthy way to the discipline of the Lord. Very few people I know have had positive disciplinary experiences with the primary earthly authority figures in their personal histories. It is natural to transfer these unpleasant experiences to the Lord, thereby getting a warped image of who He is and what He is really like.

91

It's challenging for us to believe not only that God loves us, but also that He likes us and enjoys us, even in our immaturity. Many people actually give up on their walk with the Lord because of their misconceptions regarding His nature. This is why it is crucial to meditate on what Scripture teaches about the personality of God.

We must seek the higher ground of responding properly to the dealings of God in our lives. We need to learn to take our medicine humbly in the proper ways at the proper times without becoming bitter and angry at God. We mustn't be either insensitive or hypersensitive when our loving heavenly Father points out our faults and errors.

By the way, according to this passage, one of the primary ways that God disciplines us is by allowing us to experience injustices at the hands of others. He allows us to be tested, watching for a response of trust in Him and forgiveness toward our offenders.

The Proverbs state that "reproofs of instruction are the way of life" (6:23). May God help us to learn how to honor Him when we go through our necessary seasons of discipline.

Remember the purpose of God's discipline is to equip our hearts in Christlikeness. Hebrews 12 says it clearly, "God disciplines us for our good that we may share in His holiness" (v. 10, NIV).

The prophetic message that He gives us is in essence to embrace the various dimensions of Christlikeness. His overall prophetic goal for all Christians is "to be conformed to the image of His Son" (Rom. 8:29).

God wants us to embody the prophetic message that He entrusts to us. It is never enough to proclaim a message. We must seek to live the message we proclaim before we can genuinely claim to have a prophetic message and a prophetic ministry. In one sense, God wants His Word to become flesh in our lives.

Therefore, He sends various forms of redemptive discipline to help us see the unperceived weaknesses in our lives, those hidden fault lines beneath the surface. We can despise His discipline and decide to quit pursuing the Lord as fervently as we once did. We can become bitter at God for administering it.

Or we can respond in the only right way, which is to endure His redemptive discipline, knowing that it is for our good that we might share in His holiness (Heb. 12:7,10).

CHAPTER 7

STONING FALSE PROPHETS

W hen people first hear of someone being called a prophet, they might think of a man with wild hair and fiery eyes crying out against sin and calling fire down from heaven. Others might think of someone pronouncing judgment and doom or predicting the end of the world. Though the image may be a little distorted, this is the picture many people have in their minds of prophets as they appear in the Old Testament.

The character of New Testament prophets and prophecy is, however, somewhat different from that of the Old Testament. Some people have difficulty with the idea of modern day prophets and prophecy because they are looking at them through Old Testament spectacles and with an Old Testament understanding. We live in a new era, and our relationship with God is under the New Covenant. All this calls for a rethinking of our concept of New Covenant prophetic ministry.

In Old Testament times there were usually only a few prophets in the whole earth at any one time. Sometimes prophets were contemporaries (Haggai and Zechariah, Isaiah and Jeremiah), but for the most part they operated in isolation as the lone mouthpiece of God. They often were not incorporated into the daily religious life and traditions but stood apart, separated unto God.

No prophet exemplifies this more than Elijah, who stood alone against King Ahab, the prophets of Baal and the sins of a rebellious people. John the Baptist fits that mold as well — the man of God coming out of the wilderness to proclaim repentance because the day of the Lord was imminent.

In their understanding, the day of the Lord was a day of judgment that would signify the end of the present evil age, usher in the Davidic Messiah and inaugurate the eschatological kingdom of God. Most of the people in Judea came to think of John as a prophet in the Old Testament sense.

These prophets spoke with a clear and unmistakable, "Thus saith the Lord!" The authority of God's prophets was not limited to the general content or the main ideas of their message. Rather, they claimed repeatedly that their very words were the words which God had given them to deliver.

> I will be with your mouth and teach you what you shall say (Ex. 4:12).

> Behold, I have put My words in your mouth (Jer. 1:9).

> And Balaam said to Balak, "Look, I have come to you! Now, have I any power at all to say anything? The word that God puts in my mouth, that I must speak" (Num. 22:38).

We do not find in the Old Testament any instance in which the prophecy of someone who is acknowledged to be a true prophet is evaluated or discerned so that the good might be sorted from the bad, the accurate from the inaccurate. Because God was thought to be the speaker of all that a prophet spoke in His name, it was unthinkable that a true prophet should deliver some oracle which was a mixture of accurate and inaccurate information. There was no middle ground.

94

They were true prophets who spoke the very word of God and should be obeyed as such, or they were false prophets and should be put to death.[1]

In the Old Testament prophets were frequently representatives of the Lord in the presence of kings — those who had the power to punish them if they falsely prophesied. There was never a question about accurately discerning the genuine word from God. For the prophet, it was only a matter of whether he had the courage to deliver it.

The essence of Old Testament prophetic ministry was a chosen vessel delivering what he had received as *direct revelation.* Old Testament prophets didn't struggle in their attempt to discern the still small voice or sort out the subtle impressions from their own thoughts. The message was clear and unmistakable.

Can you imagine Noah saying, "I feel the Lord is impressing upon my heart that He's going to destroy the world with a flood and that I should consider building an ark." Stepping out in faith for them was not a matter of proclaiming with confidence what they only remotely sensed. It was repeating what God clearly said regardless of the consequences.

NEW TESTAMENT PROPHECY

Prophecy in the New Testament has a different character. There are not merely one or two prophets for a nation, but the gift of prophecy, the prophetic ministry and the word of the Lord are *diffused* and *distributed* throughout the entire body of Christ. I believe there are people with prophetic giftings residing in most cities of the earth where the church is being established. They may be immature, but they are probably present.

Under the New Covenant we don't usually see prophets who live by themselves in the wilderness. The prophetic ministry is a vital part of the greater body of Christ. Prophetic ministers are validated by their involvement in and with the local church, not by their separateness.

The church becomes evangelistic through its evangelists, caring through its pastors, serving through its deacons and prophetic through its prophets. Prophetic ministers serve within the church to help it fulfill its function. They are one of the "joints that supply" (Eph. 4:16) the church, enabling it to be the prophetic voice in the earth.

But just because we have called and ordained evangelists, pastors

95

and deacons doesn't mean every believer cannot share the gospel, care for others and serve the church and the world. In the same way, the prophetic word can be manifested through any believer, not just those called by God as prophets.

In the New Testament, the prophetic ministry is directed less to the national leaders and more to the church. In the Old Testament prophets often, though not always, spoke of judgment. Prophecy today is primarily for edification, exhortation and comfort (1 Cor. 14:3).

Although New Testament prophecy does at times come by way of dreams, visions and the audible voice of God, much prophetic revelation can be more subtle. More common forms of revelation are impressions by the Holy Spirit — the *still small voice,* so to speak — as opposed to the always unmistakable audible voice of God.

New Testament prophecy is different because we have a New Covenant: one in which the Holy Spirit dwells in each believer; one in which God has designed for the full expression of His purpose to be revealed through the local church.

Though the office of the prophet in the Old Testament existed in a higher realm in many ways, the New Testament gift of prophecy is a *better* gift based on a *better* covenant because all have the potential to prophesy (1 Cor. 14:31). The "lone ranger" is rare because the Holy Spirit brings the whole body into the process of giving and receiving the prophetic word.

There is another major difference between Old and New Testament prophets. Because Old Testament prophets received direct and unmistakable revelation, they were 100 percent accurate. They did not need to have the others discern the prophetic word they gave. The only way they missed it was by blatantly changing what God had said or deliberately making up a false prophecy. Consequently, the Old Testament judgment on false prophets was to stone them to death.

> I will raise up for them a Prophet like you [Moses] from among their brethren, and will put My words in his mouth, and He shall speak to them all that I command Him. And it shall be that whoever will not hear My words, which he speaks in My name, I will require it of him.
>
> But the prophet who presumes to speak a word in My name, which I have not commanded him to speak, or who speaks in the name of other gods, that prophet shall die.

96

> And if you say in your heart, "How shall we know the word which the Lord has not spoken?" — when a prophet speaks in the name of the Lord, if the thing does not happen or come to pass, that is the thing which the Lord has not spoken; the prophet has spoken it presumptuously; you shall not be afraid of him (Deut. 18:8-22).

In the New Testament, instead of stoning prophets when they make mistakes, the leaders are instructed to "let two or three prophets speak, and the others judge" (1 Cor. 14:29). The Revised Standard Version translates the passage: "let the others weigh what is said." Paul gives similar instructions to the church in Thessalonica:

> Do not quench the Spirit. Do not despise prophecies. Test all things; hold fast what is good (1 Thess. 5:19-21).

We don't stone people if they miss it once; neither do we believe everything they say, whether they are accurate 51 percent or 99 percent of the time.

This idea of prophetic people with subtle impressions of the Holy Spirit making mistakes some of the time is difficult for many conservative evangelicals. The reason, of course, is that they have failed to understand the transition in prophetic ministry. While they clearly see other aspects of the Old Testament changing under the New Covenant, their understanding of prophetic ministry is still based on an Old Testament model.

PRIESTS AND PROPHETS UNDER THE NEW COVENANT

The first individual referred to in the Bible as a priest was Melchizedek. He was "the priest of God Most High" (Gen. 14:18). Following the Exodus from Egypt, God instituted a priesthood after the order of Aaron.

Until that time, all references to priests referred to those of other ancient religions, primarily the priest of the occultic religion in Egypt. One of Joseph's wives was the daughter of the priest of On (Gen. 46:20). So the office and ministry of the priesthood was a well-established religious tradition long before God's instructions to Moses on Mt. Sinai.

Three months after being miraculously delivered from Egypt, the children of Israel arrived at Mt. Sinai. Through Moses God declared His intentions to them:

> Now therefore, if you will indeed obey My voice and keep My covenant, then you shall be a special treasure to Me above all people; for all the earth is Mine. And you shall be to Me a *kingdom of priests* and a holy nation (Ex. 19:5-6, italics mine).

The people were instructed to prepare for the day when God would speak in such a way that each one of them would hear His voice. They sanctified themselves and gathered at the foot of the mountain on the third day. That morning the thunder and lighting began, and a thick cloud descended upon the mountain. When the Lord descended upon Sinai in fire, the smoke went up like the smoke of a furnace and the mountain quaked. Heavenly trumpets began to blow and continued for a long time growing louder and louder.

Apparently, all the people heard the voice of God as He proclaimed to them the Ten Commandments. Here is how the people then responded:

> Now all the people witnessed the thunderings, the lightning flashes, the sound of the trumpet, and the mountain smoking; and when the people saw it, they trembled and stood afar off.
>
> Then they said to Moses, "You speak with us, and we will hear; but let not God speak with us, lest we die" (Ex. 20:18-19).

That is the last time that God spoke in an audible voice to the people as a whole. From then on He used prophets and priests as mediators between Himself and the chosen people. But it was clearly God's purpose from the beginning for the children of Israel to function eventually as a kingdom of priests, a kingdom in which every person had direct access to God in hearing His voice.

God's purpose for His people, that they should be a kingdom of priests, was fulfilled in the New Covenant. In his first epistle, Peter called the saints a holy and royal priesthood (1 Pet. 2:5,9). John wrote to the seven churches: "[Jesus] has made us to be kings and priests to His God and Father" (Rev. 1:5). In his vision, John also heard these words in the new song sung to the Lamb by the four living creatures: "[You] have made us kings and priests to our God; and we shall reign on the earth" (Rev. 4:10).

In the New Covenant, we are priests because the veil has been removed, and we each have direct access to God, to the throne of grace (Heb. 4:16). We need no man or priest to intercede for us because Christ Himself is our constant mediator (1 Tim. 2:5).

In the same way, we do not need to have someone seek God for us in the way that Saul asked the prophet Samuel to inquire of God on his behalf. In the New Covenant, we can do that ourselves.

Jeremiah prophesied about a New Covenant in which each person had the ability to hear from God through the indwelling Holy Spirit:

> Behold, the days are coming, says the Lord, when I will make a new covenant with the house of Israel and with the house of Judah — not according to the covenant that I made with their fathers (Jer. 31:31-32a).
>
> I will put My law in their minds, and write it on their hearts; and I will be their God, and they shall be my people. No more shall every man teach his neighbor, and every man his brother, saying, "Know the Lord," for they all shall know Me, from the least of them to the greatest of them, says the Lord (vv. 33a).

In the Old Covenant priestly and prophetic ministries: 1) the calling was reserved for a select few; 2) the requirements were clear and unmistakably defined (the priest's duties were spelled out in detail and the prophets received direct revelation); and 3) the judgment upon them was severe. Prophets were put to death (Deut. 18:18-22) and the priest died in the presence of the Lord if the sacrifice was unacceptable (Lev. 10:1-3).

The New Covenant is different. The emphasis of Peter's sermon in Acts 2 was that sons and daughters, old men and young men, menservants and maidservants — *all* were going to prophecy in this New Covenant because of the outpouring of the Spirit. Instead of a limited few, everyone is a priest, and the gift of prophecy is diffused through the entire body. Instead of the direct, audible-voice-of-God revelation, much prophetic ministry is imparted by impressions of the Holy Spirit upon our own hearts. Instead of stoning prophets, we are instructed to judge and discern that which they speak, to know if it is from God.

In the generations that followed the beginning of the church, some appeared to revert to the Old Testament understanding of the priesthood. This not only robbed an essential truth of the gospel from the church, but it empowered the priests to an elevated position that became to some a corrupting influence.

Martin Luther, an Augustinian monk and a priest, was troubled by the understanding of the priesthood. The priests were few and exclusive, the requirements were structured and ritualistic, and the judgment for failure was severe.

Early in the sixteenth century, Luther began to teach a doctrine that we know today as the *priesthood of the believer.* This New Testament understanding of priesthood is an accepted foundation of evangelical theology, but in his day it was radical enough to get him condemned to death.

Luther also taught the doctrine of *private judgment,* the principle that every person can hear God and interpret the Scriptures for himself. That was another radical idea for the sixteenth century, but it is the starting place for the New Testament understanding of prophetic ministry. Every Christian can hear from God, exercise discernment and be led by the Holy Spirit. Ministry that was exclusive in the Old Testament (prophet and priest) is now diffused and common in the New.

From one perspective, the New Testament doctrines of the priesthood of all believers and of private judgment (hearing God for oneself) certainly complicate things. In fact, these doctrines can make things downright messy. The human fallout from Luther's emphasis on these doctrines has caused innumerable arguments, denominational splits and even wars. To some, it would seem simpler and neater if we had a hierarchy of priests and a single person who spoke for God. But God's plan all along has been to have a kingdom of priests and a prophetic church made up of His very own sons and daughters.

Though it can sometimes be messy, unpredictable and hard to control, the doctrine of the priesthood of all believers is here to stay. No evangelical is going to deny it. All of us agree that this is an issue worth defending.

New Testament prophetic ministry is an extension of the idea that we all can hear from God. However, prophetic ministry in the church is extremely difficult for some fundamentalists and conservative evangelicals simply because they embrace an Old Testament understanding of the prophetic in which only a few receive direct revelation that is 100 percent accurate — otherwise, they are stoned.

PACKAGING PROPHETIC MINISTRY

For the most part, the same New Testament prophetic gift can operate in very different packages. Usually people have no problem with the woman in the prayer group who feels a burden to pray for someone, who senses the Holy Spirit leading her prayer, and who states that God is "impressing" something on her heart. All of this is in a package that most people are familiar with and understand.

But if she speaks up during the Sunday morning service in her non-charismatic church and loudly proclaims her revelation interspersed with "Thus saith the Lord," she could get a significantly different response. Here are the same words and the same message, but delivered in a very different package.

Sometimes I think we are too concerned about the package and not concerned enough about the message.

It bothers me when prophetic people preface everything with "Thus saith the Lord." They may say this because they have heard others do it. Or perhaps it is an attempt to be more dramatic or to increase the chance of being heard. Sometimes it may come from an Old Testament understanding of the prophetic. Whatever the case, I think it is important that we encourage people to dial down the drama and mysticism when they proclaim that God has spoken.

Because there are many levels of personal revelation in the New Testament church (from slight impressions to audible voices to angelic visitations), the messenger needs to be clear about what he or she has received. Slight impressions don't need to be punctuated in the same way as an open vision. A person may eventually find himself sounding like the boy who cried, "Wolf!" when he says, "But I *did* hear something this time. Thus saith the Lord — *really!*" And all the people yawn.

Many prophetic ministers I know act on prophetic revelation by making suggestions or asking questions of the person being ministered to. For example, if you feel impressed by the Spirit that a person you meet has a particular illness that God wants to heal, you can simply ask them if they have the problem. The gifts of the Spirit can operate in the course of natural dialogue. We don't have to roll our eyes back, speak in King James English and end with "saith the Lord." Tone it down. It will still work!

I think that sometimes a personal motivation is involved if a person is reluctant to dial down the Old Testament prophetic tone. Some people may be too interested in "hitting a homerun." They want to impress their audience. They fail to understand that God gives them revelation through Holy Spirit impressions not so they can be known as a prophet, but in order to help other people.

Even if someone asks a person about his illness because of revelation from the Holy Spirit, and the person acknowledges the illness, there is still the temptation for the prophet to add the comment: "Well, the Lord told me that." Sometimes we want to establish that we were responsible for hearing the word rather than just letting God do His will in other people's lives.

Prophetic revelation in the New Testament is often based on impressions given by the Holy Spirit that have to be properly discerned. Therefore, we have to reel in the Old Testament ministry style to reflect the more subtle nature of New Testament revelation.

There's not as much personal glory associated with that more subdued style, but we don't stone prophetic people who make mistakes, either. Prophetic people need to understand that this is not about personal recognition and glory. The gift is diffused throughout the body of Christ in order that He alone will be uplifted.

CORRUPTING POWER OF THE PROPHETIC

If you could raise the dead on only one out of ten attempts, you could gather a crowd of one hundred thousand people anywhere in the world on twenty-four-hour notice. If you could raise ten out of ten, you could rule and control any nation on earth.

Remember, they tried to make Jesus king because He healed the sick and multiplied the fish and the loaves. The release of any type of supernatural ministry with overt demonstrations of power puts a lot of attention on the people God uses.

Because genuine miracle ministry is so unique, the millionaires and kings will come to serve such anointed vessels. There are a lot of millionaires in the world, but how many people can hear from God like the prophet Elijah? A prophet of the stature similar to those in the Old Testament would face incredible temptations and pressures.

William Branham's prophetic ministry in the 1940s and 1950s was so unique that he came to be revered by some on a level with the Old Testament prophets Elijah and Elisha. Regretfully, some of his followers referred to him as Elijah. Branham died in 1965, yet a group of churches made up of his followers still gather on Sundays to hear his teaching tapes from the 1950s.

Branham himself, wanting to be a teacher, ended up promoting certain heresies. His ministry stands forever as a warning for prophetic people to submit to the local church and its teaching ministries.

A lone ranger prophet is susceptible to many heresies, just as is a lone ranger evangelist, pastor or teacher.

CONTEMPORARY PROPHETIC MINISTRY WITHOUT CORRUPTION

Because of his prophetic gift, Paul Cain has had the opportunity to meet with and declare God's Word to two presidents of the United States and several heads of state in Europe and the Middle East. I believe this will become increasingly common as God raises up more prophetic people like Paul who receive clear discernment into the secrets of people's hearts and clarity about future events. This type of prophetic ministry gets the attention of people from all walks of life, including presidents and kings.

Generally, the gift of the prophetic in the New Testament is dispersed throughout the body of believers. However, there are people whom God raises up with special giftings. Though such people may appear to have the anointing of an Old Testament prophet, that is, having direct and unquestionable revelation, both they and the people who hear them must remember they are New Testament prophets. They are subject to error, to correction and to the body of Christ. They are not to be lone voices in the wilderness, but gifts to the body serving to further the ministry of the church

CHAPTER 8

GOD'S STRATEGY OF SILENCE

Tremendous pressures weigh upon people who are called to prophetic ministry. Whether their prominence is a result of God's promotion or man's, the pressures increase with their notoriety. And it doesn't take a very high success rate to gain a huge following.

Any kind of regular supernatural manifestations and giftings must be accompanied by a great measure of spiritual maturity, or the pressures will become a stumbling block surely to be tripped over.

THE PRESSURES OF SILENCE

One of the more difficult things to deal with as a prophetic minister is coming face-to-face with people in great need only to find God completely silent on the matter. God's heart and mind may have previously been revealed to the prophetic minister with great clarity and astounding detail concerning a dozen other people in the same congregation. Then, when confronted with a person in a desperate situation who obviously has more need for a word from God than anyone else, the same prophetic minister may sense nothing from the Holy Spirit — complete silence.

This awkward situation, which will inevitably arise, presents a real test of character and maturity for the prophetic person. If he or she says, "I have no word for you," people will be disappointed, if not angry, at this response. The minister's reputation may be on the line. If he or she is a full-time prophetic minister, future invitations and honorariums may be affected. People's faith in him or her will be diminished since prophetic words are received only occasionally.

The pressures of people's expectations and assumptions push many prophetic ministers into dangerous waters that can eventually shipwreck their integrity as well as their ministry.

The great temptation is to give a word they don't have in order to release the pressure of the moment. It is the same temptation that provokes the teacher to answer a question citing information of which he is not certain. The teacher desperately hopes no one listening realizes that he's way beyond what he actually knows. But for many teachers, it's just too hard to say, "I don't know."

The same immaturity and pride that causes the teacher to think his credibility is based on his ability to know it all prevents the prophetic minister from saying in a despairing situation in which his or her reputation is on the line, "I have no word for you."

Notwithstanding the pressure of people's expectations or his own desire to help a person in need, a prophetic minister must discipline himself to remain silent when God is silent. Manufacturing a word in his own mind, whether it is out of compassion or the pressure of our ministry credibility, can work directly against the purpose of God in the life of a church or an individual. A lack of integrity never builds people's faith over the long haul, even though the people may be excited for the moment over a man-made prophetic word.

BAILING OUT GOD

Sometimes prophetic people add to what God says because they are trying to be more loving than God by quickly answering people's questioning hearts and giving them a word even when God is silent. I call this a "hamburger-helper" prophecy — giving in to the temptation to add filler.

Though this can cause significant problems, it is not what I consider false prophecy or a false prophet.

Jeremiah 23 contains the Lord's condemnation of those who prophesy out of their own imagination, who "speak a vision of their own heart, not from the mouth of the Lord" (23:16). The pronouncement of judgment on these false prophets is frightening indeed.

Consequently, it really bothers me when this passage is used to criticize prophetic people who don't discern the voice of the Lord accurately or give in to pressure to embellish the word out of their own heart and mind.

The condemnations of Jeremiah 23 are directed to prophets who deliberately changed the specific pronouncement of the judgment God gave to them for Israel's national rebellion. And they knew it. They disregarded God's warning to the nation and fabricated a prophecy proclaiming only wonderful things, assuring the Jewish people that God would protect their nation from judgment.

This is the context of Jeremiah's dirge against the false prophets. It is quite different from a situation where an immature prophetic person erroneously prophecies out of his own heart of compassion for a person in need.

God never said to kill prophetic people who err in this way. The threat of death was to the prophet who opposed God's discipline on an entire rebellious nation. The context of Jeremiah 23 is not primarily directed as a warning to sincere young prophetic people who are new and unskilled in prophetic ministry.

People are constantly thrust into ordeals in which they agonize over the question: "Why would God allow a certain person to continue in suffering?" In order to "bail out" God and His reputation, some pastors, teachers or prophetic ministers rush to provide the answer. Maturity as it relates to prophetic ministry is not only the willingness to speak a difficult word when God gives it, but also the willingness to be silent, even when offering a "prophetic word" might seem appropriate.

The temptation to manufacture a word is the same for the individual as it is for the prophetic minister, only from a slightly different perspective. Some people find the circumstances they are in so acute that they absolutely *have* to receive a word from God, and they *must* have it immediately. Their situation may be desperate, or they may just be weary of waiting for God to answer.

In either case, sometimes there is no word from God, no confirming circumstances that suggest an answer — and even the famous prophet who gave almost everyone else a word says he has received nothing from God for them. Having spent all their perseverance waiting for God, they manufacture a word for themselves and then take off with it.

The impatient King Saul tarrying for the prophet Samuel, who seemed in no particular hurry, is a prime example of this. King Saul had gathered the people at Gilgal to fight against the Philistines, but Samuel delayed in arriving to offer the sacrifice.

Seeing that after seven days of indecision and inaction his army was beginning to desert, Saul could wait on the prophet no longer. A full-scale national crisis was at hand. He went ahead and broke God's law by offering the sacrifice himself, even though Samuel specifically warned Saul to wait for him to do it.

Of course, as soon as he had finished, Samuel showed up. Saul tried to explain his actions:

> The Philistines will not come down on me at Gilgal, and I have not made a supplication to the Lord. Therefore I felt compelled, and offered a burnt offering (1 Sam. 13:12).

Samuel, who was long overdue (at least by Saul's watch), offered no apology, but chastised Saul for his foolishness in disobeying God by failing to wait on God's prophet to come in God's timing. Samuel told Saul:

> The Lord would have established your kingdom over Israel forever. But now your kingdom shall not continue (1 Sam. 13:13b-14a).

It was a serious sin against God's law for a king to offer the sacrifice — a job strictly reserved for the prophet and priest. Saul refused to wait on God, which resulted in a time of personal crisis. He went on without God, creating a far greater crisis.

WAITING ON GOD REVEALS THE HEART

God's silence or inactivity at a time when *we* desperately want God to act or speak serves to reveal the spiritual maturity of both the people and the prophet. This was Saul's first major test after becoming king, the first of many that he would fail.

Another example of this impatience with waiting on God happened with the children of Israel. The delay of Moses revealed that the golden calf was "hiding in the hearts" of the children of Israel.

On the other hand, disillusioning questions about God's lack of intervention and what seemed to be God's inattention caused a totally different reaction in King David. He poured out his soul in the writing of the Psalms; he did not move on without God.

In the instance of the golden calf, waiting revealed the inclination to idolatry in the people; in David's case, waiting revealed that his heart was truly after God.

Each believer must go through the struggle of learning to walk with God when He is silent. It's an inescapable part of spiritual growth, and a prophetic minister must understand God's strategy of silence.

As one who supposedly speaks for God, a prophetic minister must understand that God does not always speak, even in the most desperate of situations. If he cannot grasp this, he will inevitably manufacture words for people when God's specific purpose is for him to say nothing. Regardless of his well-intentioned efforts to make God *look good,* he becomes a stumbling block for those whom he seeks to help.

WALKING CONFIDENTLY IN DARKNESS

Part of the process of spiritual maturity is coming to the edge of our understanding, then walking on ahead without knowing what will happen next. God sometimes calls us, as He called Peter, to walk on water — to proceed in faith, but with uncertainty.

Isaiah 50 describes the person who walks in the fear of the Lord:

> Who among you fears the Lord?
> Who obeys the voice of His Servant?
> Who walks in darkness and has no light?
> Let him trust in the name of the Lord
> And rely upon his God (v. 10).

Walking in darkness as it is used here doesn't refer to moral darkness that comes from sin or demonic oppression. It simply means walking in unknown territory without clear light and reassuring direction. Isaiah continues in the next verse:

> Look, all you who kindle a fire,
> Who encircle yourselves with sparks:
> Walk in the light of your fire and in the sparks
> you have kindled —
> This you shall have from My hand:
> You shall lie down in torment (v. 11).

This verse highlights the peril and torment of those who refuse to wait for God's light, instead creating their own fire in an attempt to manufacture some light. This fire speaks of fleshly activity, a man-made counterfeit fire which can never substitute for God's light. People who resort to this counterfeit will lie down in turmoil instead of lying down in the safety of peace. This is a warning not to manufacture prophetic words!

Isaiah warns the person who fears the Lord not to kindle his own flame. Do not manufacture an artificial light out of your frustration with the darkness. Or, as it relates to the prophetic ministry, do not manufacture the light for someone else.

God's silence forces us to grow in our confidence in Him as a Person while we walk through the darkness, lacking a sense of direction. We eventually realize He was nearby all along. In this way, we develop our own personal history with God.

In my years of relating to prophetic people, I have observed that this is one of the major ways that God tests and refines them. This challenge could be called "learning the art of dangling." It seems as though God holds out to the last possible movement to reveal whether we will panic or trust Him in our times of uncertainty.

MISUNDERSTOOD SILENCE

God's personality is infinite in its complexity and creativity. We think of God as being *perfect* in every way. God has a divine personality, perfect in His wisdom, love and goodness. His dealing with each of us is in terms of building a relationship of love.

But more often than not, our monolithic misunderstanding of how

God *should* act in a given circumstance sometimes causes His action to seem contrary to our way of thinking.

One of the things we should learn from the Gospels is that Jesus often did not answer people in the way we think our Lord should have. Then, when we think He should have answered, He was silent. At times when we suppose He should have intervened, He was inactive. If for no other reason than this, prophetic ministers should be careful not to presume what God should say or do in any given situation.

As Jesus passed through the region of Tyre and Sidon, He was confronted by a Syrophoenician woman who was crying out, "Have mercy on me, O Lord, Son of David!" Though Jesus must have recognized that she was desperate to see her demon-possessed daughter set free, He seemingly *ignored* her and did not initially answer a word.

As she continued to cry out, He apparently *refused* her, saying, "I was not sent except to the lost sheep of the house of Israel."

She still pursued Him, yet Jesus seemingly *insulted* her: "It is not good to take the children's bread and throw it to the little dogs." The woman would not be denied.

Jesus finally *rewarded* her and said, "O woman, great is your faith! Let it be to you as you desire" (Matt. 15:21-28).

We would have been astounded if we had witnessed this encounter. Jesus' initial lack of response, lack of action and even His "rude" behavior certainly does not fit in with the model of how we believe the God of love should or would act. But from our perspective today, we see that Jesus was probing her, testing and drawing out her faith.

Because of our preconceived notions, we sometimes draw wrong conclusions from God's silence or His presumable lack of intervention on our behalf. We often conclude that God's love for us has waned or that we are unworthy of His attention or perhaps that we are being punished for something.

But that was certainly not the case with Lazarus. The Scriptures say several times that Jesus loved Lazarus along with his two sisters, Mary and Martha, but His delay in coming to help Lazarus in his greatest need was precisely calculated.

> Now Jesus loved Martha and her sister and Lazarus. So, when He heard that he was sick, He stayed two more days in the place where He was (John 11:5-6).

110

We know that Jesus' seeming lack of response had nothing to do with lack of love, but had everything to do with fulfilling the redemptive purpose of God. The ensuing miracle was a prophetic sign to many of His own resurrection. But for Lazarus, Martha and Mary it was something more — a lesson to trust God always, even when they must walk in darkness beyond the edge of their understanding.

From prison John the Baptist sent his disciples to inquire of Jesus. After sending them back to John, Jesus commented:

> Assuredly, I say to you, among those born of women there
> has not risen one greater than John the Baptist (Matt. 11:11).

John was the greatest, yet Jesus did nothing to prevent him from being beheaded by King Herod. Jesus' inaction was neither from lack of love for John nor lack of worthiness in John himself. It is obvious that God had appointed John to experience the honor of a martyr's death and that this would bring the most glory to God and His kingdom in the bigger picture.

We stumble over the fact that God doesn't speak or act the way we think He should. But from Isaiah we learn not to manufacture our own light when we walk in darkness. From Saul we learn not to run ahead of God when the answer is delayed. From the Gospels we learn that God's silence does not mean we are rejected or unloved; it must be understood in the light of God's redemptive purposes.

Our "Why, God?" questions are a normal part of the walk of faith for all of us until the very end. For those who have allowed the Holy Spirit to perform His work in their lives, the "Why, God?" questions are accompanied by a growing peace and trust rather than disillusionment and unbelief. God wants us to learn to be at peace in our souls by virtue of our relationship with Him, not by virtue of the information about our circumstances that we sometimes receive from Him.

People searching for God's peace and comfort often look for it by asking God for information about their future. But He wants our peace to come first by fixing any problems in our personal relationship with Him.

A prophetic person must understand that often people desperately want the prophetic word that God Himself refuses to give. They ask for information about circumstances, and God gives information about their relationship with Him. They want peace and assurance, but God has a different way for them to receive peace. If God is not answering, sometimes we are asking the wrong questions.

A FAMINE OF THE WORD OF THE LORD

There can be a variety of reasons known only to God for His silence or for the times He withholds the sense of His presence. Perhaps He is teaching us faith, training us in His wisdom or even bringing judgment for those who have deliberately rejected His words. Amos declared the following to Israel:

> "Behold, the days are coming," says the Lord God,
> "That I will send a famine on the land,
> Not a famine of bread,
> Nor a thirst for water,
> But of hearing the words of the Lord.
> They shall wander from sea to sea,
> And from north to east;
> They shall run to and fro, seeking the word of the Lord,
> But shall not find it" (Amos 8:11-12).

It seems strange to us that God would withhold His word from Israel when they seemed to be searching so hard to find it. What actually happened was that Israel had consciously ignored and rejected God's word already spoken to them through the prophets. They wanted very much for God to speak, but they didn't want to hear what God had to say. So they sought hard to hear Him say something else.

What happened to Israel as a nation takes place in the lives of stubborn individuals. Sometimes in a counseling session every possible solution that can be offered is met with the reply, "I've already tried that," or "I already know that." Counselors find themselves under pressure to come up with some exotic answer which the person has never heard of or never tried. The reason that the wisdom and word of the Lord is not clear is that the answer to the problem is sometimes the most fundamental one — and the first one considered.

For example, to a man who has been greatly hurt and offended, God's specific word to him is that he should fully forgive. But having refused and rejected that simple but challenging answer, he begins a long process of running to and fro seeking the answer to his growing problem.

Even though he is apparently seeking diligently, a famine of the word of the Lord has resulted because he deliberately rejected what God already said clearly. God's word was simply too unpleasant for him to receive.

Whether God's silence or inaction is a part of the normal maturing process or is a judgment from God is not always easy to know, but it is discernible.

Many who are sincere, though immature, are deceived by the powers of darkness into thinking that the silence of God is a sure sign of His displeasure and abandonment. God's silence as divine judgment comes only as a result of conscious rebellion against the clear conviction of the Holy Spirit. Although mankind's heart is deceitful and desperately wicked (Jer. 17:9), unless you are in the last stages of reprobation, you usually know the sincerity or the resistance of your own heart to the Holy Spirit. Though in our own hearts we try to rationalize our way out of things, usually deep down inside, we know the reality of our insincerity.

On one hand some people get the idea that God is a "blabbermouth" — that He is talking to all of His children most of the time. Yet because people experience long periods of silence from heaven, they wrongly conclude that God has withdrawn from them, that they must have sinned grievously in some way. They fall prey to the railings of the accuser of the brethren and live under a cloud of condemnation and rejection.

One the other hand others fantasize that God is talking to them when He is not. These people continually utilize "the Lord told me" preambles to their own opinions and actions. After a little while, that phase gets a hollow ring to it. They fall prey to a hyperspiritual religious trap.

We encourage people to minimize their use of this kind of language. Even if the Lord actually does say something to us, it is not always appropriate or wise to inform everyone around us of that fact.

I don't believe that God is talking to us all the time — that if we just "get on the right frequency" we will constantly hear His voice. Paul Cain has said, "God isn't talking half as much as people think He is, and when He does talk, He means it twice as much as people think He does!"

God does speak to some people quite frequently, but even they wish He wouldn't be so silent on many issues that concern them. We just can't manipulate God to talk to us if He is determined to be quiet. Yet it is not wrong to ask Him to reveal His will and wisdom to us. We just don't control the means He uses or the timetable He is on.

BE SILENT WITH REVEALED KNOWLEDGE

A vital test of a prophet is in his willingness to speak a hard word from God, then his willingness to accept the resulting reproach and persecution which is the normal burden of prophetic ministry. This is a test of surrender and consecration to God.

Another vital test is being able to remain silent when God has not spoken, regardless of the apparent need of the moment. This is a test of honesty and integrity before God.

A third vital test is the willingness to remain silent about something God has clearly revealed to you, yet requires your silence on. This is a test of maturity and security in God.

Some prophets want to ensure that they are always credited with having received revelation from God. Sometimes they're like children who know a secret and just can't stand it; they have to tell it to someone.

Just because God divinely opens your eyes to a certain revelation doesn't necessarily mean you are supposed to share it. I think some of the prophetic words that people submit for the entire church are actually words meant only for themselves.

CAUTION WITH CORRECTIVE WORDS

We also encourage prophetic people, especially if they are new in this ministry, to be very careful in delivering prophecies that call for a group or individual to pursue a different direction (directional prophecies) or prophecies that imply people are missing the will of God (correctional prophecies). This category of prophecy obviously has the potential of causing more pain and confusion than any other.

If someone does receive what they believe is a direction or a correction for someone else, I would recommend the following steps:

1. Without necessarily revealing the identity or identities of the people in question, share the revelation with a more mature prophetic leader for his or her counsel.
2. Pray for the person and his situation, and ask God to give you insight on the right time to share it

3. If you deliver it to him, do so in a nonauthoritative style so that he can have an easy out and so he doesn't have to reject you if he can't receive the message. If it is a true word, and his heart is right before God, it will make its impact even if you share it in a nonauthoritative style.

Also, the principles of Matthew 18 and Galatians 6 must be carefully followed when it comes to correcting someone who is in sin, even if his sin has been revealed through the operation of prophecy. These principles instruct us to go to a person privately about his sin before going to him publicly, and they tell us to go gently after examining ourselves in trial regard first.

THE DIFFICULTY OF SYMBOLIC PROPHECIES

Interpreting a prophetic word can be difficult because of the highly symbolic word pictures that are often involved. People who are immature in the prophetic ministry may also need to restrain themselves for a season from sharing their insight in order to watch how their word comes to pass. This will help them learn how to interpret and apply what they are receiving.

They may first have to learn the ABCs of how prophecy functions and how on-the-job training can be effective. This is one reason why recording and journaling prophetic words is important. Many times a prophecy or spiritual dream can make an impact on someone after the scenario has already played out if it has been recorded and dated in a prophetic person's journal beforehand.

It takes a mature and seasoned prophetic minister to be silent when God is silent, and then at times to be silent when God has shared something that is for his ears only.

The Lord is longing and looking for humans to be His partners in ministry. He wants to engage in a true friendship with us that is governed by the same kinds of things we value in our intimate human relationships — faithful representation of our friend to others, the freedom to speak and listen to each other, the ability to relax in each other's presence, the commitment to hold a confidence and to defend both our friend's honor and integrity when it is called into question or our friend's action or inaction when it is being misunderstood. May we rise up to become the friends of God.

CHAPTER 9

ORIGINS OF THE PROPHETIC CALL

I usually use the term *prophetic minister* instead of the term *prophet.* It's not that I think it is always wrong to refer to someone as a prophet. However, it is be wise to do so cautiously and sparingly because there are great differences among people's prophetic giftings as well as their levels of experience, maturity and credibility.

CONTEMPORARY PROPHETIC MINISTRY GIFTS

My friend Wayne Grudem, Ph.D., a professor at Trinity Evangelical Divinity School, has written one of the best books on prophecy I've ever seen. Grudem's book *The Gift of Prophecy* should be studied by all serious students of the prophetic ministry.

One of the major stumbling blocks many people first face when investigating the validity of prophecy is the question of its authority. If prophecy is some kind of "divine utterance," why does it often sound sc pitifully weak? Why aren't we recording the people speaking "the word of the Lord" and including it in our Bibles?

Grudem does an excellent job of answering these questions. He explains that the Old Testament prophets were called and commissioned to speak "God's very words," which carried an absolute, divine authority. He argues that in the New Testament, only the twelve apostles had that same authority to speak and write "God's very words." All other prophecy was and is simply "A very human — and sometimes partially mistaken — report of something the Holy Spirit brought to someone's mind."[1]

What this accomplishes for Grudem is a helpful distinction between the divinely authoritative "very word of God" that became our Scriptures and the words of New Testament prophets which must be sifted (1 Cor. 14:29) and were at times neglected (v. 30). He argues convincingly for a qualitative difference between the "very words of God" spoken only by those with apostolic authority (New Testament scripture) and the inspired messages of the prophets in the New Testament.

However, I would like to suggest adding a dimension to Grudem's argument. While Paul and the other writers of the New Testament did at times write "God's very words," it must be acknowledged that they did not always speak "God's very words." While personally affirming the divine inspiration and infallibility of Scripture, I believe that Paul could have written additional letters which were not necessarily "God's very words."

What about other people? Can people today speak "God's very words" occasionally? Can prophecy be 100 percent accurate? Is all prophecy, as Grudem argues, only "human words reporting something God brings to mind," and therefore a mixed-up combination of divine inspiration and the human spirit?

While affirming the value of the "mixed lot," Grudem argues from 1 Corinthians 14:36 that no prophets can ever speak "words of God."[2] Grudem has been very helpful in making a clear distinction between the authority of Scripture and prophetic utterances.

However, I do not believe he convincingly eliminates the possibility of a person speaking a prophetic word or words that are 100 percent accurate in every detail and, as such, are God's words.

In saying this, I do not mean to suggest that any contemporary prophetic word should be treated in the way in which we treat Scripture. However, I do believe that some individuals may be peculiarly gifted in the prophetic and may on occasion speak the words of God with complete accuracy.

As Grudem states, in most cases prophesy is reporting "in human words what God brings to mind." God conveys to our mind thoughts which we communicate in contemporary language. They are a mixture of God's words and man's words. Some "prophetic words" may be 10 percent God's words and 90 percent man's words, while others have a greater revelatory content.

Nevertheless, I have found that people who move with a remarkable degree of accuracy in the prophetic do so by receiving revelation from God by means that go beyond the "reporting in human words what God brings to mind." On occasion God speaks to His servants in an audible voice. Clearly these are His "very words" that may be reported with 100 percent accuracy.

Additionally, open visions of the spiritual realm or of future events are familiar modes of communications to those who move in the prophetic realm with a remarkable degree of accuracy.

All this helps to explain why some prophetic utterances "ring more true" than others. I have attempted to graph this phenomena of mixing our thoughts and ideas with God's words:

God's Words		Man's words
Strong prophetic	Average prophetic (mature)	Weak prophetic (immature)

What I am trying to illustrate is that while it is possible to speak words from God which are 100 percent accurate, most often prophecy is a mixture. Sometimes this yields a "mature" word that reflects ideally what God would like to communicate, and sometimes His word is communicated in a much less than ideal fashion, yielding a "weak" word of lesser value, but still not to be despised.

Whatever the case, and however good or reputable the prophet or prophesy may be, we are called to weigh what is said (1 Cor. 14:29-30). Paul instructs the Thessalonian church:

Do not despise prophesies. Test all things; hold fast to what is good (1 Thess. 5:20-21).

If the prophetic utterance is from God, then the Holy Spirit will bring the words home to our hearts and give us an internal witness of the fact that it is indeed something God is saying to us.

WHO CAN PROPHESY?

The church, from its very inception on the day of Pentecost, was to be of a prophetic nature. It would appear that the gift of prophecy is potentially available to all (Acts 2:14-18). Paul urges the Corinthians to seek this gift (1 Cor. 14:1,39) while acknowledging that not all are prophets (1 Cor. 12:29). What is going on?

Again, I find Grudem helpful, but not adequate. His definition of prophesy as "speaking merely human words to report something God brings to mind" allows for a type of prophetic utterance that is possible for every believer, and rightfully so. He also acknowledges that in the New Testament some people ministered more regularly in prophecy and were called "prophets" (Agabus in Acts 11, 21; Philip's daughters in Acts 21; Barnabas in Acts 13:1).

Grudem does not, however, acknowledge that there was an "office" of prophet, something Pentecostals and charismatics have argued over for years. He argues that the term *prophet* is more of a description of function rather than an office or title.

> "The distinction between function and office would be reflected in the greater and lesser degrees of prophetic ability, all ranged along a wide spectrum in any given congregation. Prophets would differ in ability among themselves, while they would also see changes in the extent of their own prophetic abilities over a period of time. Those with a high degree of prophetic ability would prophesy more frequently, at greater length, with more clear and forceful revelations, about more important subjects, and over a wider range of topics."[3]

Grudem points out that some people, like Agabus in the book of Acts, ministered regularly in prophecy, and while we may not want to give him the *office* of prophet, he had an acknowledged and reputable ministry in prophecy.

I would like to expand on this idea of a continuum and suggest that there are levels of prophetic ministry.

FOUR LEVELS OF PROPHETIC MINISTRY

At our church we have felt it necessary to define our terminology to distinguish among the different levels and types of prophetic callings and anointings. We use four levels to define prophetically-gifted people in our church.

1. SIMPLE PROPHETIC

A simple prophecy is given when any believer speaks something God has brought to mind. This is usually within the scope of encouragement, comfort and exhortation explained in 1 Corinthians 14:3, and it doesn't include correction, new direction or predictive elements of prophetic words.

2. PROPHETIC GIFTING

Believers who regularly receive impressions, dreams, visions or other types of revelation have prophetic gifting. These are usually symbolic, being in the form of parables and riddles. This group receives more regular prophetic information than the first group, yet lacks clarity in understanding what they receive.

I have met many people at levels 1 and 2; these groups account for the vast majority of those who prophesy in charismatic-type churches.

3. PROPHETIC MINISTRY

Believers whose gifting has been recognized, nurtured and commissioned for regular ministry in the local church are in prophetic ministry. There is still a strong symbolic or allegorical element in what they receive, but through the process of team ministry, it is possible to discern much of the interpretation and application of their revelation.

4. PROPHETIC OFFICE

Believers whose ministry is somewhat like the prophets of the Old Testament occupy the office of the prophet. They often minister in signs and wonders and are known to speak 100 percent accurate words from God. This doesn't mean they are infallible, but their words are to be taken seriously. Their credibility has been clearly established by their proven track record of accurate prophecies.

The following chart will hopefully illustrate the relationship between these four levels of prophetic ministry and the person's ability to speak "the very words of God."

God's words			Man's words
IV Prophetic office	III Prophetic ministry	II Prophetic gifting	I Simple prophetic

I have attempted to show that there is a type of prophetic ministry in the church today in which men and women may at times prophesy with 100 percent accuracy. While these words may or may not be mixed with the prophets' own words, I believe we should acknowledge that mature and gifted people can speak "God's words."

I have also attempted to clarify the issue regarding who can prophesy. What I have described as different levels of prophetic ministry is simply an attempt to provide labels for what most authors who have written on prophetic ministry believe.

There are really no clear-cut standards for deciding if a person is at Level I, II, III or IV, or exactly what the distinctions are. These are not biblical distinctions; they are simply categories which help us to communicate with each other more effectively. It may become apparent that more levels are necessary, but I believe that the initial groupings will provide some framework for further research.

Our church, Metro Vineyard Fellowship, has had a few Level III prophetic ministers throughout the years, and they occasionally minister together with Level II gifted people in the regular activities in the church and at special conferences. These conferences sometimes provide the emerging Level II gifted ministers with opportunities to minister side by side with the Level III prophetic ministry.

I know hundreds of people, many within our church and others outside of it, who minister in Level I, simple prophecy, and many others who could be described by Level II — being used periodically to give a strong prophetic word.

I know personally or have heard of maybe twenty to twenty-five people who have a proven prophetic ministry as described by Level III. These are men and women who regularly receive dreams, visions and supernatural encounters as a part of their lifestyle. They function in this way as a gift to the body of Christ. Many of these people may one day be recognized as being in the office of a New Testament prophet.

What I have called "the level IV prophetic office" represents a maturity and power in prophetic ministry that parallels the Old Testament ministries of men like Samuel and Elijah.

In my mind, recognizing a person as a Level IV New Testament prophet involves three issues:

1. The prophet has a certain level of *supernatural giftedness* that is evidenced by regularly receiving divine information from the Holy Spirit. The validity of this gift is proven out over time and is not an issue of having just one prophetic word, regardless of how accurate or spectacular it seems.

2. The prophet has a *godly character,* which is an essential mark of a true prophet. Jesus said that you would know true and false prophets by their fruit (Matt. 7:15-20). The fruit I believe Jesus is referring to is the kind of impact that this prophet's ministry has made on others. But having good fruit also means that the Holy Spirit's presence and sanctifying work are operating in the prophet's life — creating a brokenness, a kindness, a selflessness and a compassion that have the mark of the Holy Spirit on them. These are people who diligently seek to cultivate holiness and deep passion for Jesus in their lives.

3. The prophet has the *matured wisdom* of God that has come through experience and relationship with the Holy Spirit. This wisdom enables the person to be an instrument of the prophetic knowledge and power of God in a way that builds up the people of God and the purpose of God. This wisdom is foundational to using the prophetic in a manner that will build up the local church.

I have seen the Holy Spirit work in these three areas with the prophetic ministers I know. Some have grown more than others. Paul Cain is an example of someone whom I would consider a Level IV prophet. I suppose there may be many with that kind of calling; nevertheless, I am reluctant to refer to people publicly as being in the office of a New Testament prophet.

I personally know only a very few at the present time who could be spoken of as in the office of a prophet when measured by the maturity level of their gifting, character and wisdom.

I'm not at all comfortable with labeling most people who prophesy as "prophets." I would rather err on the side of caution. I tend first to put prophetically gifted people in a lower category until they are well-proven in the context of long-term relationships in the local church.

I think the church does itself harm when it allows people to quickly identify themselves as "apostle" or "prophet" simply because they consider themselves to be so or because it looks good on a brochure. By doing this, we trivialize the gifts and callings of God, and hinder the emerging of God's genuine ministry gifts to the church.

I feel that our generation is going to be significantly impacted by the ministry of many, many Level III prophetic ministries and more than a few Level IV prophets. Pastors will need to learn how to nurture effectively these prophetic ministries and incorporate them into the ministering life of the church.

I firmly believe that the church will yet become the prophetic community which Peter described in Acts 2. Lord, help us.

SOVEREIGN CALLING

Being called into some kind of prophetic ministry is not necessarily the reward of how diligent you have been to seek to mature in prophecy. It's not even determined by how eager you are to grow in wisdom and character. It is a matter of God's sovereign call.

The same thing is true with regard to each individual manifestation of the Spirit. Paul writes to the Corinthians:

> But one and the same Spirit works all these things, distributing to each one individually *as He wills* (1 Cor. 12:11, italics added).

We serve a personal God who has His own purposes for each individual. God is not an impersonal force. A Tibetan monk may go

123

through exercises and disciplines, thinking these will help him become an ascended master. But the gifts and callings of God are not primarily based on our striving, seeking or searching, but are based on His sovereign choice and His grace. It is not a matter of our efforts to attain or develop spiritual skills. It is all about God's sovereign calling and God's gracious giftings.

People often ask us in conferences how they can grow in the prophetic and receive more words from God. Paul Cain usually tells people, "We can only teach you what to do with the words. Nobody can teach you how to receive words from God. Those things are the activity of the Holy Spirit in our human experience. We can only teach you how to cooperate with the activity of the Spirit, not how to produce the activity of the Spirit."

I suppose that when John Wimber asked me to pray for the gift of prophecy to be imparted to people at the 1989 Vineyard conference in Anaheim, many people wanted me to pray for them to be called to the office of a prophet. Of course, there is no way I could do that. It is God's choice.

However, we have seen people who were prayed for in such conference settings suddenly begin to regularly receive an increase from the Spirit of the Lord in the area of dreams, visions and prophetic words. Many of them have continued to experience an increase of prophetic gifting from that time on.

To some extent, this kind of gifting is transferable, but only to the degree that God sovereignly ordains. I believe some measure of the calling of God to the prophetic was already present in these people's lives. There is a mysterious interplay between God's sovereign activity and human agency and responsibility. We simply open our hearts before God, seek His will and ask for what we desire. Then we let each individual experience unfold without trying to explain fully the dynamics.

The catalyst that releases or activates the gift of God in a person is sometimes a divine encounter at salvation or even years later by a sovereign visitation of God without any human agency. Sometimes it happens suddenly in childhood, or it may be after someone has been a Christian for many years. With some, a growth of the prophetic anointing occurs slowly, while with others, the gift is imparted quickly through the laying on of hands (1 Tim. 4:14; 2 Tim. 1:6).

There is a place for diligently seeking to grow in gifting, character and maturity. But while diligence causes you to grow within your calling, it does not determine your calling.

ORIGIN OF THE CALL

There are numerous ways people are called into the various types of prophetic ministry. I want to share some things I have observed concerning the origins of the prophetic call. The people I will refer to are some of those who have either fellowshipped with us or have been a part of our team. This is by no means a comprehensive list of the *premier prophets* of the land. There are many prophetic groups and prophetic ministers around the country that I don't know much about. It is, however, easiest for me to talk about the ones I know.

CALLED IN THEIR YOUTH

Paul Cain is an example of being called to the prophetic ministry while he was still in his mother's womb. The prophet Jeremiah as well as John the Baptist were called in the same way.

Paul's mother, Anna Cain, was forty-five years old and very sick when in 1929 she became pregnant with her first son. She had three terminal illnesses: heart problems, large cancerous tumors in her breasts and uterus, and tuberculosis. Plus, the tumors in her womb would prevent the child from coming through the birth canal.

Anna had been sent home to Garland, Texas from Baylor University Hospital to die. The doctors could do nothing for her. But, like Hannah, she promised to dedicate the child in her womb to the Lord (1 Sam. 1:11) — that is, if she lived long enough to deliver the baby.

Late one evening as she was desperately crying out in prayer, the Lord spoke to her through the literal appearance of an angel. In essence, He promised that she would not die and that the child would be prophetically anointed as a minister of the gospel. Anna was healed immediately and lived sixty-five more years. She died after celebrating her 105th birthday. So Anna was able to nurse her baby on the very breasts that had been so riddled with cancer.

Anna Cain never talked to Paul about the Lord's call upon his life. She wanted the Lord Himself to reveal this directly to him. That happened one night when Paul was eight years old.

Paul was in his bedroom. Suddenly, the angel of the Lord appeared to him and spoke clearly to him about His sovereign call. God called

125

Paul to prophetic ministry. The voice of the Lord was also heard by Paul's sister, who was present in the room. She became a lifelong prayer warrior on behalf of Paul and his ministry.

Immediately after this experience, the gifts of prophetic revelation began to operate in Paul's life. He received supernatural words of wisdom and knowledge and the discerning of spirits (1 Cor. 12:7-10). He also developed a passion for the Lord and a burning desire to preach. At nine years old, Paul used to set up discarded railway spikes in rows, pretending they were people sitting in pews, and preach to them. Paul also found that he "knew by the Spirit" things that were going to happen as well as information about people's personal lives.

Paul's Baptist pastor, Dr. Parish, would take him along on some of his pastoral visits during the late 1930s and early 1940s. The young boy would sometimes know by the revelatory gifts of the Spirit which of the sick people were going to be healed. Many times this knowledge came to him in the form of a vision.

On one occasion, while en route to a hospital, Paul related to Dr. Parish that he had seen a vision of a lady who was in bed dying of cancer. She was about sixty years old and was wearing a rose-colored housecoat. Standing at the foot of her bed was her brother, Tom, dressed in his work clothes.

When they arrived at the hospital, they found the scene exactly as Paul had described. Paul hadn't previously known anything about this lady or her brother, Tom. They prayed for the lady, and she was completely healed.

By the age of nine, Paul also began preaching to his young friends. He first gathered a crowd of a dozen neighborhood children along with his grandmother and his parents. They all sang praises to God, and then Paul preached. Public preaching for a boy of that age was something Paul's Baptist church found hard to handle. However, when Paul was about eighteen, the Pentecostals began inviting Paul to preach at their evangelistic meetings.

By the time Paul was twenty, he had a regular radio ministry and was conducting healing services in a small tent. He began traveling across America, ministering as an evangelist who emphasized physical healing. Those were the early days of the healing movement which swept through the Pentecostal churches during the 1940s and 1950s. Paul began to discover that he was resented and even rejected by some of the movement's leaders. This was partly because of his youth, but also because Paul had not yet gained the maturity and discretion necessary to function in such a powerful ministry.

Paul Cain's calling came while he was in his mother's womb and an angelic messenger visited her. It was later confirmed to Paul when he was eight by the Lord Himself. It had nothing to do with his personal diligence or his own righteousness. The calling was by God's sovereign grace, and the prophetic gifts immediately began to operate in Paul's life after the angel of the Lord appeared to him at the age of eight.

John Paul Jackson is a prophetic minister who was on the pastoral staff of Metro Vineyard Fellowship for about five years, and then with John Wimber and the Vineyard Christian Fellowship in Anaheim for another three years. Like Anna Cain, John Paul's mother also had an experience with the Lord indicating that her son would one day have a prophetic ministry.

John Paul was converted at an early age and began immediately to move in the gifts of the Spirit. However, he went through a period in which he did not follow the Lord fully. His heart had grown cold. During that time the revelation gifts ceased. In his late twenties when he recommitted his life to Christ, the manifestations of the Spirit returned in a very strong way. He currently pastors a church in Dallas, Texas, and he continues to travel as God uses him in the prophetic ministry.

Bob Jones, whom I have already mentioned numerous times in this book, is a man who has had a very profound prophetic ministry. His former lifestyle was that of a thief, a brawler, a bootlegger and an alcoholic. Bob had very little religious background and did not become a Christian until he was in his late thirties. Nevertheless, Bob had several angelic visitations and supernatural experiences as a boy that indicated that he would have a prophetic ministry in his adult life.

When Bob was thirteen he heard an audible voice from heaven call his name. When he was fifteen he saw himself in a vision being brought before the throne of God. These experiences terrified Bob. It took him several months to get over the vision. It never occurred to him until after his conversion that these things represented God's call on his life rather than God's judgment.

Immediately after his conversion, to Bob's amazement, the prophetic gifts began to operate powerfully in his life. Bob is another example of how the gifts of grace and the calling of God were given as a result of God's grace, not his striving.

Larry Randolph grew up in a Pentecostal home in Arkansas. He had encounters with the Lord in his childhood and grew up experiencing prophetic revelation throughout his life. He is now in his forties and travels full-time in the prophetic ministry.

SUDDEN AND UNEXPECTED CALLING

Marty Streiker spent his whole life as a schoolteacher in Canada. He had been a Roman Catholic his entire life, but in his early fifties he experienced the new birth. Marty knew nothing about prophetic gifts or ministry. Nevertheless, prophetic dreams and visions began immediately. Marty had no frame of reference for these experiences and, initially, had no understanding of why God gave him such experiences.

Those prophetic gifts that began with his conversion have continued to increase over the years. Marty is now a part of a small interdenominational prayer group in addition to his affiliation with his local Catholic parish. God has been using his prophetic ministry to bless individuals as well as a number of pastors from different churches in his area.

STIRRING UP THE GIFT

Michael Sullivant is an excellent pastor and teacher who for many years believed in the prophetic ministry. Yet Michael's function in the church, like mine, could be described as mostly in the areas of leadership and teaching. Several prophetic people told Michael that they sensed that he would have a prophetic ministry someday, but that seemed unlikely since there was no notable sign in him of any prophetic gifting or calling.

In May 1990, Paul Cain singled him out at one of the meetings in our church. He spoke to Michael about a prophetic calling and encouraged him to set aside some time to seek the Lord and to let the Lord remove some dross from his life.

Michael retreated to a cabin in Colorado for thirty days. Beginning the very first night and for the next thirty nights in a row, he had prophetic dreams. Since that time, Michael has grown rapidly in the prophetic ministry.

John Wimber was teaching at Fuller Theological Seminary when he began to teach on healing. Soon after, healings started taking place. Before long the word of knowledge, which is a function of the prophetic call, began to operate in him in a mighty way.

With John Wimber, there was no dramatic angelic visitation or voice from heaven. He simply stepped out in faith in whatever way seemed appropriate. In the process, the gifts of the Spirit began to operate through him. For these men, the manifestations of the Spirit working through them enabled them to recognize, in retrospect, that God had certainly called them to their particular type of Holy Spirit ministry.

Phil Elston is another prophetic person that I have come to know and appreciate. His birth was unusual in that his mother was not supposed to be able to conceive any children, and yet Phil was born. He was an only child.

Phil has recollections of "seeing" things as a boy and thinking that there was nothing unusual about this. He had several supernatural encounters with God. One of them led to his conversion to Jesus Christ.

Initially, Phil did not have much understanding about the prophetic gifting that manifested itself rather strongly in him after his conversion in 1976. He had many spiritual dreams and visions and heard God's voice. The most common way that this gift operates in him now is by receiving impressions from the Holy Spirit that allow him to know things he has no natural way of knowing.

In 1989 Paul Cain gave Phil a prophetic word about his life that helped him to accept the prophetic calling upon him. Since that time he has been traveling internationally in teaching and prophetic ministry.

These are just a few of the testimonies that could be offered in this book. The point of all this is that the calling of God on someone's life is a function of His divine plan, issued before that person ever lifted a finger to serve Him.

It doesn't matter if you haven't had a special divine visitation. God has gifts and callings designed for your life. Bible training, discipline, fasting and praying will not change your calling. However, these spiritual disciplines *will* enhance the release of the calling that has already been divinely determined. The goal is not to get God to call you as a prophet or to endow you with spiritual gifts. It is usually a matter of stirring up the gifts and callings already determined for you by God.

This is a paradoxical tension:

1. God knows what He has ordained for us;
2. We ultimately want only His will for us;
3. He has ordained prayer and a seeking heart as ways of releasing His will in our lives;
4. So we may ask Him for prophetic giftings, but we must ultimately be spiritually content with the measure He gives to us if we are passionately seeking His will for us.

THE PAIN OF THE PROPHETIC CALLING

There is always a temptation to want something before we understand it. Then once we have it and understand the difficulties associated with it, the temptation is to want get to rid of it.

There is a lot of misunderstanding about prophetic ministry. Spectators don't realize how much prophetic people typically wrestle and struggle with the "down sides" of their own lives and ministries. If a person has a desire to be involved with prophetic ministry, it should not be because it seems exciting. The pain, the perplexities and the attacks upon these people are far greater than on most people.

Some prophetic people I know have spent a portion of their ministry with a painful complaint, asking the Lord to lift the prophetic call off them. The glory that appears in a conference setting is untypical of their everyday lifestyle.

We encourage people to find their joy in loving God, knowing that God loves them and in being faithful servants. They should not think that some spectacular ministry will make their life happy. I have never met a prophetic person whose life was made significantly happy because of his or her gift. Typically they have experienced demonic attack, opposition from godly people and great perplexity in their own souls. They may see so much, but they often can't understand the full meaning of what they see.

Prophetic ministers seem to have more disappointment with God than the average person. They often see clearly how things should be or how God plans for them to be. But they have to wait in faith for a longer time because they have seen farther ahead. They are much more prone to the Proverbs 13:12 difficulty: "Hope deferred makes the heart sick." Because their expectations are typically higher, they are more deeply disappointed.

It's easier for other people to enjoy life as it is because they are not so burdened with how things are supposed to be, and they don't have to live in the pain of it all the time. Jonah had a big disappointment with God. So did Jeremiah who complained that the Lord had tricked him.

Every time Jeremiah opened his mouth he got in trouble. He was perplexed, he was ridiculed, and he wanted to quit. Nevertheless, the word of the Lord was like a fire burning within him, and he could not hold it back (Jer. 20:9). Some of that pain comes with the calling.

Prophetic people also have difficulties that are sometimes leadership induced, as they were in our case, because we as a church didn't know how to nurture and administrate prophetic ministry.

AN IMPORTANT REALITY CHECK

Let me offer a general encouragement to all. Through my years of being personally involved in the lives of fellow believers, I have observed a common hidden agenda that often operates within their lives. This motivation is driving many of them, but it is subtle and very hard to pin down. I would call it a commitment to avoid pain and suffering at almost any cost.

Even as committed Christians, we are tempted to invent theologies and work long and hard trying to create a painless environment for ourselves. We will use God, the Bible, other people and even spiritual gifts and power to achieve this end.

In fact, I have found that many people gravitate toward seeking out various forms of prophetic ministry for this reason. They imagine that if they could more clearly discern the voice of God, then He would surely lead them into a problem-free and totally satisfying life on earth.

The problem is that when God speaks, He sometimes tells us to believe and do things that ultimately lead us into more testings, perplexities and pain! Some of the most confusing and spiritually dry experiences and seasons come upon prophetic people directly on the heels of being used by the Holy Spirit. Often they cry out for God to use them, and when he does, they complain about "feeling used"!

The following scripture describes three categories of experience that are characteristic of genuine apostolic Christianity and are the very seal of authentic Christian leadership. I call them the negative pressures (vv. 4-5), the positive qualities (vv. 6-7) and the divine paradoxes (vv. 8-10) of life in Christ.

> But in all things we commend ourselves as ministers of God; in much patience, in tribulations, in needs, in distresses, in stripes, in imprisonments, in tumults, in labors, in sleeplessness, in fastings; by purity, by knowledge, by longsuffering, by kindness, by the Holy Spirit, by sincere love, by the word of truth, by the power of God, by the armor of righteousness on the right hand and on the left, by honor and dishonor, by evil report and good report; as deceivers, and yet true; as unknown, and yet well known; as dying, and behold we live; as chastened, and yet not killed; as sorrowful, yet always rejoicing; as poor, yet making many rich; as having nothing, and yet possessing all things (2 Cor. 6:4-10).

If we are in true fellowship with the Father and seek to live according to His Word, then all of these things will come our way in different measures from season to season. Expect these opposing and perplexing experiences to show up in your life. If we are reconciled to this reality from the outset, then we are able to respond redemptively to them as they occur.

I believe in praying for the blessings of God to come our way, and I would never encourage anyone to go looking for trials or sufferings. We really don't have to. They will automatically come just by our living in a fallen world. God intends to use the pain of these things to draw us into a relationship of mature faith and fervent dependency upon Him.

Pain and passion are inseparably linked. If there's no pain, there'll be minimal passion for God and minimal compassion for others. Pain causes us to reach fervently to Jesus and to rejoice passionately when God answers us in the midst of our pain.

Even when we enter into intimacy with God by the Holy Spirit (which the prophetic ministry is given to enhance), it will not be totally satisfying to our hungry souls. The Scripture teaches us that we are destined to live with a certain groan for more of God in our souls. Paul refers to this lack of perfect satisfaction in Romans 8:

For we know that the whole creation groans and labors with birth pangs together until now. Not only that, but we also who have the firstfruits of the Spirit, even we ourselves groan within ourselves, eagerly waiting for the adoption, the redemption of our body (vv. 22-23).

The gift of the Holy Spirit is just a down payment of the full inheritance that will be ours to fully enjoy in the age to come. Even full-blown, end-time revival is not heaven on earth — read the book of Revelation!

I find many people spending their spiritual, emotional, physical and relational energies seeking ways to escape all the pain of this "groan" within ourselves. Our deepest satisfaction and the perfection of all things is certainly promised, but its fullness is delayed until heaven.

Yet we can know some significant victory, joy and satisfaction in this age — but only in part:

For now we see in a mirror, dimly, but then face to face. Now I know in part, but then I shall know just as I also am known (1 Cor. 13:12).

Paul teaches us here that in this age, we know and see only in part. Our victory and satisfaction are not yet in fullness. But in the age to come we will see Him face-to-face, and our victory, joy and satisfaction will be in total fullness. We are called to wait joyfully and patiently for that as we love God and others in this evil age.

I certainly don't want to discourage people from getting as intimate with God as possible, enjoying the thrilling, glorious and pleasurable experiences they have with Him. But as deep and precious as these times are to our hearts, they are less than the deepest satisfaction and pleasure we will know when we see Him face-to-face.

Groaning for God's fullness and longing for heaven — these are vital for a healthy Christian life and the salvation process in which we are engaged. A healthy Christian life is characterized by genuine joy in the midst of groaning for God's fullness, which will only be fully satisfied when we see Him face-to-face in heaven.

Thus, even the greatest prophetic ministry with unprecedented power will not satisfy our deepest groan for God's fullness. We must never forget this truth.

CHAPTER 10

PASTORS AND PROPHETS:
GETTING ALONG IN THE KINGDOM

The prophetic ministry in the local church functions in an "orderly freedom" only when both the pastors and the congregation have a common understanding of how things should work. It is important for unity and peace that the church understands how the prophetic ministry functions. The principles for nurturing and administrating prophetic ministry need to be understood not only by pastors and prophets, but also by the majority of the congregation.

One of the reasons I agreed to write this book was to fill the need for a unified, systematic teaching on the prophetic that could be available to our church body. We've had new people join our church over the last years who have not understood the basic principles written in this book. It doesn't seem edifying to repeat continually

134

these principles to the church because the body then becomes too focused on the prophetic. My plan is to ask the new members to read this book so we all have the same understanding.

NON-PROPHET LEADERSHIP

Some people are surprised that I can be the pastor and overseer of prophetic people without being prophetically gifted myself. This misunderstanding has occurred numerous times. Often as a guest speaker I have been encouraged by pastors to "take my liberty." By that they meant I should feel free to single out people in the congregation and give them personal prophetic words from the Lord. When I tell them I don't usually prophesy over people, they often think I am just being falsely humble.

On several occasions I've had to insist, "Listen guys, I'm not joking. I am not a prophet." Some pastors are surprised by this, and some are disappointed. They were hoping to see a spectacular manifestation of God's power when I preached at their churches.

I have had private conversations with many wonderful pastors who were frustrated because they were not able to move in spiritual gifts as freely as some of the people in their congregation. Often, some of these prophetic-type people in the church are spiritually immature in other ways. Pastors feel insecure, thinking that these folks are *apparently* more "in tune with the Spirit" than they are. Consequently they feel too intimated to correct such prophetically gifted people.

As much as the prophetic ministry has found expression at Metro Vineyard in Kansas City, I seldom prophesy, and even then there is no "thus saith the Lord" tagged on for emphasis. If I have something I feel is from the Lord, it will usually come out in my preaching and teaching without my mentioning it as a prophetic word. While some feel pressure to sound more spiritual because of their leadership position, I am careful to *tone down* any appearance of prophetic giftings *because of* my position as senior pastor of the church.

When pastors realize that I am a pastor/teacher with very limited prophetic giftings, their response is often something like this: "I never realized you could have this kind of thing happening in your church and survive as a pastor without being a prophetic person yourself." It doesn't take a prophet to nurture and administrate prophetic ministries in your church. It takes a leader with a vision for a multi-gifted, diverse team.

PASTOR AS PROPHET: THE FOX IN THE HENHOUSE

A pastor with a strong gifting in the prophetic or the miraculous needs to understand the dynamics of his role. Those giftings, if not used with wisdom and restraint, can have a negative effect on his ability to pastor the church effectively.

I run into some pastors who want to create a mystique about their gifting in order to perpetuate the image that they live on a higher plane. Perhaps the intention is to inspire the people in the church to press on to spiritual maturity. Often the secret motivation, however, is to enhance people's confidence in their spiritual and pastoral leadership.

A pastor needs to understand that if he falls into this trap of showcasing his own prophetic giftings, it will hurt and hinder the whole church. In the end, some people will lose trust in the pastor's wisdom and leadership abilities if the pastor too often makes his case by saying that God told him to do it. Some will feel unable to relate to him on his level of exalted spirituality.

A pastor also can end up with people wrongly hooked into him as a prophetic leader instead of their being hooked into the Lord. This is evident when too many people want to be with him, hear from him and get a word from him. The insecure pastor enjoys this attention for a couple of years, but he'll eventually burn out.

Pastors wanting to lead primarily through prophesying are making a serious mistake in their leadership style, and this will have a demobilizing effect on the church. As the senior pastor, I am careful not to add emphasis to what I say with "thus saith the Lord." Only rarely can I give that kind of vital direction, warning or correction. The people will become weary of such terminology attached to the directions of the pastor if it comes too often.

A pastor in one city began to experience the gift of prophecy regularly. He saw his prophetic ministry as an extension of his pastoral ministry. Consequently, he used little restraint. His role as pastor was used as a platform for his prophesying. The fox was in the henhouse in the sense that there was not much pastoral restraint to his revelatory gifts.

As time went on, his role as pastor began to be overshadowed by his role as prophet. He was calling out people and giving them words in most services. He began to struggle and was soon prefacing most of his prophetic words with "thus saith the Lord," though many did not come to pass.

Nevertheless, he was beginning to demand the clout of one with a proven prophetic office. Everything in the church began to break down. The people were devastated, the church was a wreck, and finally, after a couple of years, the doors were closed.

Pastors and teachers serve a different purpose than prophets and evangelists who have predominantly power-gift ministries. Most who try to emphasize both get into additional pressures.

God wants all the gifts to rest in a body of people, not in just one or two leaders. One person functioning as both the head prophet and the senior pastor can present a conflict of interest similar to what would have existed in the Old Testament if a single individual were to hold the office of both high priest and king. It was forbidden within the Jewish nation for one person to serve both governmental and priestly functions, perhaps because of the inherent conflict of interest.

I'm not at all saying it is unbiblical to be both the strongest prophetically gifted person in your church and the senior pastor. I am saying that it is rare and that the situation would have added pressures.

A fresh wind of the Holy Spirit is blowing all across the world today. With each new outpouring of the Spirit comes unusual and unexpected manifestations. People receive prayer, they fall to the ground, their bodies convulse as though electricity is going through them, and they see heavenly visions or hear the voice of God. As the Holy Spirit comes upon them, they have an intoxication-type experience in which they might be healed, spiritually refreshed or somehow renewed in faith, hope or love.

This current moving of the Spirit is only a beginning of the kind of deluge prophesied in the end times. The church desperately needs wise and mature pastors/teachers who can lead, nurture and administrate prophetic people in the midst of such a supernatural downpour, or the wineskins will burst and the new wine will be lost.

Michael Sullivant is one example of a person who is called to the rare position of being both prophet and pastor/teacher. Consequently, he plays a unique and essential role in the nurturing and administration of the prophetic ministry at Metro Vineyard. Michael's ministry effectively enables the new wine to flow and increase without bursting our wineskin.

There are usually people in a church who are sensitive to the stirrings and activity of prophetic ministry. They seem aware of exactly how much "freedom of the Spirit" they felt in the last church service.

They often bemoan the fact that the pastor is not more prophetic.

Actually, a God-ordained pastor is equipped with the leadership gifting God wants him to have. He is in a strategic position to help the church succeed in becoming more prophetic if he wisely uses his gift of leadership. Often striving and insecure pastors, rejected and pushy prophetic people, and the lack of a diversified team ministry are factors that hinder the flow of power and revelation through the church. If everyone were a prophet, the church would function like a runaway train without an engineer.

THE PAY IS THE SAME

We all have to learn to be secure in what God has called us to be and realize the value and importance of each person. Paul, in his letter to the Ephesians, was explaining the different gifts and callings in the church when he wrote:

> The whole body, being fitted and held together by that which every joint supplies, according to the proper working of each individual part, causes the growth of the body for the building up of itself in love (Eph. 4:16, NAS).

Satan is a master at sowing into the people's hearts discontentment about who they are and what God has called them to do. This is a problem throughout the whole body of Christ. People are always leaning over the fence, longing for the other cow's grass.

I have met numerous prophetic people who want to be teachers. They clearly see all the pain associated with their prophetic gift, and they imagine that the teacher has only success, respect and a life of appreciation. Yet many teachers I know who have seen genuine prophetic people want to prophesy.

Paul pointed out in his letter to the Corinthians that one part of the problem is *inferiority* — "because I am not an eye, I am not of the body" (1 Cor. 12:16) — and the other part of the problem is *superiority* — "the eye cannot say to the hand, 'I have no need of you'" (v. 21). We have created a lot of this by attaching status to different ministries and giftings. Prophets are ultra-spiritual; apostles are to be super-ultra-spiritual; pastors and teachers are a little less; and so on down the line to deacons, ushers and the person who prints the bulletins.

A lot of this is magnified by Western culture. The social status associated with different functions in the body of Christ causes people to do rather eccentric and unbalanced things, and in the end it affects the way the members of body do their part to supply what is needed. We have often said at our church, "Whether you are raising the dead or taking a nap, if you are doing God's will, the pay is the same in the end."

At Metro Vineyard in Kansas City we are associated with several prophetic people of international stature. Some have lived in Kansas City, and others have been related by friendship. We also relate to about a dozen people who have full-time traveling prophetic ministries and many people who regularly have prophetic dreams and visions.

A pastor like me in this situation has to deal with his own heart about two things. First, he needs to be secure in his limited calling. I am *at peace* within my limited spiritual giftings. Actually, that was never a real big problem for me. I could see the terrible difficulties and pressures people like Paul Cain and others had experienced as a result of their prophetic ministry. I didn't covet that for a second.

One of my main callings is in the area of intercession. For years I have found grace to cry out for a revival of passionate Christianity across our nation. I was content within those limited spiritual boundaries before I had ever heard of any contemporary prophetic people. That was a real key for me, and I still identify with my intercessory burden and calling.

My first book, *Passion For Jesus,* was a clear expression of my heart and primary life message. I am still not a prophetic minister, and I probably never will be to any great degree. I am neither a really good pastor nor a really effective manager. Primarily, I exhort and encourage people, and I also lead a team of people who have gifts which are very different from mine. Their gifts are stronger than mine in many diverse areas. I love it.

One of the most important lessons I had to learn was that I did not have to be intimidated by people who heard directly from God much more frequently and much more dramatically than I did. At first this was terribly different.

I was a pastor in my late twenties relating with people like Bob Jones who received profound and accurate prophetic words. That can be intimidating. My reluctance to confront prophetic people came to a head at nearly the two-year mark of the prophetic ministry in our church.

DUELING PROPHET SUNDAY

During the second year of pastoring our new church plant in Kansas City, I noticed that five or six prophetic people regularly competed for the microphone during the Sunday morning services. I was becoming exasperated because it was clear to me that there was a lot of hype in what had been going on for the last few months. Some of the people were getting tired of feeling manipulated by these prophetic people and were starting to voice their feelings.

On one Sunday morning in December 1984, two of the main prophetic people got into a "prophetic duel" right in front of the church. One stood up and proclaimed something to this effect: "Thus says the Lord, 'A great thing is going to happen.'"

Then the second guy stood up and said, "Thus says the Lord, 'Better things are going to happen.'"

Then the first prophetic guy topped him. Not to be out-prophesied, the second prophet answered back by giving something even better. They went about three rounds each.

I was on the front row getting really angry. It was clear to me what was going on. These two guys were yielding to a common temptation among prophetic people and were competing against each other to be the top prophet of the church. It was scandalous, embarrassing and ridiculous, and everybody could see it except these two prophetic men.

A dozen people came up to me afterward and asked how much longer I was going to let this go on. Usually I tried to cover for the prophetic people by encouraging people to be patient and reminding them of all the great things that had happened through them.

But this time they had gone way over the line. The emperor, or rather the prophets, had no clothes, and the only ones who didn't know it were these two prophetic men themselves.

Bob Scott, a man skilled in administrating prophetic people, and I got both of these prophetic men together and had what turned out to be a very strong and direct confrontation. Both of them were defensive and threatened that if I didn't accept their ministry style and what they had to say, the Holy Spirit's blessing would leave our church.

I was really surprised they would resort to such fleshly means of manipulation because previously they had given prophetic words about the future that had already come to pass exactly as they had predicted. But when they issued this warning — to let them do what they wanted or the Holy Spirit would leave — it pushed a button in me. My eyes opened, and I saw the rank carnality in all of it.

I would normally have been intimidated by people who had previously prophesied with such dramatic accuracy. But I was provoked and offended, so I rose up and told them both to leave. I essentially informed them, "I am finished with you guys!"

That was such a disillusioning time for me that I was tempted to get rid of all the prophetic ministry — the miracles, the supernatural confirmations — everything. We would just no longer have prophetic ministry in our church.

I'm glad now that I didn't give in to my anger and frustration because of the marvelous things that I've seen God do in our church through the prophetic ministry. One very positive thing came out of what we call "Dueling Prophets Sunday." Something broke inside of me, and from that point on, I was no longer afraid to confront prophetic ministers, even if they previously had authority to call fire down from heaven.

Both of the prophetic ministers told me that they were finished with our church, and they assured me that God was canceling all the tremendous prophetic words spoken over the church. They assumed that God was going to leave with them.

It sounds silly to me now, but there was a time when I would have thought that God's blessing would leave if these men got their feelings hurt and left. But God doesn't abandon you because a prophetic minister gets offended. He can be used mightily and effectively by the Holy Spirit, but he is not the mediator between us and God. Only Jesus is.

These two men went out from there to complain against me to some of the key people in the church. But these people called me up and congratulated me saying, "Thank you, thank you, thank you!" That's when it dawned on me that it was *not* the prophets who had the gifting and calling of governmental leadership in our church.

I also realized that if the leaders don't stand up and speak the pastoral wisdom that God has given them, the prophetic people would not only destroy the church, they would destroy their own ministries as well.

Much of what happened on "Dueling Prophets Sunday" was my fault because I had not exercised my leadership gift and responsibility. I allowed these men to get themselves into a difficult and embarrassing situation. I realized that the team of governmentally gifted people in our church had a lot more pastoral wisdom than the prophetic men did about church life and how people respond to the Word of God. In one short week, the way I viewed my own ministry and that of our pastoral leadership team totally changed.

Within two weeks both of those prophetic men came back and repented to me of their ambition and carnal motivations. This gave me a new confidence; those deep, uneasy feelings that I had about their ministry style were really wisdom and discernment. I determined that I was no longer going to dismiss or quench those feelings again.

Since that encounter, I have decided that whenever I get a nervous feeling about what the prophetic people are doing, I am not going to ignore it. To neglect the responsibility to lead the prophetically gifted people will usually result in harm to the church and to the prophetic ministers.

THE MOTIVATION OF REJECTED PROPHETS

Most prophetic people get in touch with their giftings long before they cultivate the corresponding wisdom, humility and character that is necessary to succeed in prophetic ministry.

In the beginning, they may appear arrogant or pushy because of their zeal. As years go by, their pushiness usually comes from fear, hurt and rejection.

Most prophetic people who have been around for a few years have had their hands slapped many times. Some of them have been dealt with harshly, without proper explanation and without the security of a good relationship with church leadership.

By the time I met Bob Jones, he had been mistreated by many people and had deep ministry scars. John Paul Jackson, another prophetic minister at Metro Vineyard, was so shell-shocked by negative experiences with previous churches that he was expecting to be totally rejected by us at any time.

The average person who has been in the prophetic ministry for ten years is pretty beat up and bruised. This is especially true if the prophetic gift was active in his or her early years. By the time this person reaches forty or fifty, he or she is often very guarded and suspicious of authority figures.

Those coming into prophetic ministry later in life may also have problems with rejection. These past histories of dysfunctional relationships with leaders in the church cause prophetically gifted people to put a lot of extra effort into getting honor and acceptance. Several problems can develop if they give in to those temptations.

Many prophetic ministers are trying to build up enough credibility to ensure that they won't get ousted. Many of them just want some security. They feel that if they get enough clout, they don't have to worry so much about being rejected. Everyone knows you don't cut a great athlete from your basketball team just because he has one bad game.

Also, they feel that if they can build a reservoir of credibility, when they have something to say, they won't have to fight to be heard. Since building clout is so important to them, there is the temptation to push hard to get credit for having accurately heard from God.

I do not think it is always appropriate to acknowledge publicly the person who gave me a key prophetic word as I share it with the church. However, a rejected prophet can hardly resist proclaiming, "Oh, *I'm* the one who gave him that key prophecy!"

One temptation often leads to another, and when the prophetic person or his or her revelation is not publicly recognized, the temptation is to whisper to the influential people in the church in an attempt to get recognized. Some prophetic people are determined to be heard one way or the other. Obviously, this does not make for a good friendship with the pastor, who sees all this as selfish ambition and manipulation.

Sometimes prophetic people come into conflict with pastors because they push too hard for their revelations to be spoken at the public church services. If the pastor doesn't give the prophetic minister a public platform in the church, the prophetic person is tempted to judge the pastor as having a controlling spirit or to think he is a stiff-necked Pharisee who is always resisting the Spirit of God. Sometimes people with this attitude will gather their prophetic groupies together to pray against the pastor.

All of this and more is usually a result of wounded and rejected prophets giving in to former hurts and present temptations. The problem is amplified by pastoral leadership which does not see far enough beyond the prophetic person's pushiness to discern the fears and hurts that drive him.

If prophetic people who are misunderstood, wounded and rejected, give into their fears and temptations, they will extend great efforts to obtain credibility and acceptance. But, ironically, their efforts will always backfire on them. The harder they try, the worse it gets. The unfortunate fact is that many of them have not yet figured this out.

Pastors are usually reluctant to confront seasoned prophets. Why? Because the pastor has his own insecurities. I was very much aware of my inability to hear from God as they did. I operated on the premise that if they could receive divine information, certainly they could hear from God on how to apply it. I made a false assumption.

INSECURE PASTORS AND LEADERS

Knowing where and how to draw the line with prophetic ministry minimizes the insecurity and fear a pastor normally experiences when first encountering such people. If a pastor understands how to deal with these people, he is less afraid of them. Most pastors don't mind that things are a little messy if it is going to be profitable at the end of the day. But if they don't see the long-term benefit, they're going to say, "Enough of this!" and press the reject button.

For the most part, pastors don't want to be embarrassed, and they don't want their people becoming hurt and confused. They are trying to protect their people and keep peace in the church.

Prophetic people often have a very keen sense of being answerable to God. Pastors have that sense too, but they are also very aware of being answerable to people.

A pastor probably feels both concerns differently than the prophetic minister. The pastor realizes he is answerable to God, but he knows that if there is a problem, he's going to hear it from the elders and from half of the congregation on Monday morning.

The pastor also has the conflicts and the practical pressures of meeting the budget. When people get upset, they often leave and disrupt the economics of the church. What that means to the pastor is that he might have to fire part of the ministry staff. Prophets don't usually live in that arena or with those pressures.

Many pastors yield to insecurity and the fear of man. They've seen too many churches fail and too many people hurt by it. They sometimes get their eyes off God and yield to fear when things get beyond the comfort zone. They must learn to lead without fear and yet keep balanced in the area of risk-taking without sacrificing pastoral wisdom.

The pastor and leaders sense several things: what God wants, what the people are going to say, and a half dozen other factors that, if left unattended, may cause the wheels to come off the entire operation. It's good for prophetic people to understand all of this so they don't see pastors and leaders as people who simply want to quench and oppose the move of God.

Most pastors I know will let unusual, unprogrammed and even strange-looking things happen as long as they know it is not hype or fake. Pastors are afraid of things happening beyond what is of the Holy Spirit. They would rather cut things off a little before the danger zone.

Prophets are almost always willing to go a little bit farther than the danger zone to make sure that we do everything that might be of the Lord. If we do a little bit more, in their way of thinking, it's better than not doing all of it.

The prophet's biggest fear is that he might not get everything unloaded that God wants unloaded. The pastor's biggest fear is that he doesn't want to get the church into hype because he has to maintain a long-term relationship with them. Prophets and pastors have the same motivation, being afraid of missing God, but act from different points of view.

One of the greatest benefits of having prophetic ministry in the church is having the input from proven, gifted people who carry the prophetic burden of God's heart without the same fears and anxieties that often accompany the pastoral leadership team. Many times those fears and anxieties serve as blinders to the pastor.

It may be harder for a pastoral leader to recognize a flaw in the church if it has been there a long time. Yet this flaw seems obvious to the prophetic people. Perhaps the pastor is more acutely aware of all the problems that will arise from trying to fix the problem. On the other hand, a general understanding of pastoral and administrative problems associated with leading the church should enable prophetic people to understand the pastor's dilemma more clearly.

The church's greatest effectiveness is realized when the diversity of gifts and personalities work together as one team ministry. But it takes a lot of patience and the ability to honor one another to deal with the pressures that come from nurturing and leading a church with a variety of giftings.

Unless we learn to show honor to each other and to the unique work that the Holy Spirit is doing in each person's life, we may wind up in a holy war, especially if the gifts and personalities are strong. Without team ministry, none of these gifts would be able to prosper. I believe this is especially true for the prophetic ministry.

CHAPTER 11

THE PROPHETIC WORD
IN PUBLIC WORSHIP

The way we handle prophetic words in a regular public worship service has evolved over time. For the first two years in Kansas City, we allowed almost everything to happen spontaneously without any of the procedures we have today.

During those first years, as well as in the years that followed, there were numerous occasions when a prophetic word was spoken forth by someone in the congregation that resulted in great benefit to our church.

THE BENEFIT OF PUBLIC PROPHECY

A couple of years into the life of Metro Vineyard, one of the men on our prophetic team got up and said that the Lord had spoken to him very clearly and powerfully. It was February 1, 1985. He said the Lord was going to provide a building for this body of believers in four months — by June 1. He went on to say that two men in business suits were going to come up to us and make us an offer we could not refuse.

At that time we had a seven-hundred-member congregation and no building. The meetings were held in a high school, and we had *a lot* of meetings! Everything we owned had to be packed and unpacked each meeting. There were numerous inconveniences that made this arrangement tiresome to everyone.

This prophetic minister was telling the congregation what everyone so desperately wanted to hear: All of this was going to be over in a few months. Everyone clapped and cheered wildly at the word.

I stood next to the man giving the prophecy, feeling complete panic race through my soul. I didn't know exactly what to do. The word was so clear: two men in business suits making an offer so good that we could not refuse it. June 1. A building we didn't have to look for — and we had been looking long and hard *without any success.*

I was struggling with the idea that a great deal was at stake here. What if I let it go without comment or correction, and it didn't happen? The backlash directed at this man was going to be minor compared to what the people were going to say to me for letting them be led around by this prophetic word.

This particular minister had a lot of credibility and a fairly accurate track record with regard to some significant prophecies. Nevertheless, he still made mistakes occasionally.

All I could think about was all the people who would want to lynch me on June 2 because of their dashed hopes if a building was not provided by God on June 1. I knew that there were only four months until June 1. As the pastor, I felt that the prophetic word put me way out on a limb.

The building committee was not very enthusiastic either. In fact, I think they felt a little undermined by what had happened. They had already put in many hours of hard work looking for a permanent facility.

It was not clear to me what to do with this committee. If I believed the prophetic word, the new building committee should be dissolved, and if not, I needed to encourage them to keep working. The truth was that I really didn't believe the word. I felt that the prophetic minister probably had an incorrect interpretation of what God showed him. Thus, I told the building committee to keep searching.

I informed the prophetic minister afterward how much I would have appreciated it if he had talked to me before putting me into such a difficult position. After Dueling Prophets Sunday a few months earlier, we had begun to work out a system for administrating the flow of prophetic words in our worship services. We were only in the beginning stages of learning to give pastoral leadership in this area. Believe me, this incident helped move the process along.

The committee continued looking for a building for the next three months. As May rolled around, they had located no facilities that were even considered possibilities. I was really sweating and was already preparing my answer to the congregation for the meeting in the high school on June 2. However, on May 10, two men asked my beloved associate Noel Alexander and myself to lunch.

The first thing they did was apologize for their dress. They felt overdressed wearing suits and ties (which they rarely did) because they had just come from a special meeting. They went on to say that they had a building to offer us. These businessmen had a burden to reach young people and had bought an indoor soccer field in order to win kids to Christ, but things were not working out as they had hoped.

"We've heard about your ministry," they said, "and we want you to have our building. Our soccer schedule is over on May 28, and we want you to take it immediately so that there will be no vandalism." So three weeks later, on Saturday, June 1, we took the keys, started cleaning up and had our first church service there on Sunday, June 2.

It happened just as he had prophesied it — two men in business suits made us an offer, and they did it before June 1. A building that would seat over two thousand people was offered to us at such a low price that we were able to pay it off completely in three years. It was truly an offer too good to refuse, just as had been prophesied. I was overjoyed.

All of this could have happened without any prophetic proclamation in the Sunday morning service. I would much rather have heard the prophetic word in private and hidden it in my heart. It sure would have been easier on my nerves. But God knew exactly what He was doing.

Most of our congregation lived in a semi-affluent area of town. This new facility was ten miles south of where we had been meeting; it was located in a lower socioeconomic area. Most of the church growth

149

experts say that a ten-mile move to a different socioeconomic area would be negative for any church, normally resulting in a loss in membership.

But the prophetic word was so precise that the church accepted the new location as being from the Lord. Of the seven hundred people in our church, we lost only about three or four families. God not only prepared the building, He also prepared the people for a significant move through a prophetic word that morning.

"ANYTHING GOES" APPROACH TO PROPHETIC MINISTRY

Very often, people who are new to the prophetic ministry are concerned about the Holy Spirit being quenched. Most of them don't understand the length, height, depth and breadth of God's love and patience with His people. He is not as easily quenched as we imagine, especially with people who are sincerely trying to do His will but seem to get it all wrong.

That's the way I started out. I thought of the Holy Spirit as a sensitive, skittish dove who would fly away at the slightest ruffle. He's not that easily offended. The Holy Spirit is very secure, very powerful and very kind.

Consequently, in those first two years, except for the really flaky stuff, I would let almost any type of prophetic utterance go without correction or any attempt to administrate it. In my mind, attempting to administrate the flow of the prophetic was equal to standing in the way of what the Holy Spirit wanted to do.

We typically had three or four prophetic words and sometimes as many as eight or ten. There were a couple of instances when people were so enthusiastically charged that the prophesying regretfully continued on long after God was finished.

Many wonderful things happened in those years, but there were some negative circumstances as well. In the midst of it, some prophecies were given that were inaccurate, and some true words were misinterpreted. A true word that is not accurately interpreted or applied can be as dangerous as an inaccurate word of prophecy. For the most part, everyone was left to his own interpretation and application.

People who were around in those days can remember the liberty and excitement of the meetings. All in all, it seemed like a pretty exciting place to be. Someone titled our church *Never-a-Dull-Moment Fellowship.*

However, what I remember are the hours and hours of meetings with discouraged people who were disillusioned and hurt. I was getting a significant education about my naive approach to leadership, by which I was letting almost anything be said in the public meetings.

LIBERTY AND STRUCTURE

There are at least eight basic components that we see as edifying in a normal worship service: 1) the worship of God through music; 2) the preaching of the Word; 3) testimonies; 4) ministry time to pray for the sick, the hurting and the lost; 5) a time for God to speak to the church through the prophetic gifts; 6) fellowship; 7) baptisms and communion; and 8) church business (announcements, tithes and so on).

Some people have the mistaken idea that liberty is simply changing the order of those eight elements. Just because someone decides to preach at the beginning and have worship second doesn't mean there is a freedom of the Spirit in the church.

Liberty, in my understanding, consists of two things. First of all, it is the confidence that people have in their hearts before God — an assurance that they are forgiven and that the Lord is for them even in their weakness and immaturity. When people sense liberty in their hearts before God without any condemnation, then the church is in position to grow in the Spirit.

Second, liberty is the willingness to allow the Holy Spirit to interrupt what we have scheduled to do. If God wants to send a "Holy Spirit breeze" across the congregation in an unusual way, then we must allow it. We don't want to be in bondage to our church structure.

The church leadership has to be sensitive to the spontaneous wind or direction of the Spirit. If God does not indicate a change of direction, then be at peace with the normal format. Simply juggling the order of the service does not constitute liberty.

On the other hand, I know some people who consider any kind of structure a sign of a controlling spirit. In my opinion, God is the author of these eight components of public worship. He likes fellowship, worship, preaching and even announcements that enhance the necessary communication within a church family.

At Metro Vineyard we "put up our sail," and if the breeze of the

Spirit comes across the church, we try to catch it. We are not, however, under the presumption that an unpredictable "breeze" needs to break into every gathering. Those eight components are very biblical and represent a healthy overall diet for the church.

We have also noticed that the interrupting breeze of God often comes in seasons. At times we have gone two to three weeks with the service interrupted and redirected by the Holy Spirit every week. Then we have four to five months in a row in which this almost never happens. There are seasons in the life of a congregation when the Holy Spirit redirects the service according to His specific purposes.

He will also blow the wind of His Spirit on the preaching, the worship, the fellowship — on the whole service — in such a way that it does not redirect the order of the service but simply anoints what is already happening. Some people have the idea that liberty is to reorder the eight components each week. It doesn't take much insight to see through this superficial definition of liberty.

It is naive to believe that structure and liberty are opposites. I know a number of pastors who do not believe in conforming to a structured meeting. People are permitted to do anything they want with very few boundaries. That may seem fun for a few months, but by the twelve-month mark, it usually get wearying. After everyone has done their thing a dozen times, people aren't usually as excited about spontaneity as they once were.

God put the gift of leadership into the church for a reason. It is not to restrict true liberty, but to facilitate, direct and preserve the flow of life. Much of the flow of life can be enjoyed without changing the order of worship very week.

PROCEDURE AT METRO VINEYARD FELLOWSHIP

Most churches I've visited that allow for the expression of prophetic gifts do so by having a programmed pause for the prophetic. The service begins with exuberant praise, slows down to tender worship songs and finally slows down even more to a silent pause in the service waiting for prophetic words to be given.

There are two types of pauses in a worship service. One is a programmed silence to make room for a prophetic word. On the other hand, times of silence come because we sense the presence of God. This is a worshipful silence in which people can commune with God in a private way unrelated to the program and direction of the entire church service.

On occasion, we pause for both reasons, to receive a prophetic word and just to enjoy God's presence. We pause out of reverence for God because His presence is awakening people's hearts. The last thing we want at that point is someone shouting out a prophecy.

Throughout the week or during the worship service there are usually many people who have had some kind of prophetic dreams, visions or impressions. Many feel they have a word from the Lord that relates to the life of the church or to that particular worship service. Nevertheless, we very seldom have spontaneous prophecies voiced from the congregation.

Over the years we have developed a somewhat different method for administrating and making room for the prophetic gifts in a regular worship service. Again the purpose of leadership is to facilitate the flow of life and power. Therefore, we do not always have pauses to wait for prophetic words in our worship service, and spontaneous prophecies are almost never shouted out from the congregation.

We have a microphone down on the front row near one of our pastors who has the oversight of prophetic ministry for that meeting. We invite and encourage people to come to the front at any time during the service to speak with the pastor.

If the pastor knows the person is credible, he simply hands the microphone to them. If he doesn't know the person, he quietly helps them discern if the prophetic word is for the whole church or just for them personally.

Also, he seeks to understand if this is the right time to share it. People can have a legitimate prophetic word but the wrong timing. Maybe it should be shared after the preaching and just before the ministry prayer time instead of during the worship time.

If several people approach the pastor at once, he will usually determine in which order the words should be given. Many times several people come with the same word. In this case, the pastor sums them all up and shares it with the church instead of having each person give his word individually. At the proper time, he will get the attention of the worship leader who will make a place in the service for the prophetic word.

If it seems more appropriate, he may come up and summarize some of the different prophetic words himself, or he may also have one or two of the people come up to the microphone and speak to the whole church.

It is our presumption that in a large congregation which nurtures the prophetic ministry there are going to be fifty to one hundred different people with a dream, vision or prophetic word that they received either in the worship service or throughout the previous week. Just because someone receives a revelation from God doesn't mean it is to be spoken from the platform.

The issue is to find a way to discern what God is saying to us and then communicate it to the congregation in an orderly way. My guess is that a lot of revelation is not intended to be shared publicly, but is actually a personal word for the individual. Also there may be ten people who have the same word, dream or vision. Nine of those are not to be spoken but are God's way of confirming the facts of the one who speaks.

In our current format, there are few programmed pauses in our worship services, and a limited number of spontaneous words are given from the congregation. We have singers on the worship team who are gifted in singing the prophetic impressions they receive.

They're on the platform with microphones in hand. In the course of the musical flow of worship, they sing out spontaneous prophetic prayers, encouragements, challenges and longings. Sometimes a person from the congregation may come to the open microphone on the floor of the auditorium and sing out a prophetic message. The prophetic singers usually express God's prophetic word to us with beautiful songs and music.

Usually Michael Sullivant is the pastor responsible for the leadership of prophetic ministry during the worship services. He is supported by the other members of the leadership team, serving somewhat like an air traffic controller. The gift of leadership in operation here is to facilitate the orderly flow of prophetic revelation.

A couple hundred people in the congregation who have their spiritual antennae up and who would love to see God interrupt the normal course of every service can be a challenge to anyone's gift of leadership. The worst thing that can happen is for the leaders (who believe it is God's best to stick with the predetermined order) and the people (who desire spontaneous interruptions) to get into a tug of war over this issue!

The pastors must be willing to go with the Spirit's flow and, likewise, those sensitive people also need to recognize the legitimate need for the gift of leadership in the God-ordained functioning of the worship service.

When people come to us with some type of prophetic revelation that suggests a significant redirection in the service that is not apparent to all, we usually tell them that we are going to wait for some other confirmation. According to 2 Corinthians 13:

> By the mouth of two or three witnesses every word shall be established (v. 1).

I understand that neither this verse nor its Old Testament source (Deut. 19:15) is primarily focused on judging prophetic words. Nevertheless, we follow a principle of confirming major course corrections in our worship service by two or three witnesses. This confirming principle is alluded to in 1 Corinthians 14:

> Let two or three prophets speak, and let the others judge (v. 29).

Usually there are prophetic confirmations when God wants to change the direction of the service.

CORRECTING UNANOINTED PROPHECIES

Most pastors and leaders have at one time or another experienced the fear of strange or unbiblical words being voiced in the church in the name of prophecy. But if there is an established process of correcting such fleshly words, there will be less pressure on both the leaders and the people. Several different types of correction will periodically need to be employed.

Although most of the prophetic words in our church come through the microphone up front, that procedure is not established as a hard and fast rule. Asking the people to speak their prophetic word over the microphone serves three purposes. First, it allows the entire congregation to adequately hear the word. Second, it gives us the ability to record the word. Third, it gives the leaders a chance to talk with the person before the prophetic word is spoken.

However, someone will occasionally give a word from the congregation which does not edify the body. It seems to have no inspiration, no life or no relevance. I do not like to call this false prophecy because that might imply to some that the person is deceived by a demon. The Bible says:

He who prophesies speaks edification and exhortation and comfort (1 Cor. 14:3).

The word may not do any of those things, but if it's not a directional prophecy, and if it doesn't represent a doctrinal error, then even though it is unanointed, we treat it as a less serious problem. We will usually let it go the first time and probably the second. However, after two so-called prophetic words that seem to contain no anointing or edification, we will go to the person and gently *suggest* that they submit their word to the leaders sitting at the front.

If it happens a third time, we then *require* them to submit their prophetic word to the leadership before speaking it out in the church service. If the person does not heed this third private correction from the leadership, then we will stop them on the fourth time and correct them publicly.

This has happened only a few times. On each occasion we have taken time to explain to the entire congregation the whole process that evolved with that person. If the whole process is not explained to the congregation, then other prophetic people will have the fear of being publicly corrected.

But when the people understand the whole process, it gives them security to know that the leadership will not deal harshly with them if they make a mistake when they begin to step out. They must not be afraid that they might prophesy something wrong and be suddenly corrected for it before the church.

The church needs to be able to trust the leadership to deal with such things in a spirit of gentleness or else the spirit of faith and liberty in the church will diminish quickly. If this happens, then the prophetic ministry will surely dry up and shut down.

INSTANT CORRECTION

There are two types of prophetic words that we publicly correct *immediately* — but again, as gently as possible. The first type is a prophetic utterance given as a rebuke or correction to the church by someone who did not first go through our leadership team.

For example, I would never go to another church and give a prophetic word that was a correction or redirection without giving it first to their leadership. If the leadership of the church agrees with the word, I would ask them to present it to the church. It is usually more effective if the local leadership team speaks the corrective word instead of a visitor who is not well known by the local church.

They might ask me to share it with the church, but I would do so only after it was made clear to everyone I was speaking at their request.

If, in our private discussion, the leaders rejected the prophetic word, yet I was convinced that I had unmistakably heard from God, I might warn them in the pastor's office, "I think you guys are really in trouble." But I would never speak a corrective word publicly in a church outside their leadership and authority structure.

If a person stands up and gives a prophetic word that suggests a new direction, a rebuke or a correction for our church without first submitting it to the leadership, I gently respond in this way:

> I appreciate the fact that you are trying to hear from God for this church and that you care about us. However, I would like you to take this word, share it with the leadership team and let us discern it together. We invite you to be a part of this process if you wish, but for now we are not going to move in that direction. We will come back and give you a report later.

It is very important to teach the people to stay within proper lines of spiritual authority when bringing a corrective or directive word to a local church.

The other type of prophetic word we would correct immediately is one that contains unorthodox doctrinal implications. Again the correction must be done with kindness and gentleness. This is not the time for the pastor to look macho by showing how many bullets he has in his pastoral gun.

We must always remember that we are dealing with precious human beings who are redeemed by His precious blood. We can harshly deal with the individual's error, but with harshness we will also destroy the liberty and openness in the church.

If a person's prophecy included some kind of significant doctrinal error, then I would correct it on the spot. I would begin by saying, "I'm sure he meant well, but the word spoken calls into question a doctrine that we esteem as biblical." Then I would accurately state the doctrine that was called in question.

GOD SPEAKS THROUGH *Us*

It is such a simple idea: God wants to speak to and through the body of Christ. The power of revelation can flow through even the youngest believer in the church.

The church is made up of people who are all indwelt with the power and presence of the Holy Spirit. No one has a corner on the Holy Spirit; He sovereignly moves in and through the church as He desires. Our procedures are not perfect, but on occasion they work well to facilitate the power and revelation of the Spirit operating through the church as a whole.

Recently, a dear lady in our congregation came up to Michael Sullivant. It seemed obvious to him that she was being moved on by the Holy Spirit. She was very urgent and emotionally charged, which is not her natural inclination. She said that the Lord was showing her that there were some people present that morning who needed to come to Jesus for salvation and that the Lord was going to move upon them.

She offered to share this word publicly, but Michael didn't discern that this would be the best thing. Rather, he briefly shared with me the prophetic word and left it in my hands to administrate.

At the end of my sermon, I gave a salvation invitation based on this prophetic word, and five people immediately responded. Although this kind of thing has happened from time to time at Metro Vineyard Fellowship, it is not a weekly occurrence. I then shared with the congregation that this prophetic word had been given to one of our members earlier that morning. This just added to the joy of the whole event in the hearts of our people.

Earlier last year, a similar thing happened at the end of the Sunday morning service. After the preaching, during a ministry time, Michael was in the front of the church as usual collecting words of knowledge from the people to speak over the microphone.

People were coming forward in response to an invitation to receive personal prayer. At one point I prayed for a certain lady. As I began to pray, nothing seemed happen. This went on for five minutes or so.

At this point, Michael shared a word of knowledge over the microphone given by one of our members about a dysfunctional pancreas. The lady I was praying for told me that this prophetic word was for her. Up to this point, I was simply praying for the Lord to touch her in a general way.

Suddenly she began to feel God's power move upon her body and she became unsure of what to do. I later found out that she was a first-time visitor who had been brought to the service by a friend and that she had never seen anything like this before. That was why she was anxious.

I encouraged her to calm down and explained to her that the power of the Holy Spirit was touching her and that she didn't need to be afraid. As I spoke to her, she opened her eyes and started screaming and crying. She seemed to be looking behind me, and she started crying out, "I can see, I can see!"

I had no clue what was going on. As it turned out, she had a large blind spot over one of her eyes due to diabetes that instantly went away as we prayed that morning.

The last report we received was that this woman needed to cut back on her insulin dosage and that at least a partial healing had occurred. The Lord had used that prophetic word of knowledge from one of the people in the congregation to spark a marvelous healing. The church rejoiced greatly in praise to the Lord that day.

Despite the dangers and the historic and possible future abuses of public prophecy, it is still essential to give it its proper place within the gathered community of God's people. Paul exhorted us not to quench the Spirit or despise prophetic utterances (1 Thess. 5:19).

The Holy Spirit will bring necessary and essential encouragement to believers' hearts as they hear the word of God spoken by the "whosoevers" — young, old, male, female, trained or untrained members of the body. We must make a place for this expression because the Holy Spirit lives within and moves upon every member of the body. Any one of us is a potential vessel for a timely and vital word from our Lord Jesus, Head of the church.

CHAPTER 12

THE PROPHETIC SONG OF THE LORD

Music is a heavenly thing in its essence, a part of creation that reflects and proceeds from the very heart and personality of God Himself. This makes music prophetic in nature.

Our Father loves music. He is a singing God (Zeph. 3:17). He has a powerful and majestic voice (Ps. 29). Jesus, the Son, composed the song of all songs that will be eternally fresh — the "song of the Lamb" (Rev. 15:3-4).

The Holy Spirit inspires songs and melodies. There is a whole book of them in the Bible — the book of Psalms. The Bible also contains the greatest song in redemptive history, the Song of Solomon. The Scriptures reveal that music existed within the angelic realm before the creation of the earth (Job 38:7).

160

Music has always provided a means of communion and connection between God and His creatures above and below. Spirit-filled Christians are to occupy themselves with singing psalms, hymns and spiritual songs, singing and making melodies in their hearts to the Lord (Eph. 5:19). Music has intrinsic power to move the inner affections and the outer actions of people. It is a providential gift that God has given to all peoples and even to some of the animals. It is pleasant to hear the birds sing on a beautiful spring day.

It is also true that music is a source of power that Satan has always sought to usurp, pervert and use for his assault against God and His kingdom. This is actually a testimony to its great value. Satan has used the spiritual force and influence of music to seduce and lead people into idolatry, vanity and sexual immorality through the ages. He has used it quite effectively.

Yet God is not intimidated by this fact, and He refuses to allow the thief to possess it as his own. God still owns all the real and true life-giving music of both heaven and earth.

WHAT IS THE PROPHETIC SONG OF THE LORD?

In light of the nature and importance of music, it should not surprise us that God has used minstrels to inspire and activate the prophetic (2 Kin. 3:15). Neither should it be surprising that prophetically inspired people will be led to sing in the Spirit, communicating the heart of God to His people and the heart of His people back to God. The following scripture implies that one of the deepest longings within the heart of Jesus is to sing the praises of His Father in the midst of and through the instrumentality of the congregation of the believing:

> I will declare Your name to My brethren; In the midst of the assembly I will sing praise to You (Heb. 2:12).

This is the essence of what some have termed the "song of the Lord." This phrase, popularized by the charismatic renewal of recent decades, refers to the scriptural references to the Lord's song (Ps. 137:4), spiritual songs (Eph. 5:19) and singing a new song to the Lord (Ps. 33:3; 96.1; 98:1; 149:1; Is. 42:10). The risen Christ loves to impart some of the passion He has for His Father into the hearts of His younger brothers and sisters through giving them His songs by the Spirit.

The Westminster Catechism begins with the famous statement, "The chief end of man is to glorify God and enjoy Him forever." So much for Puritans being down on pleasure! American pastor and author John Piper has brilliantly changed this sentence to say, "The chief end of man is to glorify God by enjoying Him forever."[1]

I can't think of any better way of enjoying God than by experiencing the pleasure of mingling the very love that Jesus has for the Father with Spirit-inspired music. Surely some of the "pleasures that are at His right hand forever more" will be the heavenly music and songs that surround His throne.

Many people who have had heavenly encounters and returned to tell about them have spoken of the marvelous music they heard in heaven. People who have had experiences of having their ears open to the spirit realm have testified of hearing the angelic choirs and music. In fact, I had an experience like this myself.

Early one morning a few years ago, I arrived at the church auditorium to attend an intercessory prayer meeting. As I got out of my car and approached the building, I heard this tremendous music coming from the sanctuary. I thought that the people who had gathered were listening to some wonderful music tape like Handel's *Messiah* on the sound system at a very high volume. The sound was loud and majestic.

I continued to hear this awesome music up until the moment I opened the sanctuary door. The glorious music was instantly shut off like someone had pushed the stop button on the stereo.

To my surprise, the sound system inside was not yet on, and the few people who had arrived early for the meeting were quietly waiting for the worship team to arrive. They had heard nothing. I was stunned to realize that I had just had an encounter with the Holy Spirit.

I didn't tell anyone at the meeting what I had heard. In anticipation, I thought that surely the Lord was going to visit and especially bless this meeting in power. That must be why He let me hear the heavenly music. But to my surprise, it was just like most of the ordinary prayer meetings that we conduct each day — nothing spectacular; just some tired but sincere believers calling out to their God at an early morning hour.

Afterward, as I pondered the meaning of my experience, I realized what God was saying. He was blessed by those "ordinary" daily prayer meetings that to us often seemed weak and unanointed. The heavenly hosts, under the Holy Spirit's direction, apparently are regularly gathering at prayer meetings, unseen and unperceived, to mingle our weak prayers and praises with their strong and glorious heavenly music, worship and prayer. I figure that the angelic choir may really help our voices sound more beautiful in the rarefied air of heaven.

I am actually grateful that the prayer meeting that morning was ordinary. It built my faith and gave more significance to all the time I've spent in "dry" intercession.

This story has also encouraged other believers to persevere in prayer. Maybe the Lord always adds the voices of His angelic choir as our day's intercession reaches His throne. We aren't responsible to make our prayers anointed; we're just supposed to pray and not give up!

Jesus promises to proclaim the Father's name as He sings in the midst of the congregation (Heb. 2:12). This implies that the Holy Spirit gives the church a deeper revelation of the nature and personality of God in prophetic messages through song. It also encourages extolling and declaring the majesty and beauty of God and His ways through prophetic prayers that are sung.

Romans 8:26 states that the Holy Spirit who resides within believers helps them communicate the depths of their being to God in prayer that is in harmony with His will. The work of the Holy Spirit is also explained in 1 Corinthians 2:

> For the Spirit searches all things, yes, the deep things of God. For what man knows the thing of a man except the spirit of the man which is in him? Even so, no one knows the things of God except the Spirit of God (vv. 10-11).

The Holy Spirit is the communication link between God and His people.

Still, I think there will be an intensification of the Spirit's work in releasing His songs before the second coming of Jesus. Perhaps one aspect of the depths of God is the treasury of heavenly music that the Holy Spirit will impart to prophetic musicians within the body of Christ for the blessing of all mankind and the furthering of God's kingdom. This music will reflect a full range of the attributes of our awesome God, from His tender mercy to His terrible judgments.

This is really nothing new; He has been releasing His songs throughout the centuries. Some of these songs are spontaneous, as they

163

are sung for the first and only time in worship services, prayer meetings, home groups or in one's private devotional time.

On the other hand, many prophetic songs have been written down and even recorded to be heard over and over as worship songs or hymns used by choirs or soloists at Sunday worship services.

The book of Revelation indicates that God's work and Satan's work both take on new levels of manifestation and power just before the end of the age. I view this as a cosmic and earthly clash of holy and unholy passions.

Attending the increase of prophetic ministry will undoubtedly be an increase of inspired prophetic music to impart passion for Jesus and His Father in the hearts of believers. Undoubtedly, the enemy will increase his counterfeit anointing to musicians and songs which will draw people's allegiances after him and his unholy spirits.

The Scriptures exhort us to sing a new song unto the Lord. The Holy Spirit stands ready to anoint and inspire many prophetic musicians and singers who will risk getting so intimate with the Godhead that they will discern the fresh music of heaven and release it to us for our enjoyment, refreshment, instruction and admonition.

TWELVE PRACTICAL HELPS

We have learned several things through the years that help define the banks of this musical river of prophetic music that flows through the church.

1. Sing to the Lord in your private devotions. Sing the Scriptures. Sing in the Spirit. Sing what is in your heart. Sing your prayers. In this way you will discover if the Lord is periodically anointing you with prophetic songs. Your confidence will grow so that you may sing them out in public worship settings.

For those of us who are never called to sing publicly, singing in private will be spiritually edifying and pleasurable to the Lord, even if it could only be called at best a "joyful noise"!

2. I believe that God is pleased when we do some "holy risk-taking" in safe settings where we can sing these spontaneous songs out loud before other people. One way to

become accustomed to this type of spontaneous singing is in small group settings such as the worship times during a home fellowship group or a prayer meeting. We have found our intercessory prayer meetings and home groups a wonderful place to test the waters.

Your friends can give you loving feedback on the impact, good or bad, that you are making in your spontaneous singing. Heed their advice and encouragement.

3. If you decide to sing publicly, it is wise to start by singing songs to God rather than songs from God. You will avoid the extra pressure that necessarily comes with the claim of directly speaking on God's behalf.

I encourage the prophetic singers to sense the particular heart-cry the Holy Spirit is anointing as the congregation worships with a heightened sense of inspiration on various songs. Then they can sing a prayer back to God that captures that particular mode they discerned through the songs God anoints in that service.

The song may be a cry for mercy, a lament of failure, an expression of gratitude, an expression of joyful celebration or a search for truth. Or it may be a song that recites any number of spiritual postures and moods that occur in the lives of God's people.

People can often discern when the congregation feels that added inspiration as the worship leader touches these themes in his selection of worship songs. It is very easy to sing a spontaneous song back to God that reflects the songs and themes that the Holy Spirit has already anointed in that worship service. For instance, maybe a worship song about opening and softening our hearts before the Lord has been particularly blessed. People obviously have been moved by it.

After the song ends, a prophetic person might sing out spontaneous words and a tune that continues this theme. This song could even include a divine response about how God's heart is also moved by seeing the open and soft hearts of His people. Maybe He would issue a promise of His intervention on their behalf because He gives grace to the humble and draws near to those who draw near to Him (James 4:6-8).

4. Use the Bible as a glossary for words and phrases to draw

upon in singing prophetically. The Psalms are an obvious place in which to meditate to store up this kind of inspirational material. I sometimes encourage our prophetic singers to sing straight out of the Psalms, opening their Bibles on the spot to provide the words to sing. If prophetic singers immerse themselves in meditation on Scripture, then their prophesying in song will become richer, fuller and more anointed because God has already anointed His written Word.

5. Don't feel that to sing prophetically you must sing only spontaneous songs. God can give prophetic songs ahead of time just as well as on the spot. You may even simply sing a scripture passage that God seems to be highlighting in that moment or season. Old and well-known songs alike can often have a prophetic edge placed on them under the creative leadership of the Holy Spirit.

Many times a musical instrument can even be used prophetically. For years we have had a very anointed saxophone player in our midst named James Nichols who has blessed us repeatedly by spontaneously playing during worship services.

6. Be prepared for mistakes to occur from time to time. Usually they won't be so bad that attention needs to be drawn to them. Administrating this ministry is virtually the same as dealing with prophetic utterances in general. If leaders establish a spiritual atmosphere so tight that mistakes can never be made or tolerated, then they probably won't have anyone in their midst with the fortitude to grow in prophetic singing or in spontaneous instrumental solos.

7. The church leaders need to teach publicly on prophetic singing from time to time in order to place value upon it and stir the faith and courage of the prophetic singers and musicians. If leaders will sow, then they will also reap. All things are subject to the law of entropy, and we need to put energy into the things that we believe in so that their expression doesn't fizzle out.

It can also be helpful to host a weekend seminar for your worship team. Bring in outside worship leaders who are experienced in prophetic music. Have these visiting prophetic worship leaders teach and model prophetic music. Then have them lay their hands on those who desire to be released in prophetic music. This gifting can be imparted from one believer to another by the Holy Spirit (1 Tim. 4:14).

We can assist churches in this by sending a prophetic worship leader or musician to them for a weekend. Your church will be significantly blessed once the music is edified with a prophetic anointing on it.

8. Worship leaders need to make room for prophetic songs during worship services. If they simply pause a few times during the singing part of a worship service while continuing to play a discernible chord progression, the prophetic singers will know when to sing out and will be able to sing in harmony with the instruments. As time goes by, the worship team will learn to work together in an undistracted manner.

9. We have found, as a rule, that a maximum of three to four prophetic songs is enough for most worship services. There can be exceptions. We have celebration services once a month on Sunday nights in which we worship for two to three hours, inviting the Holy Spirit's ministry to heal and refresh people. At these more intensive worship settings, we may have more than three to four songs because the worship lasts several hours.

The singers in a regular Sunday morning service should limit themselves to one to two minutes and one or two general themes. There are exceptions to this, but if these guidelines are generally followed then prophetic singing won't be overdone. If it becomes too common and overused, it can become an object of scorn.

10. Prophetic songs should be limited to the boundaries of exhortation, encouragement and comfort as described in 1 Corinthians 14:3. They shouldn't become a vehicle for bringing correction or direction to the body unless the governing leaders of the church have agreed to it in advance.

167

11. We encourage prophetic singers to seek to bring forth clear and simple messages. Prophecy in the church needs to trumpet a distinct sound. They should definitely seek to avoid overly mystical, parabolic or complicated messages. We have had to ask a few of our singers to avoid using language that is heavily symbolic in order to express themselves in simple themes that are easily understood by all.

12. Encourage the people who have a singing or instrumental gift to test the waters in this kind of ministry. God may have given them their singing voice and musical ability for a prophetic purpose. Discourage those who don't have the voice for it from singing their prophecies in public settings. They, like me, need to stick with talking!

CHAPTER 13

PROPHECY: REVELATION, INTERPRETATION AND APPLICATION

Practically everyone who is filled with God's Spirit is able to prophesy on an inspirational level (what I have referred to as Level I prophecy), especially in a worship service where the Holy Spirit's presence is more easily recognized. The result of what we call *inspirational prophecy* is described by Paul this way:

> He who prophesies speaks edification and exhortation and comfort to men (1 Cor. 14:3).

The purpose of this type of prophecy is to inspire and refresh our hearts without giving any correction or new direction. This kind of prophecy is usually a reminder from the heart of God about His care and purposes for us, and it often emphasizes some truth we already know from the Bible.

Inspirational prophecy can be a very profound revelation, or it can be (as it usually is) something very simple, such as, "I feel the Lord is saying that He really loves us." That message, if it is given at a divinely prescribed time, can be powerful and effective.

Since this type of revelation can flow through every believer, leaders may have to restrain large numbers from prophesying in a service. There are times in worship services that the Holy Spirit moves in a way that everyone can sense. If the pastor doesn't exercise some leadership, forty people will line up to give an inspirational word.

If inspirational prophecy occurs too frequently, it will become too common, and people will no longer pay attention to what is being said. They will, in a sense, begin to "despise prophesying," and not without good reason. When there is an overload of inspirational prophecy, the congregation will often miss the simple but timely word that is designed to give people a fresh inspiration from the heart of God.

Small groups provide the best opportunity for people to experience and participate in this kind of inspirational prophecy. In our larger worship gatherings, we are limited by time restraints and, at best, only a very few can participate prophetically in any given meeting.

The small group setting can also be a "safe" place for a congregation which desires to move into prophecy to begin. In an atmosphere of prayer and quiet waiting for the Spirit's stirrings, leaders can encourage their members to speak out the impressions that come to their hearts and minds. Immediate feedback and evaluation can occur in this setting, and faith for prophetic ministry can grow up gradually as people have experience with accurate and helpful prophetic revelations.

The kinds of prophecy that go beyond inspiration to include correction or direction need to be administrated even more carefully. Our church has received many significant benefits as a result of directional prophecy. However, the ability of any church to receive these benefits hinges on their willingness to wade through the process of discerning not only the initial revelation, but the proper interpretation and then the correct application.

Prophetic ministry can dynamically affect the spiritual temperature of your church, but if leaders don't concentrate on the interpretation and application of the prophecy, the church may be headed for trouble.

INTERPRETING DIVINE INFORMATION

We use the term *revelation* to refer to the essence of the information that is communicated — no more, no less. It is the raw data of divine communication.

The problems we have had to deal with have not been the result of incorrect prophetic revelation. In most cases, the divine information was right, but the problems began when someone went on to interpret incorrectly what the prophetic revelation meant.

This misinterpretation can begin either with the person receiving the prophetic revelation or with the person to whom it is directed. Let me give an example.

In a public meeting, a prophetic minister spoke the following prophetic word to a man whom he had never met: "You have a music ministry. You're called to be a singer." What the prophetic minister actually saw in a vision was musical notes around the person. So the prophetic minister thought the man was called by God to sing or play an instrument, but the person to whom the revelation was directed didn't play or sing at all. He was the owner of a music store.

When we took the prophetic minister aside and questioned him, his response was, "Well, how was I supposed to know?"

That is precisely the point — he wasn't supposed to know. It seemed obvious to him that the person would be in the music ministry as a performer. However, when he made an assumption about prophetic revelation based on what *seemed obvious,* he got into trouble. He could have said, "I see musical notes around you; does this mean anything to you?"

It is easy to receive a revelation and then, without even realizing it, cross over the line to the interpretation of that revelation. Pastors and team leaders must constantly remind themselves to distinguish between the raw data (divine information) and the interpretation of its content.

Additionally, many people become disillusioned over the fact that they may not see the prophetic revelation come to pass. Often, the prophecy simply did not come to pass as they assumed or interpreted that it would. The problem was that they allowed revelation and interpretation to run together in their minds until they could no longer distinguish between what God had actually said and the expectation they created by their interpretation.

The interpretation of revelation is often contrary to the obvious. The scribes and Pharisees were perfect examples of this. The *tradition of the elders* was more than a collection of their customs; it was the theological interpretation of the Torah, the first five books of the Old Testament. As centuries passed, those traditions were written down in what became the Talmud.

To the scribes and Pharisees, Jesus was a lawbreaker because He did not keep the traditions of the elders. These religious leaders could no longer distinguish between revelation (the Torah) and interpretation (later called the Talmud). To them, the interpretations and applications were obvious and indisputable.

This tendency to mix up revelation and interpretation shows up in every generation. Many people today who are *into* end-time prophecy become so wrapped up in their charts and predictions that they can no longer distinguish between the raw data of biblical revelation and their systematic interpretations. The Pharisees also misinterpreted the prophets' revelations and missed the purpose of God because Jesus came in a way contrary to all their expectations.

One of the characteristics of prophetic revelation is that it is sometimes allegorical or symbolic, and it is fully understood only after future events have taken place. From the Old Testament perspective, it was not altogether clear what the Messiah would look like. The prophets foretold the coming of both a kingly Messiah and a suffering Servant, but no one even remotely considered that both were the same person. Obviously, kingly messiahs aren't servants, and they don't suffer.

Even the disciples had a hard time with it. The Gospels, especially the synoptic Gospels (Matthew, Mark and Luke), show how baffled the disciples were. The messianic secret is a theme that runs throughout all the synoptic Gospels. They had a very difficult time figuring out who Jesus was and the nature of His eternal kingdom.

The Gospel of John, which was probably written a few decades after the others (around A.D. 90), looks back at Jesus with greater hindsight. In John's Gospel, there is no mystery about Jesus' identity. Clear affirmations of His deity are found in the first verse and throughout the entire book.

For the disciples, and even for some of the Pharisees and scribes, the interpretation of events foretold in prophetic revelation was difficult while they were happening; but their meaning became crystal clear after the foretold events had taken place. We have to be careful about locking in on our interpretation of prophetic revelation lest we miss what God is trying to say to us and do with us.

Carelessly interpreted prophetic revelation can cause chaos in someone's life. Over time we have gained insight about the administration of prophetic ministry. In that learning process, however, we have naively allowed some unfortunate things to happen. One situation was the result of a wrong interpretation being applied to an authentic prophetic revelation, and it turned into a pastoral nightmare.

I happened to be out of town that morning, which is not to say that it wouldn't have occurred if I had been there. One of the prophetic ministers received a word from the Lord for a man in our congregation. This man was horrified as the prophetic minister publicly shared that he had no integrity in his finances.

When I returned, I went to the prophetic minister and asked him exactly what he had seen. He told me that he had seen a dark cloud over the area of the man's finances. He interpreted this to mean that the man was stealing money, but his interpretation was totally wrong!

What actually happened was that soon after this prophecy, the man's business partner embezzled a large sum of money from him. The prophetic word was a warning to the man to watch out for someone who might steal money from him, but it was mistakenly pronounced as a judgment against him. The brother was humiliated publicly by the prophetic word and a resulting shadow was temporarily cast over his integrity.

The problem was that we were naive about the process of dealing with corrective prophecies. We learned that first of all, this category of prophetic word (as it was being interpreted) should have never been given publicly. If the man was guilty of financial sin, then he should have been approached privately as called for in Matthew 18.

Next, if we had interpreted the prophetic word accurately as a warning to help the man instead of as a judgment against him, it would have been spoken differently. "The Lord is indicating there is some kind of dark cloud over you in the financial arena. Let's pray that God will protect you from an attack of any kind of evil." Then, if we had properly distinguished between the revelation and the interpretation, perhaps the warning could have prevented the financial loss.

REVELATION AND CONFIRMATION

When you receive a prophetic word from someone, you must hold it at arm's length until God *Himself* confirms it in your heart. If a prophetic minister receives accurate and authentic revelation from God that, for example, you are going to have a street ministry, all they are doing is giving you an advance warning that *you* personally are going to hear a new direction from God about a street ministry. This prophetic notification is sometimes God's way of confirming ahead of time what you will hear for yourself later on.

On other occasions, prophetic words can confirm something you have already heard very clearly. But you should not step out and act on the prophetic word alone if you haven't received the confirmation.

Often, when people act on a new direction before receiving the confirmation, they get off track. Many times the accurate and often unexpected interpretation is clarified in the process of the confirmation.

One of the reasons we require all directional prophecy to go through the leadership is that it would be awkward to go through the process of properly interpreting the word in the middle of a public worship service. I often hear prophetic words in churches or conferences I attend as a visitor. I have all kinds of questions about some of the words that go unchallenged. You can't interrogate people every time they say something prophetic, but you'd *better* question them carefully if the prophetic word involves a new direction for you.

It is important that you know the difference between what is put forth as *divine revelation,* what is *confirmed* and what is *assumed* to be the interpretation. If you don't distinguish among these three elements, you will undoubtedly trip over your own misconceptions.

If we receive a prophetic revelation which speaks about our future promotion in natural or spiritual things, we must guard our hearts. It is easy to make wrong assumptions, then run with things we have no business running with. Sometimes, our selfish ambition causes us to set our hearts on things that the Lord has not confirmed. Prophetic words that promise us future promotion can fall on us like gasoline on a fire. We so long for those words to be accurate.

The basic problem is not always with the prophetic words or with the people who give them. It is sometimes our selfish ambition that gets us into trouble. If our eyes are completely on the Lord, then we're not as prone to be a sucker for words that promise us great honor.

Sometimes I've been more interested in running with the word than really knowing if it was truly from God.

A man with an ambitious heart is always a sucker for an exaggerated or flattering prophetic word. Problems associated with prophetic ministry are sometimes rooted in ambition, either in the prophetic minister who exaggerates or in the ambitious recipient who refuses to wait for the confirmation or the proper interpretation.

If a prophetic minister adds his own commentary and interpretation to the basic revelation he has received from God, then someone is eventually going to wind up confused and disappointed. The same is true if a person accepts the word of the prophet without a confirmation.

Proverbs 13:12 says, "Hope deferred makes the heart sick." Deferred hope also makes a person angry. There are Christians who are unaware of the fact that they are angry with God. They have become cynical, critical, angry people who bite and devour others in the body of Christ. The problem is that they are heartsick over unfulfilled hopes and expectations, and in a heart that is sick with disappointment, all kinds of heartache can develop. If we are not careful to interpret prophetic revelation, we can wind up with many heartsick people.

People who are disillusioned and offended with God will eventually lose their spiritual vigor. Many times it doesn't happen overnight, but it does eventually happen. The enemy wants to drive a wedge between you and God. Remember, he tried to cause Job to be offended at God by tempting Job to interpret his circumstances incorrectly.

THE APPLICATION OF PROPHETIC REVELATION

The last step in our process of prophetic administration is application. The interpretation answers the question, What does the revelation mean? The application answers the questions, When and how will this come to pass? and What should *I* do? Application is the action that should be taken based on the interpretation.

The anointing and grace to receive revelation is not the same as the anointing and grace to discern the interpretation. We have people who interpret prophetic revelation with much greater clarity than the people who receive the revelation. The other distinct grace from God is the ability to apply what has been interpreted. We have a council of prophetic people who are regularly involved with this.

I have not met many prophetic people who have much wisdom on the application end of the process. I have seen some of the more seasoned prophetic ministers receive words from the Lord which predicted the timing of events with great precision. Nevertheless, the person with the revelation rarely knows the timing.

Bob Jones has an incredible gift of revelation, but he would tell you himself that he often tends to miss it on interpretation and application. One time Bob gave a person a word along with the phrase, "By the end of the year." Well, the end of the year came and the prophecy had not come to pass. I went back to Bob and questioned him about it. It turns out that "by the end of the year" was not a part of the revelation.

"Well," said Bob, "why would the Lord give it if it weren't going to happen by the end of the year?"

My reply was, "I can think of a dozen reasons!"

Revelation itself is not going to help the body unless it goes through the process of interpretation and application. The interpretation may be accurate, but if a person jumps the gun and gets ahead of God in the application, a considerable amount of hurt and confusion may result.

Consequently, there is as much need for divine wisdom in the interpretation and application as there is in the revelation.

God never works as fast as people think He should. Don't get involved with prophetic people and words if you are not willing to wait on God to bring them to pass. God will declare His intention through the prophetic gift, but if the application is not in His timing, you'll find yourself trying to step through a door that is not open. The way is not yet prepared, and the grace is not yet sufficient.

Another aspect of the application involves who should be told the revelation and interpretation and when they should be told. This question must be answered: Is it something for the entire congregation, for only the leadership, or is it not to be spoken at all?

Joseph learned the hard way that telling his brothers about his prophetic dreams could get him into trouble. His brothers interpreted the dreams accurately and came up with their own application — getting rid of Joseph! Like Joseph, many people have a hard time not revealing what they have heard from God. It's our nature to want others to know that *God* has a special plan for us.

The same thing is true of the person through whom prophetic revelation comes. The prophetic person often feels he should tell everyone immediately. He wants everyone to know he was the one who received special revelation. He wants the credit for it. That sounds pretty self-serving, but it is often a motive in the hearts of prophetic ministers — and they are not always aware of it.

Prophetic people who strive to get recognition usually wind up getting corrected. I understand the reasons they have that tendency, but it's still selfish ambition. The indisputable sign that a person has a wrong motivation is pushiness. Striving, pushy people with revelation are unbroken vessels. They don't care about counsel or unity or the wisdom of others. I've learned to stay clear of those kind of prophetic people. If you give them three or four times at the microphone, they will end up bringing unnecessary division to the body.

The most important thing is to get the word to the right people in the proper manner. Sometimes, the way we as leaders present things to the congregation often leaves them not even knowing who originally received the word from the Lord. This can be a protection for a person who is young and vulnerable in prophetic ministry. It can also be a test in humility for them. The prophetic person may feel let down and will try to find a way of letting people know that *he* was the one who received the word. His discernment and perspective on how to apply prophetic revelation is influenced by his need for people to know that he is hearing from God in a special way.

Unfortunately, people usually know what's really going on and will disdain the selfish ambition they see in the prophetic person. This shows that one of the reasons prophetic people need to be involved in a church that both nurtures and administrates the prophetic is that they often fall into this negative pattern without realizing it.

I've had my share of controversy over prophets and prophetic ministry. There are times when people sincerely think they are hearing from God but are completely mistaken. Nevertheless, the problems in the church caused by prophetic ministry are *almost always* caused, not by incorrect prophecies, but by presumptuous interpretations and applications.

Churches need to take the time to work through the process of administrating prophetic ministry and prophetic revelation because the benefits of prophetic revelation to the local church are too great and the consequences of shutting it out are too severe.

WOMEN AS PROPHETIC MINISTERS

T he ministry of women in the church is a hotly debated topic in many circles today. Unfortunately, the effectiveness of the church has been greatly diminished because the ministry of women has been so limited. The intransigent and sometimes chauvinistic position of some in the church is a result of long-held stereotypes about women, dysfunctional male-female relationships and a truncated view of early church history.

My purpose here is neither to put forth a comprehensive theological framework for women in ministry nor to attempt an exegesis of the New Testament texts that relate to the role of women in the church.

My purpose is to cite some examples from church history and how women function in prophetic ministry at Metro Vineyard Fellowship.

WOMEN THROUGHOUT CHURCH HISTORY

The significant involvement of women in the ministry of Jesus is well documented. Women were the witnesses of His crucifixion and resurrection when males were conspicuously absent. Luke declares that the women who had followed Jesus from Galilee still followed along as Christ was carried to the tomb (Luke 23:27-31). Matthew tells how they kept watch over the sepulcher after the men had left (Matt. 27:61). John records that the group of people immediately beneath the cross consisted of three women and one man (John 19:25-27). Though it broke all kinds of social and religious traditions, Jesus made a point to include women in His ministry.

It is little wonder that the prominence of women continued in the development of the early church. A number of women served as leaders in the house churches that were a part of the larger church in the city of Rome. Some of those mentioned are Priscilla, Chloe, Lydia, Apphia, Nympha, the mother of John Mark and possibly the "elect lady" of John's second epistle. Paul mentions Phoebe and refers to her as "a servant [literally, 'deaconess'] of the church in Cenchrea" (Rom. 16:1).

Paul also talks about Junia, referring to her as being "outstanding among the apostles" (v. 7, NAS). Some have debated the exact meaning of this verse. Until the Middle Ages, the identity of Junia as a female apostle was unquestioned. Later translators attempted to change the gender by changing the name to Junias.[1]

Women also functioned as prophetic ministers. Philip, who was selected to serve the apostles as one of the seven men appointed to the administration of feeding the poor (Acts 6), was head of the church in Caesarea. He had four virgin daughters who were recognized as prophetesses in the church (Acts 21:8-9). Some believe that these prophetesses became the standard and model for prophetic ministers in the early church.

When Pope Militiades proclaimed that two female followers of Montanus were heretics, he contrasted them with Philip's daughters. Militiades explained that their problem was not that they were women prophets (for this is what Philip's daughters were), but rather that they were false prophets. Eusebius mentions one Quadratus, a man famous in the second century, who "shared with the daughters of Philip the distinction of a prophetic gift."[2]

The church quickly spread from its birthplace in Jerusalem into areas where the predominant culture was pagan, Greco-Roman or both. In these settings, women commonly held high positions and influence in social, political and religious circles. The idea of women having a leading influence in the church was therefore not thought of in negative terms.

About A.D. 112, the Roman governor, Pliny the Younger, wrote about his efforts to deal with the Christians in Bithynia. He found it necessary to interrogate the leaders of the church, two slave women called *ministrae,* or deaconesses.[3]

There are countless examples of women who served the church with complete and tireless devotion or who, without flinching, endured terrible tortures and martyrdom. A significant step in the process of Christianity's gaining political and social dominance in Rome was the large number of female converts among the upper class.

Men were less likely to become Christians because doing so would cause them to lose their status in society. The inordinate number of upper-class women is perhaps the reason that Celestas, bishop of Rome in A.D. 220, attempted to give women of the senatorial class an ecclesiastical sanction to marry slaves of freedmen.

These highborn women seized the opportunity to become students of the Word. One of these was a fourth century woman named Marcella. The great scholar Jerome, who translated the Bible into Latin (known as the Vulgate), did not hesitate to refer church leaders to Marcella for help in solving their hermeneutical problems.[4]

Women enjoyed great freedom of expression in the earliest days of the church. However, because various kinds of problems arose, the original freedom and liberty afforded them in the church's ministry were replaced by a more precisely defined code of conduct that was reactionary in nature. With each new and more detailed explanation of what was and was not acceptable, the role of women was restricted and diminished.[5]

Nevertheless, even through the Middle Ages there were women who were outstanding examples of spirituality and dedication. The Waldensians, a group beginning in the twelfth century that could be described as Protestants four hundred years before the Reformation, were charged with, among other things, allowing women to preach. Catherine of Siena (1347-1380) was a resolute servant to the poor, a doctor of the church and a lover of God whose theology and piety were revered even by the Reformers.

One summer when Joan of Arc was about thirteen, she suddenly saw a bright light and heard voices while working in the fields. The voices, which Joan thought were either angels or saints, continued after that day, instructing her to help the dauphin (France's rightful king) and to save France. With six knights she road over three hundred miles across enemy territory to tell Charles the dauphin of her plans.

When Joan entered the large hall, the dauphin had disguised himself as one of those in the crowd. Joan walked right up to him and addressed him.

"I am not the dauphin," Charles replied.

Joan responded, "In God's name, gentle sire, you are."

Then she proceeded to reveal to him his private thoughts. The nineteen-year-old girl led the French forces and saved France, and Charles was restored to the throne. Mark Twain studied the life of Joan of Arc for twelve years and concluded that her life was "the most noble life that was ever born into this world save only One."

Though it is impossible to discern between legend, facts and spiritual anointing, Joan's prophetic experiences seem somewhat similar to others I know who have been called to the prophetic ministry.

Women have also played a significant role in the spread and development of Protestantism, particularly in the area of foreign missions. In the twentieth century, women began to emerge in ministry and leadership roles, first in the holiness churches and then with the Pentecostals. The examples are numerous, the two most notable being Aimee Semple McPherson, the founder of the International Church of the Four Square Gospel, and Kathryn Kuhlman.

David Yonggi Cho has released women into ministry and leadership positions in the Full Gospel Central Church in Seoul, South Korea, and with their help has built the world's largest church with over a half million members.

WOMEN'S MINISTRY AT METRO VINEYARD

We have had a number of women in our midst who have made profound, accurate and edifying contributions to our prophetic ministry. While much of this has been behind-the-scenes service to our leadership team, we are enthusiastic about women moving in the prophetic arena. The limits and extent of a woman's function on the prophetic team at Metro Vineyard Fellowship is the same as that of a man. We no longer give prophetic people a prominent public platform — men or women.

Paul Cain, whom we regard very highly, speaks to our church about two to three times a year. However, he gives most of what he receives for us to our main leadership group either in person or by telephone.

If a woman has the same level of prophetic revelation that Paul Cain has, she will be given the same honor and platform as Paul Cain, whether that platform be public or to our main leadership group. Any woman preacher who has the anointing to teach will get some opportunity based on her proven teaching gift. Over the years, we have had several woman preachers speak to our whole church when we've discerned in them the gifting to preach.

At Metro Vineyard Fellowship we have identified a prophetic network of about 250 people who regularly receive dreams, visions and prophetic words from the Lord. They meet periodically with Michael Sullivant as the leader. Michael also gives pastoral oversight to the itinerant ministries and the established prophetic ministries in our church.

There is a prophetic council made up of about thirty people, many of whom are women. This council leads the larger prophetic network. They help nurture these people in their gifting, listen to their prophetic revelation and help them with the interpretation and application.

This prophetic fellowship legitimizes what they are doing and provides a place for encouragement, correction and judgment within a community of people who have the same type of giftings. They feel free to express themselves in a friendly atmosphere where they can receive both direction and correction.

STEREOTYPICAL WOMEN

Stereotypes, prejudices and unfair biases are commonly directed against women. This powerful reality throughout the Western world hinders the work of God. Our deeply imbedded stereotypes primarily come from our culture. They exist in our church as well, and we need to strongly address them on the proper occasions.

We realize the vast importance of a woman's impact on the present and future generation, and we therefore highly honor and esteem the ministry of a mother in the home. But we do believe that women are often called to function outside the home to serve the kingdom of God.

There are also stereotypes about women and their psychological makeup. One common stereotype is that they are very intuitive, but don't have the proper restraint to control the emotional side of their nature. I don't think this is a fair stereotype. I believe some women certainly can be described that way, but some men are like that as well. I think it is too generalized a stereotype and should not be the reason used to hinder women from ministry.

Both men and women are intuitive, but my experience is that more women than men have a strong intuitive aspect in their nature. A man's stereotype is that he is always in control, but out of touch with his and other people's feelings. That's not always true either.

Dysfunctional relational skills among men and women have always caused many problems both in society and in the church. Some men have unfounded fears about women in ministry, for example, that women will lose their femininity if they lead and that women are more prone to deception (both of which are untrue). So they are afraid to allow women to prophesy or to preach. The problem is exacerbated by some of the radical feminist movements. Consequently, some men tend to dig in their heels and resist valid biblical expressions of women in ministry.

I do believe that if men had been honoring women in the church all along, it might have diffused some of the radical feminist movement in our society. If the church had been leading the way by honoring women in the church, it might have had an impact on the entire society. If there had been more women prominent in society because of the strength of affirmation by men in the church, the negative effects of the radical feminist movement could have been minimized.

This is one practical way that the church functions as a prophetic standard bearer to society — by honoring both women and children in a way befitting the grace of God (Mal. 4:6; 1 Pet. 3:7).

THE JEZEBEL SPIRIT

One of the most misunderstood issues relating to prophetic women in the church is the idea of a "Jezebel spirit," particularly when the term is defined as a controlling woman who dominates men. "Jezebel spirit" is not a biblical term. However, there is a powerfully negative Jezebel-type spirit or attitude in which some people seem to be immersed.

When a woman stands up to a man and confronts him in any way, even if the man has major problems with insecurity and leadership ability, the woman is sometimes referred to as having a "Jezebel spirit." Some women do have an inappropriate, domineering spirit. Some men in the church have the identical problem. But too many women who have a legitimate leadership gift are labeled Jezebels simply because they clash with a man who has a controlling personality.

Sometimes these women are a little wounded. Perhaps their social and relational skills need refining, but men need improvement in their social skills, too, especially those who are insecure and try to manipulate women.

Some women simply won't allow such men to dominate and hinder their place of service in God's kingdom. These women can really suffer from unrighteous judgments against them because they simply spoke up and challenged a man who had a wrong spirit. This type of action does not make a woman a Jezebel.

It trips a wire in my own soul when I hear a woman quickly written off as a Jezebel. It can be a crushing emotional blow to a woman. It is usually an unfair judgment that can unjustly cause her to repress or neglect her ministry gift for years.

I believe that both domineering women and dominating men need to be confronted and then hindered from having too much influence in the church. But when some leaders see domineering men, they tend to wink at the problem and say, "Well, you know he has that strong personality, and that's just the way he is." But when women do the same thing, all kinds of unjust spiritual implications become attached to it.

JEZEBEL — SEDUCTION TO IMMORALITY

I believe the idea of a Jezebel-type spirit *does* involve an element of domination and control. Between Queen Jezebel and King Ahab, Jezebel clearly seemed to be the more dominant (1 Kin. 18).

However, Jesus defined a Jezebel-type spirit very specifically in terms other than domination.

> You allow that woman Jezebel, who calls herself a prophetess, to teach and seduce My servants to commit sexual immorality (Rev. 2:20).

A Jezebel-type spirit then can be described as one who leads the

184

people of God to embrace immorality in a carefree way. This primarily refers to someone with a seducing spirit. When we talk about being seduced these days, we tend to think of it as something women do to men. But some strong male leaders, even within the body of Christ, have a potential to seduce women. They can have a powerful sensual or emotional impact on women. In this way, men can be as seductive as women. Consequently, a man can thus be likened to Jezebel.

I think the most seductive Jezebel-type spirit in the world today is found in certain aspects of the media industry, which is very effective in desensitizing and beguiling the nations to commit acts of immorality. They have promoted the prostitution racket and the X-rated — and worse — film industry. These certain members of the entertainment industry are the ones who perpetuate the stereotype of the woman as the seductress, but it is really their love of money that pours the fuel on the fire of seduction in our society. They, more than anyone else, have the characteristics of Jezebel.

If women should get a break anywhere, it should be in the church. The prejudice toward women is often due to dysfunctional relational skills that exist with both men and women. In these negative situations, the pastors are sometimes called controlling by the women, and the women are sometimes called Jezebels by the pastors. This is all ridiculous. Both the men and the women need to be healed.

We need to esteem and make room for women with valid leadership gifts in the church. Some pastors need to be less defensive and insecure in their leadership style. We need to replace the harsh judgments between men and women with the honor and patience that Jesus lavishes upon each of us who are still immature in our character, wisdom and gifting.

Acts 2:17-18 says that God shall pour out his Spirit on his sons *and daughters,* and they shall prophesy. The church in the end times will flourish as both men and women receive powerful dreams and visions that bring others to deep relationships with Jesus.

We will never be fully effective if one half of God's army is kept out of the battle against Satan's onslaught. We need the men and women both to take their place boldly before God's throne and function together with confidence and security in the body of Christ.

Together we can experience the passionate love of God for us and then use our authority in Jesus to plunder the kingdom of darkness in our generation.

CHAPTER 15

EIGHT DIMENSIONS OF
THE PROPHETIC CHURCH

T he term "prophetic" is used by some in the church to refer either to the fulfillment of end-time events or the speaking forth of revelatory messages. The New Testament church is to be a prophetic servant community, not only in these areas, but in a much broader and multi-dimensional way.

Being prophetic is not simply something "charismatics" do; it is essential to the very nature and mission of the entire body of Christ on earth. Those involved in prophetic ministry need to view what they do in the larger context of all the other dimensions of the church's calling as a prophetic servant community.

People who receive dreams and visions do not comprise *the* prophetic ministry in its entirety, but are really only one expression of

186

a community that is prophetic in at least eight dimensions.

Some of these eight categories or dimensions of prophetic expression may overlap in the same way the gifts of the Spirit do. The list of the nine gifts of the Spirit (1 Cor. 12:7-11) is simply a description of how the person of the Holy Spirit moves through individuals in the church. Sometimes it is hard to categorize and define certain manifestations. Was it a word of wisdom, a prophecy or the discerning of spirits?

In the same way these eight dimensions of the church as a prophetic servant community may overlap in some aspects. The point is that prophetic ministry is not just something the church does, but something it *is* by its very nature.

1. REVEALING THE HEART OF GOD

> The angel of God told the apostle John, the testimony of Jesus is the spirit of prophecy (Rev. 19:10).

This means that the fresh revelation of Jesus' heart is the essence of His testimony. This includes the revealing of who He is along with what He does and how He feels. The spirit (purpose) of prophecy is to reveal these aspects of Jesus' testimony. Passion for Jesus is the result of this prophetic revelation. Such holy passion is the highlight of the prophetic church.

The prophetic ministry is to be stamped and sealed with an affection for and sensitivity to the heart of God. It is a ministry that passionately *feels* and *reveals* the divine heart to the church and the world. Prophetic ministry has to do not only with information, but also with the ability to experience in some measure the compassion, grief and joy of God, and then to gain a passion for God. Out of experiencing God will come the revelation of some of His future plans and purposes.

If you "desire earnestly to prophesy" (1 Cor. 14:39) by merely seeking information from the *mind* of God, you have bypassed the cornerstone and the essence of prophetic ministry — the revelation of His heart. The apostle Paul said:

> Though I have the gift of prophecy and understand all mysteries and all knowledge, and though I have all faith, so that I could remove mountains, but have not love [for God and people], I am nothing (1 Cor. 13:2).

Prophets in the Old Testament often prefaced their message and ministry by declaring, "The *burden* of which the prophet Habakkuk saw" (Hab 1:1, italics added). The word *burden* implies emotional and heartfelt issues are at stake — not abstract truth.

So then, one prophetic dimension of the church's ministry is to proclaim, reveal and call to remembrance the intimacies and affections of God. That includes, of course, His jealous longing over His people, His magnificent compassion and His intense grief over our sin that separates us from Him.

The outcome of this revealing of God's heart is the stirring of people's passion for God. The response to such great love is to worship Him and love Him in return.

Kevin Prosch, Daniel Brymer, David Ruis, Chris DuPré and others at Metro Vineyard have been used splendidly as prophetic worship leaders who have fanned the flames of people's spiritual passions through worship. Through their worship tapes and worship leading at conferences, these prophetic men have been the source of refreshing for many. This revealing of God's heart and stirring of the church to worship through anointed music fulfills a prophetic dimension of the church.

My favorite message is that our passionate affection for Jesus is the result of an ever-increasing revelation of the loveliness of His personality that is filled with passion for us. Though I rarely voice a prophetic word in the church, I seek to contribute to the mission of the church as a prophetic servant community by teaching on the passionate heart of God.

2. THE FULFILLMENT OF BIBLICAL PROPHECY

For thousands of years the prophets foretold of the Messiah who was to come and of the kingdom that He would establish. Jesus spoke of it sometimes in the sense that the kingdom had come with the advent of His public ministry and at other times as if the kingdom was "not yet." In whatever sense and to whatever extent the kingdom *has come,* those to whom it has come are the living fulfillment of what the prophets had spoken. Jesus said to Peter:

> On this rock I will build My church, and the gates of Hades
> shall not prevail against it (Matt. 16:18).

188

Throughout the last two millennia all the powers of hell have been unable to eliminate the gospel or the church. It has only continued to grow. Jesus described the expanding kingdom of God like this:

> It is like a mustard seed which, when it is sown on the ground, is smaller than all the seeds on earth; but when it is sown, it grows up and becomes greater than all herbs, and shoots out large branches, so that the birds of the air may nest under its shade (Mark 4:31-32).

The church in its survival and growth is living out the prophetic word. Its very presence is a continuing witness to prophecies fulfilled.

The church is also a prophetic witness in its mission. Just as the apostles were in the early days, the church today is *the* witness to the death and resurrection of Jesus Christ. Its primary task has always been to preserve and proclaim the good news of His death, resurrection and His coming again to judge the world. The church is both a living testimony of prophecy fulfilled and a prophetic voice of what will come in the future. By this the church functions as the salt of the earth which restrains it from plunging headlong into corruption.

As the bride of Christ, all that the church does in order to make herself ready — gathering together, worshiping, celebrating communion, witnessing, preaching the gospel, casting out demons, healing the sick, being peacemakers (Eph. 5:27; Rev. 19:7-8) — is a prophetic trumpet to the world of the relationship of Christ to His church and of the fact that Christ is coming again. The next time you are sitting in a church service, remember that even though we are almost two thousand years removed from the first-century church, the very fact that you are gathering with others in His name is both a prophetic fulfillment and a prophetic statement to the world.

3. THE PROPHETIC STANDARD IN THE SCRIPTURES

One of the most vital prophetic realities is Scripture itself. It is a trumpet of God's heart, purpose and will. How precious to the body of Christ is the fact that God gave us the Scriptures.

For each of the eight prophetic dimensions of the church, God raises up leaders who are equipped by the Holy Spirit and who have worked hard to equip themselves. For us at Metro Vineyard, people like Wes Adams, David Parker, Sam Storms, Michael Kailus, George

LeBeau, Bruce McGregor and others have made a vital contribution over the years within the context of our prophetic community. They have extensive seminary degrees and are skilled in exegesis, hermeneutics, systematic theology and the history of the church. Prophets and exhorters among us sometimes want to interpret or apply a scripture in a particular way because it proves a point or simply because it "preaches well." For them these "doctors of the Word" serve as a balance and a plumb line.

Dr. Sam Storms is not a prophet in the same sense as Paul Cain is. Nevertheless, he serves an essential part in the prophetic ministry of our church as the president of Grace Training Center and as the one leading the equipping and training aspects of our pastoral strategy at Metro Vineyard. People such as Dr. Storms who have a thorough understanding of the historical context of the New Testament writings (to whom they were written and why) as well as the extra-biblical tradition of the second-and third-century church fathers (their historical recollections) play an essential role in kindling the church's self-awareness as a prophetic community.

The New Testament epistles were not written like lessons for a Sunday school curriculum. They were written as letters to people like us who were at times going through very difficult situations. When we as a church hear about the conflicts that caused the writing of 2 Corinthians or discover the drama which is the background of the letter to the Hebrews, we begin to identify with the *people* of the New Testament, not just with the exhortations to them.

Not only does this make the New Testament come alive, but it gives the church a sense of connection with those who began the race. The church as a prophetic community must realize that we are a continuation of what they began. We must feel that connection.

The torch has been passed so many times, it is easy to lose sight of the fact that we are running the same race they started. Their leg of the race has been completed, and they have now gathered at the finish line to cheer us on. The church is the living testimony of the prophetic purpose of God in history. It is also a prophetic community which is to preserve and proclaim accurately the Word of God.

4. MOVING WHEN THE CLOUD MOVES

The fourth way that the church must be prophetic is that it must discern the current move of the Spirit, the "present truth," as well-known

190

respected pastor and church leader, Dick Iverson, calls it. Just as the children of Israel followed the cloud through the wilderness, the church needs to move when the Holy Spirit says to move (Deut. 1:33).

This is in contrast to the aspect of the prophetic community we just discussed. While the truth that the church preserves and proclaims from the Scriptures is unchangeable and immovable, the relationship that exists between the church and the Holy Spirit is not static. The Spirit is forever doing a new thing with the church as a whole and, separately, with each congregation. The ten commandments given on Sinai are forever true and unchangeable, but the people of Israel were changing locations constantly as they moved around in the wilderness.

The kind of moving I am referring to is the changing emphasis placed on elements of truth, structure and strategy. We are, so to speak, moving around within the boundaries of the unchangeable truth of God's Word.

The leaders of various new movements are not necessarily those who exercise the gift of prophecy as mentioned in 1 Corinthians 12, but instead are people who can clearly sense the direction the cloud is moving. They might be compared to the sons of Issachar who "had understanding of the times, to know what Israel ought to do" (1 Chr. 12:32).

There is nothing more prophetic than the church of Jesus Christ "following the cloud," that is, the current emphasis and leading of the Holy Spirit. This is a prophetic dimension that can be entirely distinct from dreams, visions or the manifestation of the gift of prophecy. It is an expression of prophetic leadership.

A lot of people proclaim they *know exactly* what the Holy Spirit is saying to the church; many of these are saying opposite things. But it is when *the people* sense the witness of the Holy Spirit in those proclamations that the benefit begins. Those prophetic-type leaders who accurately discern the movement of the cloud are essential to the church.

The church's history is filled with examples of how part of the body of Christ discerned the present emphasis of the Holy Spirit as it related to the structure, strategy or particular elements of truth. However, some have followed the cloud to the next place in God, then never moved again. After camping around a certain structure, strategy or truth for a period of time, they become less of a prophetic community and more of a prophetic monument to something the Holy Spirit did long ago.

This doesn't mean we should abandon all the older traditions with

191

every new move of the cloud. The greatest expression of the church as a prophetic community is in those congregations or denominations that move on with the cloud, but carry with them all the wisdom, experience and maturity of their history with them.

5. DEMONSTRATING THE POWER OF GOD

Elijah is symbolic of the prophet of God who calls down fire from heaven as a sign of God's power. In the New Testament, attesting miracles are not limited to the prophets. The Holy Spirit distributes the gifts "individually as He wills," one of those being the gift of the working of miracles (1 Cor. 12:10-11).

Nevertheless, in a general sense the demonstration of the supernatural power of God in and through the church is a dimension of the prophetic ministry.

As in the days of Elijah, miracles attest to the truth of God's Word. Some have said that the church doesn't need the miraculous today since we have the written Word. But the written Word includes the witness of the apostles, and if attesting miracles were needed when they personally testified within a few years of the resurrection, how much more are attesting miracles needed today to confirm the veracity of their written accounts.

Attesting miracles are also valuable as a dimension of the prophetic community because, more than anything else, they make people aware that God is actually present with them. The death and resurrection of Jesus, by the way we estimate time, was *very* long ago. Without a renewed awareness of His presence, the church sometimes takes on the air of a society gathered to venerate the memory of Jesus who died two thousand years ago.

The working of miracles jolts our sensibilities and makes us joyfully (or frightfully) aware of the fact the He is in our midst by the presence of the Holy Spirit and that He is very close to each of us. A hundred sermons on God being with us may not awaken our hearts as much as a personal encounter with the manifestation of His presence and power through the miraculous.

This in no way diminishes the power or authority of the written word. It simply means that in the miraculous the living God of the written Word shows up in a powerfully personal, intimate and tangible way. Through the miraculous, the church prophesies and proclaims that He is alive!

6. PROPHETIC DREAMS AND VISIONS

The majority of this book is dedicated to nurturing and administrating the prophetic ministry as it receives revelation from God. God raises up and endows people with gifts to see and hear things that most people do not see or hear. The term *seer* carries with it some very negative connotations because of its modern-day, non-Christian applications. Consequently, when referring to someone as a "seer," one must be careful to qualify and define this term in the light of 1 Samuel 9:

> Formerly in Israel, when a man went to inquire of God, he spoke thus: "Come, let us go to the seer"; for he who is now called a prophet was formerly called a seer (v. 9).

> And Samuel answered Saul and said, "I am the seer" (v. 19).

Prophets like Ezekiel and Zechariah who are known for seeing profound visions of God are not known for demonstrations of power like healing the sick or raising the dead.

Often these type of prophetic people are not gifted with great demonstrations of miraculous power, but they regularly see things by the Holy Spirit — things such as future events, the secrets of people's hearts and the calling of God on people's lives. Like the things in Ezekiel's visions, the things prophetic people see are sometimes as baffling.

Nevertheless, the prophetic ministry has been a part of the New Testament from the very beginning.

7. CRYING OUT AGAINST SOCIAL INJUSTICE

The church has the responsibility to be a "prophet to the nation" concerning injustice, repression and the unrighteousness that eventually causes a nation to provoke the judgment of God. One of the more stellar examples of this was the prophetic outcry from the Rev. William Wilberforce (1759-1833) working within the church and, previously, Lord Shaftesbury (1621-1683) crying out in the British House of Lords. These two men, denouncing injustice on two different fronts over two centuries, are due most of the credit for the British Parliament's outlawing the trading of slaves in England.

Many times prophets to the nation speak from a secular platform, not necessarily as those who represent the church. Joseph and Daniel were two biblical examples of people who represented God in a position of secular power. Abraham Lincoln and Martin Luther King prophetically stood for justice and righteousness in our social order. Yet they were not seen as prophetic from the traditional position of being on a church staff.

The church must be careful not to undermine its prophetic ministry to the nation. Hopefully, many members of the church will be actively involved in civil government and even in party politics. However, the church and those who speak for the church *must* understand where to draw the line.

If and when they enter politics, they do so as godly individuals, not as members of the pastoral staff who are financed by the local church. It is my conviction that the church as an institution should be as a prophet standing for the advancement of righteousness without indebtedness to political party affiliations.

8. CRYING OUT FOR PERSONAL HOLINESS AND REPENTANCE

God has raised up leaders in the church throughout the generations who have functioned as prophets of God crying out against the sins of the people. John Wesley, for instance, turned England back to God when the people's personal unrighteousness and apathy had brought them to the edge of societal chaos.

This outcry is similar to the prophetic cry against social injustice, but different in that it is specifically directed to the people in the church. It is less like Jonah prophesying against Nineveh and more like Isaiah and Jeremiah prophesying to Israel and Judah.

People such as Billy Graham, Charles Colson, John Piper, David Wilkerson and A. W. Tozer stand out in my mind as prophetic ministers raised up to cry out against unrighteousness in the church as they revealed the deep things about the knowledge of God. Their words have been anointed by the Spirit to awaken hearts to holiness and passion for Jesus. God uses such prophetic voices, just as he used John the Baptist, to prick the conscience of believers unto full revival.

SERVING IN THE PROPHETIC COMMUNITY

It is the nature of the church to be the prophetic expression of the kingdom of God on earth, to represent, preserve and proclaim the truth of God to this world. All the members who serve the church or function as a ministry of the church are themselves involved with the ongoing prophetic plan and purpose of God in the earth.

Those particularly gifted with dreams, visions, prophecies and revelation need to be careful not to think of themselves too highly, as being *the* prophetic group. They serve only one dimension of the church's greater calling as a prophetic community.

My prayer and earnest expectation is that God will work mightily in our generation to help the church more and more to live up to and express its prophetic nature and calling among the nations of the earth. The proclamation and demonstration of the word of God through a Spirit-filled church is the true hope for mankind. May the Holy Spirit come upon us in unprecedented measure for the glory of God and Christ Jesus.

GOD'S MANIFEST PRESENCE

UNDERSTANDING THE PHENOMENA
THAT ACCOMPANY THE SPIRIT'S MINISTRY

INTRODUCTION

When God chooses to show His power in and through the body of Christ, opportunities are provided for both tremendous spiritual growth and tragic confusion and stumbling.

Throughout both biblical and church history, strange and even bizarre physical phenomena have accompanied outpourings of the Holy Spirit's power. In the beginning of 1994, numerous reports and testimonies began to circulate across the U.S., Canada and in several other nations concerning widespread and often spontaneous, unrelated occurrences of manifestations of the Spirit and the physical phenomena that often accompany them.

Since that time, many believers have continued to be blessed, refreshed and rejuvenated through this international spiritual renewal. Other believers have not been so blessed! They are skeptical and are

196

questioning whether these kinds of things can actually represent a genuine work of God. And what about the apparently fleshly behavior in which some engage and try to blame on the Spirit? What shall we do with that stuff?

Church leaders have been both perplexed and challenged regarding how to view these things and what to encourage, discourage or simply endure and overlook in the midst of this movement.

Believers need to pray for their leaders and try to be patient with them as they seek wisdom as to how to properly respond and lead in a way that honors God and builds up the whole church. We hope that this essay will help provide a biblical/theological framework through which these manifestations and physical phenomena may be viewed and interpreted.

When this current move of the Holy Spirit was publicly noised abroad in 1994, we remembered that God had given a number of people prophetic insight concerning it. In April of 1984 an amazing thing happened to Mike Bickle and another prophetic man, Bob Jones (who was functioning in our midst at that time).

Mike was lying in bed early one morning when suddenly he heard the audible voice of God. He later discovered that Bob had also had an open vision and had heard God's audible voice that same morning. The summary of the message that God spoke to them and supernaturally confirmed was that in ten years God was going to "begin to pour out the wine of His Spirit on the nations." God also said that He was going to bring discipline on ministries that were not preaching and producing humility before God in their constituencies and that He was going to raise up ministries that were teaching and modeling it. He even said that He would work to correct wrong theological ideas within ministries if they valued true humility.

This word was actually quite difficult for Mike to receive because at that time he so longed and believed for God to send a visitation much sooner. Through the years we have had contact with a number of prophetic ministries who, back in the eighties, had spoken to us and others about how God had shown them that He was planning to send a significant wave of His Spirit across the nations in the mid-nineties. We don't believe that this current movement is by any means the only wave of the Spirit that will come in to prepare the earth for the second coming. Yet, we do feel it is vital that we all earnestly seek to be good stewards of God's grace. May God help us to welcome, move into and glean all that He intends for us through this beginning of an outpouring.

THE MANIFEST PRESENCE OF GOD

It is to this often misunderstood and controversial concept of God's manifest presence that we now turn our attention. Visitations of God's manifest presence upon individuals, movements and geographic regions have often occurred in the history of Christianity. They have often been disdained for various reasons.

Sadly, they have most often been opposed by religious leaders who are not humble enough to admit that there might be some legitimate spiritual experience and knowledge beyond their own. This opposition can arise when leaders have been lifted up as having all the answers about God, His Word and His ways.

We must all continually seek to take the posture of being learners before the Lord and acknowledge that no one has covered all the possible ground of spiritual wisdom and experience in Christ. No matter how mature we become in the Lord, we are all still His children and therefore must remain childlike in our relationship to Him as our Father. There is only one "know it all" in the kingdom!

Someone once asked the intriguing question, "Where does God live?" Another with a sharp wit answered, "Anywhere He wants to!" A good answer indeed. When Solomon dedicated the first temple, he said, "Heaven and highest heaven cannot contain you, how much less this house I have built for you" [1 Kin. 8:27].

There is mystery to the dwelling place of God. In fact, there is mystery to God Himself as a Person and as Persons of a trinity. There is something about the mystery of God with which we are not naturally comfortable. Is it not easy for us to believe that this is by design? Yes — a divine design to keep us humble and worshipful. After all, we are the creatures, and He is the Creator.

God has left the philosophical explanations of many of His attributes and ways unsatisfying to our finite minds. How could it really be otherwise when finite minds are trying to comprehend infinity? Human language falls short in fully conveying the nature of God. We see the glory of God through a mirror, but only dimly (1 Cor. 13:12). Mystery such as this confirms the reality of our faith (Rom. 11:26; 1 Cor. 2). We need to be reconciled to the mystery of God if we are going to enjoy our relationship with Him, be enabled to freely receive from Him, and freely give back to Him and to others. The secret things belong to the Lord, and the things revealed belong to us.

So where does God really live? Where is His presence? First, He lives in heaven itself where He dwells in unapproachable light. Second, He is omnipresent, and there is no place where He is not. Third, He has condescended to live within His "temples." In the Old Testament, it was first the tabernacle and then the temple in Jerusalem. In the New Testament, it is the church — the corporate body of Christ as well as each believer in Christ. Fourth, He and His Word are one and thus He is present in the holy Scriptures. Fifth, He is present in the sacraments of the church. And finally, He also periodically "visits" specific people and places by His "manifest presence."

In other words, God "comes down" and interfaces with the natural realm. This is promised particularly when believers gather together in the name of Jesus Christ. This also is the nature of revivals in the history of the church.

God "draws near" and the normal working order of things is disrupted. When the omnipotent, omniscient, omnipresent, eternal, infinite, holy, just and loving God condescends to come down and touch weak and finite humans, what would you expect or predict might happen to the natural and normal order of things? Might it be something other than "business as usual"?

We are called to value and esteem every dimension of the presence of God — we don't have to choose one above the other as each truth and experience imparts special blessings to enhance our understanding and spiritual growth. Following are four NT passages that refer to the reality and biblical concept of the manifest presence of God:

> Again, I tell you that if two of you on earth agree about anything you ask for, it will be done for you by my Father in heaven. For where two or three come together in my name, there am I with them (Matt. 18:19-20, NIV).

In these verses Jesus gave a specific promise concerning the power of what is known as the prayer of agreement. When believers are gathered together under the authority of Christ and the banner of His name, the Lord here promises to be "present" among them in a certain qualitative way in which He is not with them at other times through His indwelling and His omnipresence.

> When you are assembled in the name of our Lord Jesus and I am with you in spirit, and the power of the Lord Jesus is present, hand this man over to Satan, so that the sinful nature may be destroyed and his spirit saved on the day of the Lord (1 Cor. 5:4-5, NIV).

In these two verses, Paul also refers to the assembling of believers. He is specifically referring to the spiritual authority that he wielded to bring discipline upon unrepentant church members. But the main point for our purpose is the statement that the very power of the Lord Jesus is present in a specialized way when believers are gathered together.

> One day as he was preaching, Pharisees and teachers of the law, who had come from every village of Galilee and from Judea and Jerusalem, were sitting there. And the power of the Lord was present for him to heal the sick (Luke 5:17, NIV).

This verse speaks of God's healing power being present in a specific way, at a specific place and at a specific time that was noticeable and noteworthy. It was present in a way that it wasn't and isn't always present. It also implies how even Jesus was reliant upon the ministry and gifts of the Holy Spirit during His earthly ministry.

> He went down with them and stood in a level place. A large crowd of his disciples was there and a great number of people from all over Judea, from Jerusalem, and from the coast of Tyre and Sidon, who had come to hear him and be healed of their diseases. Those troubled by evil spirits were cured, and the people all tried to touch him, because the power was coming from him and healing them all (Luke 16:17-19, NIV).

These verses describe the power of God flowing out of Jesus' body in an almost tangible way. This supernatural virtue was apparently not something that flowed out of Him continually, but at specific times and in specific situations which God ordained.

BIBLICAL EXAMPLES OF GOD'S MANIFEST PRESENCE

The basis for the occurrence of physical manifestations and phenomena is rooted in this biblical doctrine of the manifest presence of

God. Following are a few more scriptural examples of the manifest presence of God in operation:

- Daniel fell, had no strength, terrified by God's presence (Dan. 8:17; 10:7-10,15-19).

- Fire from heaven consumes sacrifices (Lev. 9:24; 1 Kin. 18:38; 1 Chr. 21:26).

- The priests couldn't stand because of God's glory (1 Kin. 8:10,11).

- Solomon and priests couldn't stand because of God's glory (2 Chr. 7:1-3).

- King Saul and his antagonistic men are overcome by the Holy Spirit and prophesy as they near the camp of the prophets (1 Sam. 19:18-24).

- Bush is burning but not consumed (Ex. 3:2).

- Thunder, smoke, shaking of the ground, sounds of trumpets and voices upon Mt. Sinai (Ex. 19:16f).

- Moses sees the "glory of God" pass by him; Moses' face supernaturally shines (Ex. 34:30f).

- Jesus and His garment supernaturally made brilliant, supernatural cloud and visit by Moses and Elijah (Matt. 17:2-8).

- The Holy Spirit descends in bodily form as a dove (John 1:32).

- Unbelieving guards thrown to the ground (John 18:6).

- Peter and Paul fall into trances and see and hear into the spirit world (Acts 10:10; 22:1).

- Saul of Tarsus saw brilliant light, thrown from his horse, heard Jesus audibly, was temporarily struck blind (Acts 9:4).

- John fell as dead, had no bodily strength, and saw and heard into the spirit world (Rev. 1:17).

- A virgin conceives the Son of God (Luke 2:35).

A CORINTHIAN CONTROVERSY REVISITED

In 2 Corinthians 5:12-13 Paul describes a controversy that existed among the professing believers at Corinth:

> For we commend not ourselves again unto you, but give you occasion to glory on our behalf, that ye may have somewhat to answer them which glory in appearance, and not in heart. For whether we be beside ourselves, it is to God: or whether we be sober, it is for your cause (KJV).

Paul was challenging the mentality of some who were looking on outward things and not properly discerning the heart of a certain matter at hand. He was exhorting his readers to make the most of a particular opportunity presented to them by God's providence.

What could this matter have been? The next verse tells us. Paul reveals that this controversy centered around two different general states of being that he and other believers were experiencing periodically. This first "mode" he called being "beside ourselves." The only other time that this Greek word is used in the New Testament is when the people of Nazareth accused Jesus of being mad.

Also, interestingly enough, we get our English word *ecstatic* from a Latin word that means "being outside oneself." Paul seems to be referring to what are classically understood as ecstatic spiritual experiences and phenomena. He was exhorting the Corinthian believers to not stumble over this genuine holy activity that didn't appear "dignified" or even always "rational." Instead he challenged them to "glory," that is to rejoice greatly, that such visitations were occurring among them and releasing greater passion in their hearts for God.

The record of church history is rife with testimonies of such experiences with the Spirit in many different centuries and among many different traditions. Paul contrasts this state of being with being "sober" — and we all know what the opposite of sober is.

Indeed, Paul knew what it was like to be intoxicated with the Holy Spirit. This is also why he would even choose to compare and contrast being drunk with wine with being continually filled with the Holy Spirit in Ephesians 5:18, "And be not drunk with wine, wherein is excess; but be filled with the Spirit" (KJV). God invented the original and legitimate "high" for mankind and it is spiritually, not naturally or chemically, induced.

"The kingdom of God is not eating and drinking, but righteousness, peace and joy in the Holy Spirit" (Rom. 14:17). Joy is one of the bottom-line issues of the Christian experience. The joy of the Lord is our strength. We are promised the oil of joy for mourning. We are to serve the Lord with gladness.

Jesus promised to give us His joy, and He was anointed with the oil of gladness above all His companions. Surely, the joy of the Lord is deeper than our feelings and behavior, but to consider that this supernatural joy should never or might never spill over into the realm of our emotions and affect our physical beings and behavior is totally ridiculous.

Visible joy upon believers is possibly the best advertisement for the gospel. Unbelievers may not take the time to listen to our sermons on righteousness. They may not have the interest to ask us about our experience of inner peace. But it is very difficult for them to ignore the joy that rests upon us through the Holy Spirit's anointing.

This is why the media has recently taken so much notice of the "laughing revival" that is occurring here in the mid-nineties. God uses the reality of joy resting upon Spirit-filled Christians as a way of intriguing unbelievers so that they will be more open to listen to the message of the gospel of our Lord Jesus Christ.

The book of Joel also uses the analogy of wine in relation to the outpouring of the Spirit. And, of course, Peter prophetically interprets what was occurring on the day of Pentecost as at least a partial fulfillment of Joel's prophecy. On that day those observing the 120 who were filled with the Holy Spirit accused them of being drunk with wine.

Probably more was going on behaviorally than some non-emotional, stoic and somber people speaking in other languages — they were seized and overwhelmed by the manifest presence of the living God! It is totally consistent with the nature of God to use something as simple and profound as joy, among other things, and its effects upon His people, to get the spiritual attention of burned-out, bored and hardened unbelievers of our generation. "More, Lord!"

Let us also note that we do not in anywise think that this present, fresh move of the Spirit is going to be limited to the experience of joy. The account in Acts 2 is not just a historical account of what happened in Jerusalem in the first century, it is also a divine revelation of what occurs when the fullness of the Holy Spirit descends on a particular time and place.

In that visitation of God there was the manifestation of the wind, the fire and the wine of the Spirit. Before it's all over there is going to be "blood, fire, and vapor of smoke."

The "fire of God" in conviction of sin, passionate intercession and the fear of the Lord, combined with the "winds of God" in miraculous public events and the resulting mass conversions are also going to be restored to the church.

In addition to seeing God's people refreshed, we also want the blind to see, the deaf to hear, the lame to walk, the dead to be raised and the gospel preached in power to the poor. We should long to see mature, self-perpetuating and church-planting communities of believers who walk in the love of God to be left in the wake of spiritual revival.

If any visitation of God goes no deeper than "holy laughter," then we are of all people most to be pitied. Let us not settle for a little when God is offering much more.

TESTING SPIRITUAL MANIFESTATIONS AND PHENOMENA

The Bible does not record all possible divine or legitimate supernatural activities and/or experiences that have occurred or may yet occur among men and nations. Rather, it records examples of divine activity and legitimate supernatural experiences that fall into broader categories that are typical of how the Holy Spirit works. This concept is taught in John 21:25, in which John states that if all the wonderful works that Jesus did had been recorded, all the books in the world could not contain them.

The Bible nowhere teaches that God is bound to do only what He has done before. In fact, there are many prophecies of Scripture that speak of God doing things He has never done before.

God is always and forever free to do unprecedented things that are consistent with His character as revealed in Scripture. One friend of ours has said, "God has this 'problem' you see — He thinks He's God!" Truly, He is God and He can do anything He wants to.

The only thing the Bible says that it is impossible for God to do is lie. We must be very careful when suggesting that God would never do or could never do this thing or that. He has never made it His habit to ask our permission about anything He chooses to say or do. Let us remember how He confronted and dealt with Job when he challenged the wisdom of God's ways. Western Christianity has too often been stripped of the supernatural side of faith and the sense of the mystery of God.

Sometimes people become overly zealous and/or possess deficient biblical hermeneutics and therefore twist and stretch scripture passages in order to try to prove the validity of some spiritual manifestation or physical phenomenon that is not explicitly referred to in the Bible. For example, many people have attempted to defend the experience of uncontrollable laughing by this kind of "proof-texting," yet this phenomenon it is not specifically mentioned in Scripture.

However, a broader category of the Spirit's work, "joy unspeakable and full of glory," is referred to in 1 Peter 1:8. Why should it be a surprise to anyone that a person or whole groups of people might experience an aspect of this kind of joy that could lead to the experience of uncontrollable laughter?

Some sincere Christians panic when they hear of such reports and instantly conclude that a spiritual deception must be at work. But — just maybe — their view of God, His ways, and the Bible is too limiting. Ironically, it may be their deficient biblical hermeneutics that lead them to such biased conclusions.

There is a vast difference between behaviors that violate scriptural principles about the nature of God's work among people and behaviors to which Scripture does not explicitly refer. Stating that it is impossible for God to do a certain thing or to dogmatically and judgmentally forbid or call evil anything that Scripture does not is a rather dangerous practice for mortal men. Besides, there are many things we all engage in that are "extra-biblical" but which we would never consider "unbiblical."

We even consider these to be things with which God has blessed the earth through His providence. So are we left unable to discern between good and evil? Certainly not. However, we must find more than an overly simplistic approach to judging what is valid or invalid.

To reject or call invalid a spiritual experience, the primary onus must be upon the skeptic to show biblically that something would be either contrary to the Scripture or somehow impossible for God to do. It does not first of all rest upon the one who has an experience to prove to others that it is valid.

If the skeptic cannot do so, then he must at least remain open that God could be at work; therefore he should be cautious about condemning something without praying and thinking more deeply about it and interviewing people who claim an experience is of God.

This is especially true when people who really love God and the Bible claim that the Holy Spirit is moving among them. Many believers testify to at one time coming against something the Holy Spirit was doing, only later to discover that it was a genuine work of God. Just the fact that, generally speaking, the scribes and Pharisees missed the Messiah should put the fear of God in our hearts about how easy it is for dedicated and sincere religious people to miss God.

Unfortunately, many people have a bias that nothing outside of their personal experience could possibly be from God — otherwise why didn't God do it for them or to them? This is especially true for religious leaders who often feel the pressure, whether self-imposed or from their constituency, to have "all the answers."

Can we not perceive the arrogance and presumption of this mentality? We must all stay child-like before God as learners to enter and progress in the kingdom of God.

To test the validity of a spiritual manifestation or phenomenon, we should look at a number of factors. First, we should examine the overall belief system and life-styles (and changes in them) of those affected by them. Second, we should look at the overall beliefs and life-styles of those being used to impart the experience, if human mediation is a factor. We should test the short and long-term fruit of the experiences on both individuals and churches. Finally, we need to evaluate overall glory given to Jesus Christ in the general context in which the phenomena are occurring.

Jonathan Edwards, the eighteenth-century American churchman and theologian, referred to five tests to determine if a particular manifestation was to be regarded as a true work of the Holy Spirit. He stated that Satan cannot and would not, if he could, generate the following kinds of things in people.

If we can answer "yes" to one or more of these questions, then it is to be regarded as genuine "despite any little objections (criticisms), as many make from oddities, irregularities, errors in conduct, and the delusions and scandals of some professors" (people who claim to be believers).

In other words, Edwards was saying that the presence of some human mixture does not, in general, invalidate the divine stamp upon any work within a true revival. Indeed, the presence of considerable human elements in and around a spiritual revival should always be expected. Following are the five tests:

- Does it bring honor to the person of Jesus Christ?
- Does it produce a greater hatred of sin and a greater love for righteousness?
- Does it produce a greater regard for Scripture?
- Does it lead people into truth?
- Does it produce a greater love for God and man?

HISTORICAL PRECEDENTS FOR MANIFESTATIONS OF THE SPIRIT

Extraordinary physical phenomena caused by the operation of the Holy Spirit's presence upon people is fully documented and affirmed throughout the history of revivals in virtually every branch of the Christian church.

Following are just several of hundreds of possible quotations substantiating this fact. Sam Storms has edited and published the remarkable story entitled, *Heaven On Earth*, of Jonathan Edwards' wife, Sarah, and her encounter with the Holy Spirit.

St. Teresa of Avila (1515-1582), on being rapt in ecstasy, wrote "The subject rarely loses consciousness; I have sometimes lost it altogether, but only seldom and for but a short time. As a rule the consciousness is disturbed; and though incapable of action with respect to outward things, the subject can still hear and understand, but only dimly, as though from a long way off."[1]

Jonathan Edwards, regarded to be one of the greatest theologians of history, lived during the time of the Great Awakening in America in the 1730s and 1740s. Edwards provides the most thoughtful and comprehensive biblical evaluations, reflections and writings about the manifestations of the Spirit.

> "It was very wonderful to see how person's affections were sometimes moved when God did as it were suddenly open their eyes, and let into their minds a sense of the greatness of his grace, the fullness of Christ, and his readiness to save...Their joyful surprise has caused their hearts as it were to leap, so that they have been ready to break forth into laughter, tears often at the same time issuing like a flood, and intermingling a loud weeping. Sometimes they have not been able to forbear crying out with a loud voice, expressing their great admiration."[2]

"...some persons having had such longing desires after Christ or which have risen to such degree, as to take away their natural strength. Some have been so overcome with a sense of the dying love of Christ to such poor, wretched, and unworthy creatures, as to weaken the body. Several persons have had so great a sense of the glory of God, and excellency of Christ, that nature and life seemed almost to sink under it; and in all probability, if God had showed them a little more of himself, it would have dissolved their frame...And they have talked, when able to speak, of the glory of God's perfections."[3]

"It was a very frequent thing to see an house full of outcries, faintings, convulsions and such like, both with distress, and also with admiration and joy."[4]

"...many in their religious affections being raised far beyond what they ever had been before: and there were some instances of persons lying in a sort of trance, remaining for perhaps a whole twenty-four hours motionless, and with their senses locked up; but in the meantime under strong imagination, as though they went to heaven, and had there a vision of glorious and delightful objects."[5]

The following was the report of an atheist "free thinker" named James B. Finley, who attended the Cane Ridge, Kentucky, revival in 1801:

"The noise was like the roar of Niagara. The vast sea of human beings seemed to be agitated as if by a storm... Some of the people were singing, others praying, some crying for mercy in the most piteous accents, while others were shouting vociferously. While witnessing these scenes, a peculiarly-strange sensation, such as I had never felt before, came over me. My heart beat tumultuously, my knees trembled, my lip quivered, and I felt as though I must fall to the ground. A strange supernatural power seemed to pervade the entire mass of mind there collected...At one time I saw at least five hundred, swept down in a moment as if a battery of a thousand guns had been opened upon them, and then immediately followed shrieks and shouts that rent the very heavens...I fled for the woods a second time, and wished I had stayed at home."[6]

A CATALOGUE OF SPIRITUAL MANIFESTATIONS & PHENOMENA

The Hebrew and biblical model of the unity of personality implies that the spirit affects the body. At times the human spirit can be so affected by the glory of God that the human body is not capable of containing the intensity of these spiritual encounters — and strange physical behavior may result. Sometimes, though certainly not always, physical responses are simply human responses to the Spirit's activity and are not directly caused by the Holy Spirit.

At other times physical reactions may be caused by demonic powers being stirred up by the manifest presence of God. It seems to be common in NT narratives that demons would be forced to "blow their cover" when Jesus or the apostles came around (for example, the Gadarene demoniac; the fortune teller at Philippi). Some of these strange experiences might be best considered as "revival phenomena" rather than "manifestations of the Spirit." However, this does not imply that they are therefore carnal and should be forbidden.

Following are phenomena and/or manifestations that have been observed in contemporary experience:

Shaking, jerking, loss of bodily strength, heavy breathing, eyes fluttering, lips trembling, oil on the body, changes in skin color, weeping, laughing, "drunkenness," staggering, travailing, dancing, falling, visions, hearing audibly into the spirit realm, inspired utterances (that is, prophecy), tongues, interpretation; angelic visitations and manifestations; jumping, violent rolling, screaming, wind, heat, electricity, coldness, nausea as discernment of evil, smelling or tasting good or evil presences, tingling, pain in the body as discernment of illnesses, feeling heavy weight or lightness, trances (altered physical state while seeing and hearing into the spirit world), inability to speak normally and disruption of the natural realm (for example, electrical circuits blown).

DIVINE PURPOSES FOR OUTWARD MANIFESTATIONS

The Scripture states that God chooses foolish things to accomplish His work.

> For the foolishness of God is wiser than man's wisdom, and the weakness of God is stronger than man's strength. Brothers, think of what you were when you were called. Not many of you were wise by human standards; not many were influential; not many were of noble birth. But God chose the foolish things of the world to shame the wise; God chose the weak things of the world to shame the strong. He chose the lowly things of this world and the despised things — and the things that are not — to nullify the things that are, so that no one may boast before him (1 Cor. 1:25-29, NIV).

God often offends the mind to test and reveal the heart. In the account of the outpouring of the Spirit at Pentecost in Acts 2:12-13, some people were amazed, some were perplexed, and some mocked. We continue to see these three responses to the work of the Spirit and some consequent events today. This "way of God" challenges our improper "control issues" and is intended to break down our unsanctified inhibitions and pride.

> For the Lord shall rise up as in mount Perazim, he shall be wroth as in the valley of Gibeon, that he may do his work, his strange work; and bring to pass his act, his strange act (Is. 28:21, KJV).

Following are some of the reasons why God might choose to utilize strange and/or bizarre events to further His kingdom among men:

TO DEMONSTRATE HIS POWER THROUGH SIGNS AND WONDERS

Signs are given to point beyond themselves to the God who is there. Wonders cause intrigue concerning the mystery of God's ways. God wants our faith to rest upon His power and not the wisdom of men's words (1 Cor. 2:4-5).

Scripture validates the concept of trans-rational impartations of the grace, power and wisdom of God. Sometimes, but certainly not always, God bypasses our minds when His Spirit moves upon us and within us. Praying in tongues is the clearest example of this in the NT.

> For if I pray in an unknown tongue, my spirit prayeth, but my understanding is unfruitful. What is it then? I will pray with the spirit, and I will pray with the understanding also: I will sing with the spirit, and I will sing with the understanding also (1 Cor. 14:14-15, KJV).

Some of peoples' experience with manifestations and renewal phenomena fit into this category of thinking.

To deepen experiential intimacy with God — knowing God and being known by Him

To impart grace and power to overcome inner bondages — fear, lust, pride, envy, greed, deceit, bitterness and so on

One sister in Christ we know had an encounter with a release of joy and laughter one particular evening. She was rejoicing in the Lord as she went home that night. What surprised her was that as she walked into her dark house, she realized that a fear of the dark that she had lived with and which had tormented her since childhood was absolutely gone.

She had no clue that this bondage had been broken before this. No one had prayed for her concerning this problem. Somehow it was trans-rationally removed as a by-product of an encounter with the joy of the Spirit.

To impart love, peace, joy, fear of God and the like

Sue is another girl in our fellowship who recently fell to the floor under the power of the Holy Spirit, and in the course of time, she saw a vision of a rope being pulled out of her belly by the Lord Jesus. She knew that this represented "worthlessness," and since that time she has had a flooding into her being of the love of Christ and peace like she has never known in all her years as a believer.

TO EFFECT HEALINGS — PHYSICAL AND EMOTIONAL

Jill is a lady in our church that has had a remarkable physical healing touch. She recently received intensified prayer ministry that was attended by her falling to the ground under the Spirit's power a number of times. The only thing that she was aware was happening to her was that she felt great joy and peace.

However, she had been suffering from a severe eye disease as well as Parkinson's disease. The eye condition caused her body to be unable to produce tears normally. She had to take eye drops hourly.

On the way home from the conference where these experiences occurred, suddenly realized that she hadn't needed her eye drops for four hours. Since that day she hasn't needed any eye drops at all. In addition to this, she is able to walk and talk normally as the severe symptoms of Parkinson's disease are up to this point being alleviated.

TO BOND WITH OTHER BELIEVERS — RELATIONAL BARRIERS FALL WHEN PEOPLE EXPERIENCE THE SPIRIT'S PRESENCE TOGETHER

TO IMPART ANOINTING FOR SERVICE

Scott is one of our pastors whom, before he came onto staff, God took through many trials, breakings and disappointments related to ministering to God's people and life in general.

He had gotten to the point where he was so spiritually "shell shocked" that for a number of months after being released into full-time ministry he was still looking over his shoulder, wondering when things were going to fall apart around him.

The Holy Spirit has gripped him in some of the most unusual and strange ways. He has spent many hours on the floor being moved upon by the Lord in the last year, both in public meetings and in the privacy of his home.

Some of his experiences seem to have been intercessory and prophetic in nature, but many of them have simply been physical phenomena with no apparent spiritual connection. But over the course of this year, Scott has been powerfully transformed both internally and in his ministry to others. It's hard to question the genuineness and holy nature of Scott's strange encounters.

To release God's word — prophetic sensitizing, powerful preaching

JoAnn has had several encounters with the Holy Spirit in the last couple of years. She has shaken and laughed and wept in God's presence and has watched others do the same in renewal meetings. She came to the point where she was asking the Lord, "What is all this 'unto'?"

Then, recently, she had another encounter of shaking during a conference and suddenly there was an anointing for prophetic proclamation upon her at a level of accuracy and revelational depth beyond any she had experienced in many years of moving in inspirational prophecy.

To inspire intercession — apprehended for effective, Spirit-led prayer

To enlarge and liberate spiritual capacities

It seems that the manifestations associated with renewal ministry are given primarily for refreshment, encouragement, and healing. This should lead to deeper discipleship (growth in faith, hope and love).

This should then lead to more powerful and effective witness for Christ, evangelism, church growth and church planting. Hopefully, full-blown revival will issue forth out of the kind of renewal that is taking place. Already this pattern of divine strategy and activity has been playing out in parts of South America over the last ten years.

Exposing False Equations about the Manifestations

If I was more devoted, then I would experience these manifestations of the Spirit. The experience of these things is not related to our spiritual passion and diligence, but are the operation of the grace and providence of God.

Many people were visibly touched by the Holy Spirit. Revival is here! Actually the classical understanding of revival goes far beyond the experience of manifestations to deep and far-reaching spiritual and practical transformations of individuals, spiritual movements, geographic regions and whole nations. The terms "refreshing" and "renewal" are more appropriate for the work of the Spirit that encourages and inspires existing believers. Hopefully renewal will lead to

213

full revival. All the more, then, let us keep praying and believing for it!

Those people God is using to impart His power are really mature and sensitive to God. God must really love them a lot more than He does me. But if I'm diligent enough, maybe I'll become qualified to do those same things. People who have moved in "power ministry" have often unwittingly conveyed the notion that the power gifts are merit badges of spirituality. This has brought many dedicated and sincere believers into condemnation. These gifts and callings are free gifts of grace, and God gives them as He wills to various members of the body of Christ. In times of spiritual visitation, more members than usual are used to impart the Holy Spirit.

Just be open and sensitive to the Holy Spirit and you will get visibly touched, too. It would be much less perplexing if this were the way it works, but it isn't. Although people may have emotional barriers that hinder the work of the Spirit, many who are skeptical and cynical have been powerfully and visibly touched by God. Others who are very open and hungry for a touch are not powerfully affected, at least outwardly. We must refrain from judging who is "open" and who is "closed" and assuming this may be aiding or hindering a person from receiving from God.

Certainly people often have barriers that hinder them from freely receiving from God's Spirit. They can be things like fear, pride, unconfessed sin, unforgiveness, unbelief, false guilt and the list goes on. If you believe you have such a barrier, ask God to reveal the nature of it to you. He will be faithful, in His time, to answer such a request. In the meantime, do not assume that it must be a barrier that is keeping you from receiving from God.

If it is truly the Holy Spirit touching and moving upon these people, then there will instant and/or lasting 'fruit' in their lives. Actually, God moves upon and woos many people closer to Himself who never bring forth the fruit that He intends through these encounters with His grace. There are no guarantees that "fruit" will result from these "divine invitations." People are free to respond fully, partially, or even ignore such spiritual opportunities.

If it is really the power of the Holy Spirit on these people, then they should not have any control over their responses and behavior. There is such a thing as uncontrollable experiences with the Spirit; however, these are actually more uncommon than many people think. There is a mysterious combination of divine and human powers surrounding the Spirit's work. Peter knew how to walk and had the power to do so when Jesus invited him out onto the water.

The supernatural side of the event was that he didn't sink as he walked. On the front end of welcoming the Spirit's manifest presence, there is more control at our disposal to respond to His activity. In the middle of a welcomed experience with the Spirit, there is typically less control on the human side, but even still, there remains an ability to "pull out" of the experience if the need or desire is present. There are exceptions to this general rule and we must learn to recognize them.

"There is a time for everything," said Solomon. The Holy Spirit knows this (He wrote it!), and He is not necessarily quenched when those in authority in the church or a given meeting discern, for instance, that the time for quiet, attentive listening to the preaching of the Scripture has come and they therefore ask the assembly to respond accordingly. This is not automatically to be considered the manifestation of a "control spirit"! Loving community implies individual restraint. Absolute freedom is absolute nonsense!

EXPOSING DANGERS REGARDING MANIFESTATIONS

There is a possibility of divisions and judgments within the body as a result of manifestations — we must seek to avoid the "have's" and "have not's" mentality at all costs. This will truly grieve the Spirit of God (see Rom. 14 and 1 Cor. 12-14). Love for God and one another must remain the preeminent value of our community.

- *Fanaticism* — in their enthusiasm, people can get carried away into excesses of behavior and be deluded into embracing strange and unbiblical ideas. This problem must be addressed as it arises. We should seek to do this with compassion, both privately and publicly. This is a very delicate procedure, for the true fire of the Spirit will always be attended by a measure of "wild fire" introduced by the fleshly elements still resident within imperfect believers.

- *Neglect of the less intoxicating and less noticeable aspects of our faith* — things such as: daily devotions, secret prayer, humble service, helping the poor, showing mercy, loving enemies, suffering patiently, honoring parents and other authorities, restraining appetites, training children, working 8 to 5, doing chores and errands; paying tithes, bills, and taxes; resolving relational conflicts and being faithful friends.

- *Casting off all restraints and disciplines in the name of "the liberty of the Spirit."* This tension between liberty and restraint must be embraced by the whole church. We will not always agree with how this tension should be stewarded by the members of the body. Be prepared to "swallow some gnats" to avoid "swallowing camels"!

- *Becoming distracted from focusing on God and other present purposes* (that is, passion for Jesus, small groups, community, intercession, evangelism) by undue time, fascination and attention given to the manifestations themselves.

- *Falling into the pride of grace* — there is no uglier form of pride than the arrogant boastings or subtle self-righteousness of people who have been blessed by the Spirit. These graces are dispensed to magnify the grace and mercy of God and lead us into gratitude and humility. If we do not humble ourselves, God, in His love, will at some point allow us to be humiliated.

- *Spreading of rumors and misinformation* — although some of this is unavoidable, with good communication and proper qualifiers, they can be reduced. Take no delight in — and work at doubting — bad reports!

- *Exalting outward manifestations above the inward and hidden work of the Spirit within people's hearts* — progressive, internal transformation into the image of Jesus is the ultimate goal of the Spirit's work.

- *Exalting the weak human instruments that God is especially using as catalysts in the work of the Spirit* — we must avoid any kind of "hero worship" within our hearts. However, the "facelessness" of God's army does not mean that there will not be any visible leaders or prominent members with public ministries within the body. It refers to the attitude of humility, submission and deference that

216

all the members and leaders embrace within their hearts.

POSTURING OURSELVES TO RECEIVE THE SPIRIT'S MINISTRY

> So I say to you: Ask and it will be given to you; seek and
> you will find; knock and the door will be opened to you.
> For everyone who asks receives; he who seeks finds; and to
> him who knocks, the door will be opened. Which of you
> fathers, if your son asks for a fish, will give him a snake
> instead? Or if he asks for an egg, will give him a scorpion?
> If you then, though you are evil, know how to give good
> gifts to your children, how much more will your Father in
> heaven give the Holy Spirit to those who ask him! (Luke
> 11:9-13, NIV).

In this passage, Jesus is both inviting and challenging His disciples to pray in a specific way and for a specific thing. The verbs translated "ask," "seek" and "knock" are in a continuous tense in the original manuscripts. This gives the phrases the sense that the desired blessings must be pursued with repeated action and with perseverance.

God wants us to really want what we desire and not be passive or nonchalant about it. Any temporary denial serves only to deepen the hunger for the thing denied.

He also reveals that the requests for the good things of His kingdom can be summarized by asking for the release of the ministry of the Holy Spirit. God is a generous and wealthy Father who truly wants to give the Holy Spirit's ministry to us, but He also wants us to earnestly desire the Holy Spirit to come upon us with His gifts, fruit and wisdom.

> "Have faith in God," Jesus answered. "I tell you the truth, if
> anyone says to this mountain, 'Go, throw yourself into the
> sea,' and does not doubt in his heart but believes that what
> he says will happen, it will be done for him. Therefore I tell
> you, whatever you ask for in prayer, believe that you have
> received it, and it will be yours" (Mark 11:22-24, NIV).

This passage instructs us to pray in a spirit of faith and expectancy. When we set this promise in the broader context of scriptural teaching about prayer, we understand that the scope of what we might pray for in this way is also qualified by it being something that is the will of God for us.

However, when it comes to the issue of praying for the ministry of the Holy Spirit, we know from the earlier passage cited that it is clearly God's will to give us as believers in Jesus the person and ministry of the Spirit. So, we should ask confidently and boldly for His presence and purposes knowing that, in time, it shall be done — if we don't faint or doubt.

> On the last and greatest day of the Feast, Jesus stood and said in a loud voice, "If anyone is thirsty, let him come to me and drink. Whoever believes in me, as the Scripture has said, streams of living water will flow from within him." By this he meant the Spirit, whom those who believed in him were later to receive. Up to that time the Spirit had not been given, since Jesus had not yet been glorified (John 7:37-39, NIV).

> Be not drunk on wine, which leads to debauchery. Instead, be filled with the Spirit (Eph. 5:18, NIV).

These two passages give us further instruction about posturing ourselves to receive the Spirit's ministry. Jesus spoke again of our need to desire earnestly — to thirst. They also compare receiving to drinking in the Spirit. As we combine the instruction within these passages and apply them to receiving the Spirit's ministry, especially in thinking of renewal services, we encourage people in the following ways.

Come with desire and intent to receive more of and from the persons of the Trinity — the Father, the Son and the Holy Spirit — not to receive outward manifestations. If manifestations begin to occur to you or others:

- Don't be afraid of them;
- Welcome them instead of quenching them;
- View them as tokens that the Lord is truly present;
- Believe that you are receiving what you are asking for, even if there are no outward manifestations; and
- Stay in a loving, worshipful and grateful orientation as you wait upon the Lord to bring renewal into your life.

Some people seem to be more susceptible to the occurrence of outward manifestations. Other people seem less susceptible. Still other people have various kinds of barriers that hinder the flow of the Spirit into and through their lives. Bring the burden of possible barriers honestly to the Lord in prayer and trust Him to reveal if there are any. This is an easy prayer for God to answer! Once you have done this, don't become too introspective about the issue — it may be that you will not experience much of the outward-type manifestations or phenomena.

This does not mean that you haven't received from the Holy Spirit. Many people have reported having much fruit and power of the Spirit being released through their lives after "soaking" in the presence of God in renewal settings without having any outward awareness that they were being filled up.

There is a chemistry experiment called a titration. In this experiment, there are two clear solutions in separate test tubes. Drop by drop, one solution is mingled with the other. There is no chemical reaction until the one solution becomes super-saturated with the other. The final drop that accomplishes this causes a dramatic chemical reaction that is strikingly visible.

Some people we know have waited in renewal meetings for many hours with no apparent spiritual reaction taking place. Then, suddenly, they have a power encounter with the Spirit that radically impacts them. In retrospect, they come to believe that a spiritual "titration" was going on through the many hours of waiting on God and through soaking in the invisible and hidden ministry of the Holy Spirit. Whatever the case, it is not the outward effects of spiritual renewal that we must focus upon or draw attention to, but rather the inner transformation of our souls into the likeness of Jesus.

RECOMMENDATIONS FOR CONDUCTING RENEWAL MEETINGS

Dr. Martyn Lloyd-Jones said concerning the danger of being presumptuous about the mysterious work of the Holy Spirit, "Never say 'never' and never say 'always' concerning what the Holy Spirit might do or not do." The Lord, on purpose, doesn't submit to the boxes in which we try to confine Him!

- Plan on an extended and undistracted time of waiting on God with nothing else planned in case He doesn't "show up" in a manifest way. Determine that it will possibly have to be a dry and uneventful session if He doesn't. Speaking more positively, it can be viewed as a corporate devotional discipline. A few of those kinds of meetings can be beneficial in the life of a church in order to put people in touch with their deeply buried spiritual hunger and thirst. A few more of them can even make you desperate for God.

- Focus on the Lord Himself through worship and/or devotional reading of Scripture.

- Only periodically give explanation about manifestations. It is better to explain about them if and when they actually begin to happen, to take away the accusation that the power of suggestion is operative. Having literature available that explains these things can be very helpful.

- Often give a simple, Christ-centered devotional or exhortation. Regularly give invitations for people to receive salvation, as there are often unbelievers coming into renewal meetings out of curiosity's sake if for no other reason.

- If testimonies are given, which can be very encouraging and inspiring, they should focus on how relationship with God and the fruit of the Spirit have been enhanced rather than drawing attention to phenomena that may attend renewal.

- Avoid giving the impression that the Holy Spirit is under human control through a style of ministry. We humbly ask for His ministry. We boldly call for the release of His power. But we must not dishonor Him by pridefully commanding and demanding that He do this or that. He makes Himself available, but we must not take advantage of His divine humility by ordering Him around. If we abuse His presence and power long enough, He may withdraw His manifest presence. The history of divine visitations confirms this reality.

- If you draw attention to what is happening with an individual or a section of the congregation, do it for the specific intention to edify the whole group. Being sincere and more clinical in your communication as a leader and a facilitator is far better than being silly and fascinated with manifestations. Even when the Spirit imparts uncontrollable laughter to a person or group, it is a special and holy thing that is occurring. We must be serious about the joy of the Lord even while enjoying and reveling in it. After all, it is heavenly joy, and heavenly stuff is awesome by nature.

- Don't be afraid of extended silence. The Lord will often not submit Himself to our harried lifestyles and impatient ways. He wants to do the leading and initiating. We must wait for Him to move upon us and then learn to follow His movements.

- Often leave room for the Lord to touch people without direct human mediation. As this happens, faith begins to build and fears of manipulation are quenched. Allow those gathered to soak in the presence of God for a while before prayer ministers are released to go and touch them.

- Give people gracious "outs" if they do not want to receive the laying on of hands. Tell them how to signal you or respond if they are interested in receiving personal prayer or if they simply desire to commune with God alone.

- Be sensitive to the use of music and singing during personal ministry times. Sometimes total silence can be good. At other times background music may be best. If music is dominating personal ministry time, it can often be quite distracting.

- Fight against the pressure to try to make things happen. Seek to be supernaturally natural and naturally supernatural. Renewal is God's business, and we need to trust Him to accomplish it.

- Receive the measure of power that God releases and express thanks for it. If we are grateful, then He may show us even greater things.

- If renewal has not been occurring in your setting, consider inviting someone whom God has already been using as a catalyst for spiritual renewal into your fellowship to help impart the Spirit's ministry to a greater measure.

We recommend Sam Storms' booklet entitled *Manipulation or Ministry* for further insights on conducting ministry times.

FORMING A PRAYER MINISTRY TEAM

To facilitate renewal ministry, it is important to equip a group of prayer ministers who will be deputized by the leadership to help pray for others. The qualifications should not be too stringent, but, unfortunately, it is necessary to weed the few who will "prey" upon others rather than "pray" upon others!

We therefore need to set forth a model of corporate and personal ministry in the Spirit that will be imparted to others in the course of time. The model needs to be simple enough to be user-friendly and easily transferable.

The greatest challenge comes when people should be excluded from praying for others for various reasons. We need to be clear on what qualifies and what disqualifies someone from this kind of prayer ministry and muster the courage to talk about this in our teaching and in our personal responses to individuals. This becomes a bigger issue as time goes on and those who have received "more" have a desire to "give it away."

We must be willing to deal with specific situations that arise in which people are uncomfortable with certain people praying for and laying hands upon them. There is quite a bit of fear of evil things being communicated in receiving ministry from people who have substantial personal and spiritual problems.

People need to go through an informational orientation and training class, but many may "graduate" from such a course and still not be qualified to be a part of the ministry team. Some kind of finer screening needs to come into play.

Once an official team is selected, then we need to utilize them and make only very rare exceptions, if any, of bypassing the system we have created.

Following are the kinds of characteristics we believe should qualify someone to participate on a prayer ministry team.

- Happy and active member of the church
- Testimony of godly character and pursuit of spiritual growth
- Not in known need of deliverance from demons

- Not affected with glaring socially unacceptable behavior, appearance, speech, or habits
- Recommendation from a staff pastor with approval from the rest of the pastoral staff
- Completed a training course on personal prayer ministry
- Accountable to receiving correction in the midst of functioning on the team without getting "hurt feelings" and going away

As we pondered the things that seem most important to us about personally ministering to others, we came to realize that the basic values tend to fall under the same general categories as the various aspects of the fruit of the Spirit that Paul mentions in Galatians 5:22-23. Let's look at each fruit of the Spirit and consider how it might apply to prayer ministry.

- *Love.* Love can be viewed as the overarching characteristic from which the other aspects of the fruit of the Spirit flow. Really, the fruit of the Spirit is nothing less than the character of Jesus Christ being manifested in and through believers. As we pray for others, we must view ourselves as servants and not heroes. The spirit of servanthood is the most outstanding sign of true love. As we pray for others, we should be conscious that it's much more their moment than ours. A spirit of love will help keep this in view.

- *Joy.* "The joy of the Lord is our strength." "Serve the Lord with gladness." We need to approach praying for others with the joyful awareness of the privilege we have been given. Even if you aren't emotionally "up," you need to draw on the waters of joy that reside within you. You might do this by meditating and focusing upon the fact that you are a Christian, a temple of the Holy Spirit, forgiven of your sins, destined for heaven, useful to God, the recipient of many blessings and so on. In other words, try to back up and get the big picture of who you are in Christ and who He is in Himself. Then we are able to put our personal pressures temporarily behind us, and focus on the needs of the one before us. Seek to let His joy show through your eyes and on your countenance. If you are still unable to draw such joy forth, then confess your

223

weakness to the Lord and ask Him to graciously compensate for it on that occasion and pray about it later.

- *Peace.* We have been given the authority to impart the blessing of peace to others in the name of Jesus. We should seek to lead others into the experience of being at peace with God, themselves and others. We should seek to approach them with a peaceable spirit — a heart that is at rest in God's ability to work through us, weak though we are.

- *Patience.* We need to slow down and take our time in praying for others. The Holy Spirit doesn't like to be pushed — He wants to do the leading. Usually, He takes His time in showing His power. In quietness of soul we are able to better receive the impressions of the Spirit upon our spirits, minds, emotions and bodies. "Soaking" prayer is often very necessary to remove stubborn strongholds of the evil one.

- *Kindness.* We will often be praying for people whose lives have been wrecked by sin. Many haven't been taught social skills and they have unlovely characteristics about them. Many have embraced wrong teachings and even are oppressed by demons. We must be braced to gracefully absorb some of their immaturity and deal kindly with their deception. We must overcome evil with good and be kind to those who are unkind to us. This honors the Lord and gives them the best chance to get His help.

- *Goodness.* We need to genuinely care for the needs of others and, therefore, we should seek to be willing to show that care to them in practical ways on the heels of praying for them. We may not have the resources ourselves, but maybe we know others who might, to whom we can direct them. We must seek to break the cycles of injustice in people's lives rather than perpetuate them, especially in the name of serving the Lord. Also, we must never take advantage of the sacred trust that others are giving us when they make themselves vulnerable by allowing us to pray for them. Evil things, behind the guise of "ministry," have been perpetrated on vulnerable people before in the history of Christianity. Let us make sure that we don't add to the list.

- *Faithfulness.* We must become involved in personal prayer ministry knowing that it will call for perseverance on our part. We will often have to pray more than one time for the same people with the same needs. We mustn't become intimidated by apparent failure. We also need to remember the truth that if we are faithful in little, then God will give us more with which to work. The anointing of the Spirit grows stronger upon us as we put into practice what we have. Commit yourself to praying for hundreds of people for the rest of your life and see what God will do.

- *Gentleness (meekness).* We need to approach praying for others with a fresh awareness that we don't have the answers for them, but that we know Someone who does. This keeps us from presumption and platitudes. Our movements, both physical and verbal, need to be gentle rather than abrupt or harsh. If we can help set them at ease by knowing that they are safe in our presence, then they will be able to receive more easily from the Lord.

- *Self-control.* We encourage people to "dial down," both emotionally and physically, as they go to pray for others. If you are being outwardly and manifestly influenced at the moment and involved in an uncontrollable experience with the Spirit, then seek to stay in a receiving mode and wait until you can calm down to get into a giving mode. We must recognize that the danger exists of unwittingly manipulating others by putting a wrong pressure on them to respond to us if we violate this principle. There are exceptions to this general rule. One is if a person specifically asks you to pray for them while you are in such a state. Another could be if the other person is a friend and you know that they would welcome such an experience. And there may be others.

If we pray for others with these values deep in our hearts, it is very hard to do it wrong. Even though personal ministry was not intended to be an exact science, there are no laws against praying for others if these things reside in us (Gal. 5:23). These should be considered as the first steps of beginning a lifestyle of praying for others. By these ways and means, we minimize, without eradicating, the risks associated with praying for others with grace and power.

As specific individuals develop a track record for being exceptionally anointed in personal ministry, their leaders may give them more liberty to take bigger risks with prayer and/or prophetic ministry.

PROPER RESPONSES TO SPIRITUAL RENEWAL

So how do we courageously go forward, seeking to be good stewards of both the manifold grace of God and human weaknesses that are strangely mingled within a renewal context? We end with seven suggestions for how to honor the Lord in the midst of spiritual renewal.

- Take the posture of being "learners" rather than "experts" in the ministry of the Spirit. There really aren't that many of our generation who have gone before us in some of these things. We must continue to become like little children before our heavenly Father, the Lord Jesus and the Holy Spirit. We must be more confident in their ability to teach and lead than in our ability to learn and follow. Fortunately, their commitment to us is stronger than ours is to them. And this reality is truly the source of our strength.

- Be gracious, kind and patient with differences in perspectives within the community of believers and various streams of the body of Christ. If God is the true source of a move of the Holy Spirit, then He is well able to act independently of our judgments and criticisms to defend His honor and will raise up creditable witnesses and advocates. We don't have to prove to anyone that something is of God, if it really is!

- Give proper liberty and create sufficient opportunities for the Spirit to manifest Himself in the settings that are specifically intended to welcome renewal ministry and its attending activity. Of course, God may Himself break into any gathering with His manifest presence without human mediation. However, if only isolated individuals are being affected, then the leadership needs to make a "judgment call" if the course of any particular corporate meeting needs to be altered.

- Model and teach proper restraints, and seek to be sensitive to the specific situation and context. What does love "look like" or require in this particular setting? Seek to submit to those in authority for the sake of peace and unity. Mistakes in discernment are bound to happen in the midst of renewal when the heightened fear of both "missing God" and "being deceived" are present. Encourage people to appeal to leaders in private if they disagree with the direction they have given or are giving to the body.

- Search the Scriptures and look for new insights into the ways of God with His people.

- Study the history of revivals. Wisdom and errors are easier to perceive with the luxury that hindsight affords.

- Encourage people to rejoice in that, whether or not they have personally been manifestly touched by the Spirit, God is visiting the body in general. Let us not be so individualistic in our thinking. May we all trust the Lord to give us our personal portion in any visitation and be glad for what He is doing in others. This attitude puts us in the best possible condition to be able to receive what God does have for us as individuals.

Notes to Appendix I

1. Francis MacNutt, *Overcome by the Spirit* (Old Tappan, N.J.: Chosen Books, 1990), 35.

2. Jonathan Edwards, *The Works of Edwards,* "A Narrative of Surprising Conversions and The Great Awakening," (1736; reprint, Carlisle, Pa.: Banner of Truth, 1991), 37-38.

3. Ibid., 45.

4. Ibid., 547.

5. Ibid., 550.

6. John White, *When the Spirit Comes With Power* (Downers Grove, Ill.: InterVarsity Press, 1988), 70.

METRO VINEYARD FELLOWSHIP'S MISSION STATEMENT

METRO VINEYARD FELLOWSHIP IS:

• Calling people into the love of God resulting in passion for Jesus and compassion for people (Eph. 3:17-19; Matt. 22:37-40).

• Becoming a New Testament church that functions as a prophetic servant community that evangelizes the lost (Matt. 28:19-20).

ESSENTIAL FACTORS

PASSION FOR JESUS — JOHN 17:26

BRIDE

- Freely receiving God's extravagant affection through the finished work of the cross (Rom. 5:6-11).

- Because God first loved us, we desire to passionately love, know and enjoy Jesus (Song 8:6-7).

DISCIPLESHIP

- Equipping and discipling believers to believe and obey the Scriptures fully in the fear of God (Matt. 28:19-20).

- Knowing how to control our speech and bodies in moral purity and honor (1 Thess. 4:3; James 3:2; Eph. 4:29).

COMPASSION FOR PEOPLE — MATT. 9:36-38

KINGDOM

- Actively exercising the authority of Jesus over all the works of darkness as we heal the sick, deliver the oppressed, comfort the broken-hearted and serve the poor (Luke 4:18; 1 John 3:8).

ARMY

- Actively extending the kingdom of God in the home, marketplace and abroad through intercession, evangelism, good works, church planting and extravagant giving (Matt. 10:8; 11:12).

PROPHETIC — ACTS 2:17-21

EMPOWERED

- Fully embracing the Person, revelation and power of the Holy Spirit (Acts 1:8).

- Seeking to walk and worship in the fullness of the Holy Spirit (Eph. 5:18).

RESPONSIVE

- Fully yielding our plans to the present-tense direction of the Lord (Deut. 1:33).

- Embracing the Scriptural order for the local church as modeled by New Testament church values, practices and principles (Matt. 9:17).

SERVANT COMMUNITY — ACTS 2:43-47

FAMILY

- Nurturing a kingdom community of healthy friendships and loving families through a small group structure (Eph. 5:22-6:9; Rom. 12:15).

- Seeking to be a friendly church that joyfully welcomes and embraces others in the grace of God (Rom. 15:1-7).

BODY

- Seeking to function as a unified body whose various members honor and serve one another in the love of Christ.

- Rejoining the generations of young and old (Mal. 4:6), helping men and women to function fully in their giftings and cultivating ethnic diversity (1 Cor. 12).

GRACE TRAINING CENTER

A BIBLICAL FOUNDATION FOR A LIFETIME OF PASSION, PURITY AND POWER

PURPOSE STATEMENT

Grace Training Center (GTC) is a full-time Bible school based in Metro Vineyard Fellowship (MVF) of Kansas City. It offers one-, two- and three-year programs for full-time and part-time students.

The Grace Training Center, a ministry of Metro Vineyard Fellowship, is committed to both the centrality of Scripture and the power of the Holy Spirit. Our goal is to equip men and women for service in God's kingdom by nurturing a biblical harmony between theological integrity and Spirit-empowered passion for Jesus.

Our School of the Word (Division of Biblical Studies) instructs students in the interpretation of Scripture and the essentials of evangelical theology. The School of the Spirit (Division of Christian Ministries) provides training and experience in the application of biblical truth to life and ministry.

SAM STORMS, PH.D., PRESIDENT

Daniel tells us that "The people who know their God will display strength and take action" (11:32). GTC exists for this purpose. Our desire is to impart tomorrow's leaders with fresh power and a new vision through the life-changing knowledge of God.

MIKE BICKLE, DIRECTOR

"Grace Training Center was birthed with a vision to combine serious academic study in the Word of God with practical ministry training from humble yet gifted and experienced servants of God. Our desire is that you leave GTC more in love with Jesus and better equipped to serve Him through the church."

JOHN WIMBER, ASSOCIATION OF VINEYARD CHURCHES

"One of the pleasures in a growing movement is the emergence of training opportunities such as that occasioned by the Grace Training Center in Kansas City. I am proud of Sam Storms' and Mike Bickle's leadership in this regard."

JACK DEERE, TH.D., AUTHOR, *SURPRISED BY THE POWER OF THE SPIRIT*

"I heartily recommend the Grace Training Center to anyone hungry for more of God's Word and the skills to minister in the power of the Holy Spirit. The leadership and faculty at the Training Center are committed to fervent passion for Jesus and compassionate love for His people. Grace Training Center provides a unique opportunity for depth in biblical studies and growth in devotion to God."

WAYNE GRUDEM, PH.D., TRINITY EVANGELICAL DIVINITY SCHOOL

"I am happy to recommend Grace Training Center to people who are seeking deeper training for ministry but are unable to attend a theological seminary. I am confident that GTC, under the capable leadership of Mike Bickle and Sam Storms, will provide sound training in the Bible and theology, mature instruction in practical ministry skills and scripturally-guided experience of ministry in the power of the Holy Spirit. GTC would be especially helpful for people who want to combine academic teaching with guided experience in

Vineyard-style ministries of healing, prophecy, worship, spiritual warfare, intercession ministries of compassion and the use of other spiritual gifts."

TEN DISTINCTIVES OF GRACE TRAINING

1. CULTIVATION OF A HOLY PASSION FOR GOD

The Training Center seeks not only to provide a solid foundation based on sound biblical theology and the wisdom of seasoned ministers, but also to impart a passion for intimacy with the Lord as the foundation of all ministry.

2. COMMITMENT TO THE WORD OF GOD

The Scriptures are taught from a scholarly evangelical perspective, but with an emphasis on practical application to ministry. Students in our leadership training programs all major in the Bible as it is through God's Word that God's servants are fully equipped for every good work (2 Tim. 3:17).

3. COMMUNITY OF BELIEVERS

We believe training for ministry cannot be divorced from practical commitment to fellowship and ministry in a local church setting. Metro Vineyard Fellowship provides a dynamic and exciting environment for personal spiritual growth and practical ministry experience.

4. CONTINUAL INTERCESSION FOR REVIVAL

Metro Vineyard Fellowship maintains a strong commitment to unceasing intercession for the outpouring of the Holy Spirit to revive the church, to change the expression and understanding of Christianity in our generation and to usher in a great harvest of redeemed souls.

5. CHARISMATICALLY GIFTED MINISTRY

Our faculty is committed to ministry in the power of God's Spirit through all the gifts He graciously bestows. Our Christian Ministries division is called the School of the Spirit because we seek to train people to minister with sensitivity to His guidance and through His anointing rather than in human wisdom and energy.

6. CELL-GROUP BASED MINISTRY

Life and ministry at Metro Vineyard Fellowship are based on a network of small home gatherings that we call Friendship Groups. We believe this will develop the depths of a caring community and an every-member ministry that will be necessary for the church to fulfill God's purposes in the earth.

7. CHURCH PLANTING VISION

The Vineyard movement is committed to evangelism and church planting at home and abroad. We share that commitment and believe involvement in teams starting new congregations holds great opportunity for the expansion of God's kingdom.

8. CALLED TO THE NATIONS

GTC has been formed to equip people to touch the nations and ultimately to serve as an international training center to help fulfill Christ's Great Commission to make disciples of all nations.

9. CONTEXT FOR PROPHETIC NURTURE

MVF and GTC share a deep commitment to the restoration of the prophetic ministry to the church. Students will gain a biblical perspective on this dimension of the Spirit's work as they grow in hearing God's present-tense voice.

10. CHARACTER FORMATION

Power and wisdom are only part of the essential ingredients to a fruitful ministry. Students are challenged to deeper levels of holiness, humility and compassion through the Grace Training Center curriculum and the ministry values of MVF.

Metro Vineyard's Master's Commission

The Master's Commission is a nine-month resident discipleship training program for men and women between the ages of 18 and 24. It serves as a "boot camp" of intense Christian life training combining solid biblical teaching, life-challenging curriculum and practical experience. This program is an opportunity for students to broaden the foundation of their lives by giving themselves to serving the body through a practical daily lifestyle and learning about the lordship of Jesus. During this training time the student will experience many ministry opportunities, with training concentrating on:

- Servanthood
- Ministry of the Word
- Character Building
- Worship and Intercession
- Studying and Applying the Bible,
    Evangelism and Outreach

For more information about the Master's Commission, please fill out the form on page 237 and send it to us.

PERSONAL PRAYER

You've probably just finished reading this book by Mike Bickle and may be wondering how you can get other resource materials by Mike. Well, we want to give you a gift by sending you a copy of his *Personal Prayer List*. Through this book he offers practical suggestions for turning Scripture to prayer and offering it back to the Lord as a powerful tool for advancing the kingdom. Mike's years of experience in the prayer closet make this a valuable tool for helping you develop your own devotional prayer life. Just copy and fill out **in full** the form on the following page and mail it to:

Grace Ministries
P.O. Box 229
Grandview, MO 64030-0229

We'll send you a copy of his *Personal Prayer List* along with a coupon good for 35 percent off your next tape order from our catalogue of Mike's ministry resources. Quantities of this booklet are limited and will be filled on a first-come, first-served basis.

Passion for the Lord Jesus (A7PLJ) $33.50

Kiss the Son (A2KTS) $10.50

Overcoming Spiritual Mid-Life Crisis (A3OSM) $15.00

The Passions of God's Personality (A2PGP) $10.50

When Anointed Leaders Fall (A3WAL) $15.00

Lessons in the Prophetic (A2LINP) $10.50

A Song of Love (A2SOL) $10.50

Overview of the Song of Solomon (A2OSS) $10.50

If you would like to order any of the tapes, call:

(816) 763-3070 OR
in the U. S. (800) 552-2449

REQUEST FOR INFORMATION

Name _____

Address _____

City/State/Zip _____

Church you attend _____

Church address _____

City/State/Zip _____

____ Please send information about the Master's Commission.

____ Please send information about Metro Vineyard Conferences with Mike Bickle.

____ Please send information about Grace Training Center of Kansas City.

____ Please send a resource catalog of Mike Bickle's ministry resources.

Chapter 1
"There's Been a Terrible Mistake"

1. I highly recommend Jack Deere's book, *Surprised by the Power of the Spirit* (Grand Rapids, Mich.: Zondervan Publishing House, 1993), for those who want more teaching on this subject.

Chapter 2
The Coming Great Visitation

1. George E. Ladd, *The Presence of the Future* (Grand Rapids, Mich.: William B. Eerdmans, 1974). Ladd was for many years professor of New Testament at Fuller Theological Seminary in Pasadena, California.

2. I highly recommend Iain H. Murray's book called *The Puritan Hope* (Carlisle, Pa.: Banner of Truth, 1979).

Chapter 3
Confirming Prophecies Through the Acts of God in Nature

1. Marquis Shepherd, "Gentlest of Winter Goes Out With a Blast of Snow, Cold," *Kansas City Times,* 21 March 1983.

2. "Comet's Path to Give Close View," *The Examiner* (Independence, Miss.), 7 May 1983.

3. "Introducing Prophetic Ministry," *Equipping the Saints* (fall 1989): 4-5.

4. Ibid., 5.

5. Eusebius, *Ecclesiastical History* (Baker Book House, Grand Rapids, Mich.: 1981), b. 3, chap. 5, 86.

Chapter 4
False Equations About Prophetic Giftings

1. David Edwin Harrell Jr., *All Things Are Possible* (Bloomington, Ind.: Indiana University Press, 1975), 38.

Chapter 5
God Offends the Mind to Reveal the Heart

1. "Samuel Johnson to George Berkeley, 3 October 1741," *The Great Awakening at Yale College,* ed. Stephen Nissenbaum (Belmont, Calif.: Wadsworth Publishing Co., 1972), 57-58.

2. Jonathan Edwards, *The Works of Jonathan Edwards,* vol 1 (Carlisle, Pa.: The Banner of Truth, 1979), 62-70.

Chapter 7
Stoning False Prophets

1. Wayne Grudem, *The Gift of Prophecy in the New Testament Today* (Eastbourne, England: Kingsway Publications, 1988), 20-22.

Chapter 9
Origins of the Prophetic Call

1. Wayne Grudem, *The Gift of Prophecy in the New Testament and Today* (Westchester, Ill.: Crossway Books, 1988), 14.

2. Ibid., 83.

3. Ibid., 198-209.

Chapter 12
The Prophetic Song of the Lord

1. John Piper, *Desiring God* (Portland, Ore.: Multinomah Press, 1986), 14.

Chapter 14
Women as Prophetic Ministers

1. Catherine Kroeger, "The Neglected History of Women in the Early Church," *Christian History* 7 no. 17, (winter 1980): 7.

2. Ibid., 14.

3. Ibid., 8.

4. Ibid., 6.

5. Ibid., 20-24.

PASSION FOR JESUS

BY MIKE BICKLE

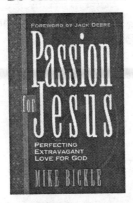

Perfecting extravagant love for God. Do you know how God feels about you? How you answer that question will determine the nature of your spiritual life.

As a young man, Mike Bickle was consumed with zeal for the gospel. Taught by his father to train hard and go for broke, it was no surprise that when Mike became a Christian, his commitment was total. He memorized whole chapters of the Bible; he prayed for hours; he fasted; he witnessed fervently to others about his faith. The ingredients to make an angry, self-righteous Pharisee were in place.

Passion for Jesus tells how the grace of God set Mike free and led him into the birthright of every believer — a knowledge of God's overpowering and intimate love.

Anyone who knows Mike Bickle knows that he has subordinated everything in his life to this one goal: acquiring a passion for Jesus. And therein lies the power of this book.

— Jack Deere, author of *Surprised*
by the Power of the Spirit

Available at your local Christian bookstore or from:

Creation House
600 Rinehart Road
Lake Mary, FL 32746
1-800-283-8494